CHICAGO PUBLIC LIBRARY

DALEY, RICHARD J. —BRIDGEPORT
3400 S. HALSTED
CHICAGO, ILLINOIS 60608

REF
B
4201
.V913
2002

HWLCPR

D1082183

THE ETERNAL IN RUSSIAN PHILOSOPHY

Chicago Public Library

C
P L

REFERENCE

Form 178 rev. 1-94

CHICAGO PUBLIC LIBRARY

DALEY, RICHARD J. —BRIDGEPORT
3400 S. HALSTED
CHICAGO, ILLINOIS 60608

THE ETERNAL IN
RUSSIAN PHILOSOPHY

B. P. Vysheslavtsev

Translated by
Penelope V. Burt

WILLIAM B. EERDMANS PUBLISHING COMPANY
GRAND RAPIDS, MICHIGAN / CAMBRIDGE, U.K.

© 2002 Wm. B. Eerdmans Publishing Co.
All rights reserved

Wm. B. Eerdmans Publishing Co.
255 Jefferson Ave. S.E., Grand Rapids, Michigan 49503 /
P.O. Box 163, Cambridge CB3 9PU U.K.

Printed in the United States of America

07 06 05 04 03 02   7 6 5 4 3 2 1

ISBN 0-8028-4952-0

www.eerdmans.com

CHICAGO PUBLIC LIBRARY

DALEY, RICHARD J. –BRIDGEPORT
3400 S. HALSTED
CHICAGO, ILLINOIS 60608

Contents

v

Russian Philosophy without Apology

Is "Russian philosophy" an oxymoron? Many people on first acquaintance seem to find that it differs so spectacularly from what they conceive to be real philosophy that they attempt to explain this difference by the cultural and historical peculiarities of Russian development. Of course, these things matter. But the problem also lies in our conception of Western philosophy. Take a look at a recent compendium with the hopeful title of *Philosophy: A Guide Through the Subject.* In the historical section, the coverage moves directly from Plato and Aristotle to Descartes, leaving out the whole of Hellenistic and medieval philosophy. The names of Pascal, Plotinus, and William James, not to speak of Ralph Waldo Emerson or Vladimir Solovyov (to give a not so random sample), are not even listed in the index.[1]

It is not just a matter of names. Problems that vex the "Russian mind," such as the concepts of truth, freedom, the absolute and the ineffable, the nature of experience, the person, are relegated in Western philosophy to the subdisciplines of aesthetics and ethics or turned over to the tender mercies of "literary theory." How has this anomalous situation come about?

No nineteenth-century Western philosopher, I think, would find the concerns of Russian philosophy alien. Nor would the ordinary person today think that these questions were not the core of anything that might be

---

1. A. C. Grayling, ed., *Philosophy: A Guide Through the Subject* (Oxford: Oxford University Press, 1995). A second volume appeared recently: A. C. Grayling, ed., *Philosophy 2: Further Through the Subject* (Oxford: Oxford University Press, 1998). Emerson and Solovyov are still missing. James and Pascal receive a couple of passing mentions.

considered philosophy — which is one reason why the precooked and re-packaged eclecticism of New Age "thought" has made such an inroad with people who certainly deserve better food with which to think. Western philosophy has relegated truth to be the object rather than the goal of inquiry. Methodology has taken pride of place, and, for all its undoubted interest and sophistication, it has had the effect of making us lose contact both with the roots of our experience and with Aristotle's "sense of wonder."[2] We have deprived ourselves of our own heritage. If we readmit some of those names and those problems, it is with an apologetic tone or with the aim of abolishing philosophy as a discipline altogether. Thus we project the limitations of our understanding of philosophy onto those philosophies that have not conformed to this understanding. No wonder the reception of Russian philosophy has often been patronizing at best. The loss is all ours. To regain what we have lost through disciplinary reductionism, we need a more open-minded approach, one that neither denies the distinctiveness of Russian philosophy nor separates it out as a culturological oddity having only a tenuous link with our own tradition. It is with the hope of contributing to a reevaluation of our situation that I have translated Boris Vysheslavtsev's *The Eternal in Russian Philosophy*.

This book was intended for a Russian audience, the narrow circle of Vysheslavtsev's fellow thinkers in emigration and their sons and daughters. It was aimed at overcoming a potential discontinuity in Russian philosophy, occasioned by the communist regime, between the work of the past (the Russian philosophical and religious renaissance of the late nineteenth and early twentieth century) and the work of the future. In this sense, the Western reader is not the intended reader: we are overhearing a message not addressed to us. The citations from Russian poetry, especially in the first two chapters on Alexander Pushkin and running like leitmotifs throughout the text, have a resonance for the Russian reader that is ultimately "untranslatable" and nation-specific. Nonetheless, it is worth our while to attend to Vysheslavtsev's message, because his book, in part a collection of essays published over the years of his exile, gives us a good overview of the kind of problems and solutions that engaged a Russian author with wide-ranging interests (psychoanalysis, Eastern philosophy, German idealism, Marxism, and religion) and an approach to philosophy that he himself describes as "intuition and dialectics." It is a book about Russian

---

2. By the later Middle Ages the passage about philosophy beginning in wonder had dropped out of the translation of Aristotle's *Metaphysics* (Lorraine Daston and Katharine Park, *Wonders and the Order of Nature* [New York: Zone, 1998], p. 120).

philosophy and at the same time an excellent exemplar of it. Vysheslav-tsev's intellectual range is a sign of both his deep immersion in his native culture and his universalism. Here the Western reader will find that Augustine is not the only church father of philosophical interest, nor is Mikhail Bakhtin[3] the only Russian concerned with the "unfinalizability" of the person.

An American reader searching for faith in (post)modern times may ask: What is the link between everyday life and the philosophical concerns, if they are indeed philosophical, of an exotic Russian thinker? But the only philosophy that could be relevant for such a reader is one that includes Russian philosophy, for Russian thinkers are existential in the religious sense: they enchurch all cultural experience — from poetry, Russian or not, to psychoanalysis to science. Enchurching and philosophizing are closely linked for all Russian thinkers, and Vysheslavtsev excels in this complex task, like his compatriot Pavel Florensky.[4] Vysheslavtsev is, however, easier to read, and serves as a good introduction to this realm of Russian thought, with its alloy of religious and existential concerns. Readers may open this book hoping to learn something about a Russian thinker, and close it having learned something about themselves and their tradition.

An example of the relevance of the Russian perspective: a popular Western view of Descartes is that he never really escaped from the solipsism that was his point of departure and has burdened us with a disembodied, relationless self — the "individual." In the Russian tradition, however, Vysheslavtsev regards the individual as a purely statistical social unit asserting its rights in a purely statistical social sense, as the antonym of the person whose personhood emanates from itself in a godlike manner. Consequently, for a Russian, Descartes's distinction between the person on the one hand and his or her attributes or functions or relatedness to the world on the other is not an isolationist recipe for self-centered Western individualism, but rather a sign pointing to that ineffable "person" quality that alone gives value to attributes, functions, and relations. Not that Vysheslavtsev is unaware of the obvious individualistic perils of Descartes, but he is capable of turning the tables on that philosopher. What

3. Vysheslavtsev probably had no regular access to work of any interest in the USSR, including the work of Bakhtin — after all, Soviet citizens had no general access to it either.

4. See Pavel Florensky's masterpiece, *The Pillar and Ground of Truth: An Essay in Orthodox Theodicy in Twelve Letters*, trans. Boris Jakim (Princeton: Princeton University Press, 1997). See also Pavel Florensky, *Iconostasis*, trans. Donald Sheehan and Olga Andrejev (Crestwood, N.Y.: St. Vladimir's Seminary Press, 1996) — a fascinating text.

enables him to do so is the characteristically Russian differentiation between the person and the individual.

A scene in Tolstoy's *War and Peace* describes the singing of the young heroine, Natasha Rostova. Her auditors are initially overwhelmed by her voice; but later, when they start rationalizing their impressions, they proclaim that it needs a "little chiseling." We do not need to purge either Russian philosophy or our own Western tradition of the rawness and freshness that makes us turn to philosophy in the first place, sometimes even before we know that such a discipline exists. As Vysheslavtsev says of Pushkin, this should not be just a matter for specialists.

Boris Petrovich Vysheslavtsev was born in Moscow in 1877. He studied at the University of Moscow, and after the publication of his thesis on the ethics of Fichte, he was appointed professor of philosophy at that institution. In 1922 he was expelled from the Soviet Union along with dozens of his fellow thinkers, and eventually settled in France, where he engaged in teaching and publishing activities. The latter included collaboration with Nikolai Berdyaev on the journal *Put'* [The Way], as well as the Russian translation of the selected works of C. G. Jung. By all accounts he was a mesmerizing and witty lecturer and conversationalist. With the advent of World War II, Vysheslavtsev moved to Geneva, where he died in 1954, one year after the death of Joseph Stalin, when there was still little hope that any of his work would reach the Russian audience at home.

Vechnoe v russkoy filosofii (The eternal in Russian philosophy) was published posthumously in 1955 by the emigré Chekhov Publishing House in New York. It was finally reprinted in Russia in 1994 along with an earlier work, *Etika preobrazhennogo erosa* (The ethics of transfigured eros) by the Izdatelstvo "Respublika" in Moscow, edited and with helpful commentary by V. V. Sapov, on which I have drawn in this translation. The two texts are basically identical.

Vysheslavtsev quotes from a great variety of sources. I have checked and profited from the standard translations of Pushkin, Descartes, the Upanishads, and so on, but the renditions are basically translations from the Russian, especially since I suspect that in at least some cases Vysheslavtsev was quoting or paraphrasing from memory. Biblical quotations are generally from the King James or the Revised Standard Versions, whichever seemed clearer or more appropriate or closer to the Russian/Church Slavonic for the context. Everything in brackets is mine.

I want to thank my husband for his encouragement, and Jon Frederickson for reading the manuscript and offering many valuable suggestions for its improvement. All the members of the seminar on Personalism and Russian Philosophy, led by Father Michael Meerson, made helpful comments about Vysheslavtsev's text and its English rendition. My greatest debt is to Professor Olga Meerson of Georgetown University. I thank her from the depths of my heart for her friendship and for the many wonderful hours we spent poring over and discussing Vysheslavtsev's book. There is no page of this translation that has not benefitted from her keen mind and her infallible ear for nuance. However, the final responsibility for this American English version rests with me.

Introduction

The basic problems of world philosophy are, of course, the problems of Russian philosophy as well. In this sense, a philosophy that is specifically Russian does not exist. There is, however, a Russian approach to world philosophical problems, a Russian way of experiencing and debating about them. The various nations perceive and value different thoughts and feelings in the wealth of material that every great philosopher provides. In this sense there does exist the Russian Plato, the Russian Plotinus, the Russian Descartes, the Russian Pascal, and, of course, the Russian Kant. Nationalism in philosophy is impossible, just as it is in science. But it is possible for different nations to have a primary interest in different world problems and different traditions of thought.

One characteristic feature of Russian philosophy is its link to Hellenism, to the Socratic method, to the classical dialectic of Platonism. It inherited this tradition along with Byzantine Christianity and the Eastern church fathers, who were themselves first-rate Greek philosophers. I think that this Hellenic-Christian tradition profoundly unites us to world philosophy, which, after all, goes back to Socrates and the dialogues of Plato. Not without reason has an English philosopher [Alfred North Whitehead] said that all new philosophy is nothing but an uninterrupted series of footnotes to Plato's dialogues.

Another basic feature strikingly prominent in Russian philosophy is its interest in the problem of the Absolute. Hegel's dictum, "The object of philosophy is the same as the object of religion," is profoundly congenial to the Russian soul, and at the same time faithfully reflects the Hellenic tradition. All of classical dialectic from Socrates to Plotinus is an ascent to the Absolute, or a quest for the Divine Being.

Dialogue as practiced by Socrates and Plato is not only an ascent to the Absolute, however, but also a plumbing of the depths of the self ("Know thyself"). The Absolute is contraposed to the relative; God is contraposed to human. Humans are comprehensible to themselves only through the contraposition of finite and infinite, temporal and eternal, perfect and imperfect. Here we come to the heart of the matter: What am I myself? What is a human being? What is a person?

These are the basic problems of Descartes and Pascal, and the Russian interpretation of them presents certain distinctive features. At the same time, this question of the person constitutes the theme of Russian literature, Russian poetry: "Who called me forth out of nothingness, filled my soul with passion, disturbed my mind with doubt?" [Pushkin, "Useless gift, chance gift . . ."]. Here we find all at once skepticism and doubt side by side with mystical feeling; we find the problem of the human being's attitude toward God, as in Derzhavin: "But if I am so wondrous a creature, and where I come from is a mystery, and I have no power on my own to exist" [Gavriil Derzhavin, "God"].

Russian literature is thoroughly philosophical: all the fundamental problems of the Russian soul are set forth in the Russian novel, in Russian poetry. If these problems were not pan-human and universal, then the universal understanding of and interest in Tolstoy and Dostoevsky would be incomprehensible. All of Dostoevsky is essentially a development of Pascal's basic theme — "the greatness and insignificance of man" — expressed with such power in Derzhavin's famous line: "I am king, I am slave, I am worm, I am god." These words contain the whole of Dostoevsky and the whole essence of the tragic conflict peculiar to humankind. "Here the Devil struggles with God, and the field of battle is — the human heart" [*The Brothers Karamazov*]. Dostoevsky is no less of a tragedian than Shakespeare, and his novels easily take on dramatic form. The classical idea of "catharsis" and the Christian idea of redemption always captured his attention. What stands out clearly here is Russian philosophy's interest in the problem of suffering, the problem of Job, the problem of tragic fate and Providence.

The whole future temperament of Russian philosophy and all of its ancient sources are expressed, right in the middle of the eighteenth century, by the man whom I consider to be the first original Russian philosopher: Grigory Skovoroda, a Russian thinker, theologian, and poet. He certainly belonged to that spiritual culture which was upheld on his native soil [i.e., Ukraine] by the Kiev Academy. This culture drew its ideas from the Platonic tradition of Greek philosophy and the patristic literature closely linked to it.[1] This amazing man, who knew Latin, Greek, and Hebrew in addition to the modern languages, traveled on foot all over Austria, Italy, and Germany. He was pan-human, a Russian European, just the kind of man whom Dostoevsky, speaking in honor of Pushkin, dreamed that everyone should be. Skovoroda's favorite philosophers were Socrates and Plato; he possessed an excellent knowledge of classical philosophy and literature. Among the church fathers he valued most Clement of Alexandria, Origen, Dionysius the Areopagite, Maximus the Confessor, and our own Nil Sorsky, that is, the fathers who were the most philosophical and the most Neoplatonic. He traveled everywhere in Russia, from Kiev and Kharkov to St. Petersburg, Moscow, the Trinity-St. Sergius Monastery and Pereyaslavl'. He also spent some time living in central Russia with his landowner friends, especially the Kovalenskys.

I will allow myself just two citations to give an idea of the starting point for his philosophy. "That most primary, ecumenical, invisible Force, which alone is mind, life, movement, existence — pouring out of the perceptibly ungraspable, out of eternity into all-encompassing time, out of numerical unity into boundless plurality, forming the sphere of humanity — this Force, by virtue of its primacy, endows humanity with its most noble benefit: free will." And here is a passage that expresses, perhaps, the essence of modern times: "My God," he exclaims, "what is there that we don't know, what is there that we can't do? We've measured the depth and height of the seas, the earth and the heavens; we've discovered a countless multitude of worlds; we construct 'incomprehensible' machines. But something is missing. You can't fill up a vacuum in the soul with the limited and the transitory."

The figure of Skovoroda embodies, in essence, all the sacred aspirations and sympathies of Russian philosophy. They were later embodied in the figure of Vladimir Solovyov, as well as in the whole pleiad of Russian philosophers at the time of the Russian renaissance — the Trubetskoi brothers, Lopatin, Novgorodtsev, Frank, Lossky, Askol'dov — and some of us who can still remind a new generation of the spirit and tragedy of Russian philosophy, and who are trying to perpetuate that philosophy in our works abroad.

Our encounter with Western philosophers immediately revealed our differing mental and spiritual mind-sets. This difference is not easy to pinpoint: in Russia the philosophy that generations of educated people and professors were brought up on was the same as in the West. But the

---

1. Cf. the excellent book on Skovoroda by P. Bobrinsky (Paris, 1929).

attitude toward it was different. In the West, philosophy was interpreted in a purely intellectual way, through the process of reasoning and the observation of facts. We Russians interpreted it more through feeling and intuition. (Tolstoy is a particularly striking example.) We also imported the "fruits of erudition" from "misty Germany," but the "fervent and rather strange spirit" of classical German philosophy was no longer to be found there: we brought it with us from Russia. We were impressed by their dry, strictly compartmentalized intellectualism, which comprehended everything, analyzed everything, laid out nicely the interconnections of ideas. But there was no way of knowing what they took seriously, what they appropriated and mastered and expounded as interesting viewpoints and combinations of ideas. Their splendid works on medieval philosophy may serve as an example. They were impressed — and sometimes incensed — by our absolutism, our maximalism, our demand for definitive solutions and our "reduction" of all problems to the ultimate meaning of existence as a whole. They had been proclaiming the "relativity" of all knowledge for so long that they at last forgot that the relative exists only in contrast to the Absolute — and then they forgot about the Absolute.

We were delighted to remind the West about the dictum of Hegel that was so dear to us: "the object of philosophy is the same as the object of religion." In other words, there is in fact an Absolute. However, a certain mutual misunderstanding persisted. Our religiosity in philosophy irritated some; our supposed "woolly" mysticism in religion irritated others, primarily the strict Thomists. Even in the West, however, an overcoming of intellectualism was effected by our favorite philosophers, Henri Bergson and Max Scheler.

The discovery of psychoanalysis, of course, forced a change in every philosophical position.[2] Psychoanalysis clarified a great deal about the Russian way of philosophizing: the collective unconscious of the Russian people lies, as it were, closer to the surface of consciousness; it is not so displaced from consciousness, not so worked over by consciousness as in the West. We are a younger, more barbaric nation and thus, to be sure, more like philosophical apprentices. Yet a little something may be learned even from us. Otherwise the Western interest in Dostoevsky, Tolstoy, even in Chekhov and Leskov would be incomprehensible.

A note about the relationship of Russian philosophy to religion and theology might be appropriate here. Russian philosophy constantly ap-

---

2. Now even the "sharp Gallic wit" [Alexander Blok] has begun to discourse about the nocturnal and diurnal.

peals to religion and theology for the solution of philosophical problems, because religion and theology were themselves the first form of philosophy and are saturated with a philosophical way of thinking. In India, Babylon, and Egypt, religion was on the whole inseparable from philosophy. In Greece, from Plato to Plotinus, philosophy always took into account the mysteries as well as the most ancient myths, such as the deeply philosophical and prophetic myth of Prometheus. This also explains why I refer so often in my articles to religious ideas and the theology of culture. For example, no philosopher can overlook the rich philosophical content of medieval theology. Nonetheless, the attitude of philosophers toward all this material differs significantly from that of ordinary believers or theologians penning their dogmatic treatises. At the time of its awakening and search for independent paths, Russian philosophy evinced an attitude toward religion that comes out clearly in the religio-philosophical gatherings in Petersburg, so vividly described by Zinaida Gippius. This attitude is even clearer and more definitive in the Moscow gatherings organized by Margarita Kirillovna Morozova, and in the publishing house, *Put'* [The Way], that she founded. However, the tasks facing the Petersburg gatherings were different: they had to do with the first exchange of ideas between eminent representatives of the Russian intelligentsia and the highest and most cultivated members of the church hierarchy. The former were members of that advanced segment of the Russian intelligentsia that had grown weary of all brands of materialism and positivism and the obligatory disregard of religious questions. They realized that the attitude of contemporary scientific psychology — and consequently of academic philosophy as well — toward myth, symbol, and religion was completely different from and even antithetical to the attitude prevalent at the time of Marx and Engels, of positivists and materialists of every shape and color. The psychologist, the philosopher, and the cultural historian now take an enormous interest in myth and symbol, as expressions of the deepest complexes of the collective unconscious.

From Derzhavin down to Tolstoy, Dostoevsky, and, of course, Dmitri Merezhkovsky (the originator of those Petersburg meetings), all of Russian poetry and literature overflows with these ultimate questions. Those who joined this group of the intelligentsia were men and women of letters, writers, often scholars, and, in general, representatives of the highest secular culture in the capital. For example, it is difficult to assign an amazingly gifted and cultivated man such as Ternovtsev to a definite professional category.

Vladimir Solovyov, beyond a doubt, effected the great revolution in the consciousness of the Russian intelligentsia. This brilliantly educated Russian philosopher, a splendid writer, began for the first time to discuss the kinds of questions that had been castigated until then as reactionary and unscientific. Nonetheless, the rapprochement of the Russian intelligentsia and the representatives of the church did not come off. Each side spoke a different language. In complete contrast to this experience was the success of the Religio-Philosophical Society in Moscow, which consciously carried forward the tradition of Vladimir Solovyov and named itself after him. Here Russian philosophers and writers met together, and a genuine philosophical dialogue ensued, which touched on ultimate themes at the border of philosophy and religion, and on current philosophical topics in general. Here Nikolai Berdyaev and Sergei Bulgakov completed their transition from Marxism to idealism, and Bulgakov his gradual transition to purely religious themes. However, Bulgakov's book *Unfading Light* is still primarily a philosophical one, like his *Philosophy of Economy*. The most talented portion of philosophical youth at the universities attended these meetings, and in those prerevolutionary years one could already feel the presentiment of a genuine blossoming of Russian philosophy and spiritual culture. This blossoming was immediately cut off by a compulsory Marxism and communism, but it continued to develop in exile among the Russian scholars, philosophers, and writers abroad. The Russian philosophers and scholars who found themselves in foreign countries carried on their scholarly and philosophical activity, and in fact wrote their most learned and mature works in emigration. Father Vasily Zenkovsky and N. O. Lossky have made a great contribution with their two wide-ranging histories of Russian philosophy, available in English, Russian, and French. These works essentially refute the view of certain skeptics that there has never been any Russian philosophy. We Russians, it is true, underwent an apprenticeship and have been conscientious pupils of all the European philosophical schools. But this is something we can only be proud of. It was our mission to make use of all the best that had been done by European philosophers.

Now that these two histories are available, there is no need for me to catalogue in precise detail what Russian philosophers have accomplished abroad. One thing is beyond doubt: it has been in emigration that they have done their best and most important work. A significant portion of these works has been translated into various foreign languages, thereby enabling Western scholarship to become acquainted with us. Thus the tradition and development of Russian philosophy has never come to a halt, and the whole problem now is one of how to pass this legacy on to the next generations. The present book is one attempt to fulfill this task.

As for the Soviet Union, the continuation and development of Russian philosophy there is even more impossible than the continuation of Russian poetry and literature. For thirty-six years now not a single independent philosophical work could be published, not a single original philosophical idea could be expressed that strayed beyond the bounds of Marxism, which, after all, is shuffling around and about on its thesis with no way of proceeding toward the antithesis. The sole contributions of Soviet scholars have been translations and editions of the classics and, aside from that, their celebrated ability to acquaint the Soviet reader with the authentic currents of free philosophy under the guise of a withering critique.

Marxism constantly chatters about a bourgeois philosophy of some kind. But there does not exist nor has there ever existed any kind of bourgeois mathematics, bourgeois science, or bourgeois philosophy. It would be impossible to concoct a more absurd expression — unless what is meant by the bourgeoisie is the well-to-do urban classes, in which case there has never been any science or philosophy that was not bourgeois. And the whole of this "bourgeois" heritage has been totally appropriated and assimilated by "proletarian" communism. But the most remarkable thing is that communism and socialism were created by philosophers who were not materialists at all, but rather idealists like Plotinus and Fichte. Conversely, materialism was created by the most bourgeois philosophers, and "economic materialism" was a genuine manifestation of the bourgeois ethos. An absolute and implacable materialist like Thomas Hobbes was also the founder of totalitarian absolutism.

CHAPTER 1

The Varieties of Freedom
in Pushkin's Poetry

The main problem in the world today is the problem of freedom and slavery, of freedom and tyranny — anyway, this has always been the main theme of Russian philosophy and Russian literature. Pushkin is, first and foremost, a singer of freedom. The philosophy of Tolstoy and Dostoevsky is a philosophy of Christian freedom and Christian love. If Pushkin, Tolstoy, and Dostoevsky express the native tradition and essence of the Russian spirit, we must allow that this spirit is antagonistic in every way to materialism, Marxism, and totalitarian socialism. Russian philosophy, literature, and poetry have always been and will always be on the side of the free world; they have been revolutionary in the deepest, spiritual sense of the word and will remain so in the face of any tyranny, any oppression, any violence. The genius of Pushkin serves as a pledge of this: "Genius and villainy are two incompatible things." Those allegations are false which claim that Russians have an aptitude for absolute obedience, that they are some kind of slave by nature, perfectly suited to totalitarian communism. If this were really true, then Pushkin, Tolstoy, and Dostoevsky would not be an expression of the Russian spirit, the Russian genius. Pushkin's poetry is a poetry of freedom through and through: "What does she [the poet's lyre] sing? She sings of freedom, faithful to herself to the end."

The first chapters of this book are devoted to the philosophical justification of freedom, and the best introduction to it is the "poetry of freedom in Pushkin." The plenitude of life and personhood is the plenitude of creative freedom. No one can philosophize about the plenitude of freedom without experiencing it. Pushkin portrays this experience at all levels:

1

from the simple "self-motion" and spontaneity of life, the unconditioned reflex of liberation possessed by every living thing, the unconscious instinct for "liberty" — right up to the higher consciousness of creative freedom as service to God, as the freely given response to the divine call.

In Pushkin's poetry there is no word encountered more frequently than "liberty" or "freedom." Human language seems to contain no word with more facets of meaning, and Pushkin truly unfolds all of its significance; he conveys the experience of freedom's many hypostases, its inexhaustibility and contradictoriness. Everything that Pushkin denies and hates is related to necessity, violence, coercion, tyranny, despotism. Everything that he loves and values, everything that excites him and captures his attention, is allied to freedom: it is the incarnation of it, the symbol of it, or the thing itself: "The sea is a free element," "the thunderstorm is a symbol of freedom," the wind, the eagle, a little bird, a maiden's heart — and finally the poet himself — all of them live and breathe only in freedom: "Because there is no law for the wind, the eagle, a maiden's heart." In response to Aleko's jealous tyranny, the old gypsy [in Pushkin's *Gypsies*] says: "Why [be jealous]? Youth is freer than a bird; who has the power to hold on to love?" This natural, elemental, cosmic freedom is an intrinsic element of Pushkin's soul. The gypsies' nomadic liberty fascinates him, and what Russian feels entirely alien to it? "Their camp for the night is merry, like liberty." When he is with them, he is a free inhabitant of the whole world. And it saddens him when the "peaceful carts of the gypsies, the humble children of liberty," head off into the distance. Every living thing seeks out freedom and suffers when it is fettered, like a bird in a cage. Pushkin senses this liberty in himself and sympathizes with it wherever he finds it: "In a foreign land I reverently observe the ancient native custom: on a bright spring holiday I set free a little birdie."

He himself is attracted to the same kind of freedom: the freedom of flight, the freedom to wander, the freedom to "see foreign lands." All his life he dreamed of seeing Italy — "sacred to the grandsons of Apollo": "the nocturnal languor of golden Italy I shall enjoy in freedom." The horizon of the sea lures him with its promise of freedom: "When will I begin my free course over the free crossroads of the sea? Will the day of my freedom come? It's time, it's time! I call to it; I wander over the sea, I wait for fair weather, I beckon to the ship's sails."

But if Pushkin was fated never to see Italy or Paris or to "taste the fruits of erudition in misty Germany," then in his native village he was seduced by "free idleness, the friend of meditation," "free and careless indolence": "Every morning I am awakened to sweet languor and freedom."

2

But for him the true significance of leisure lies, naturally enough, in creativity: "In the backwoods, the voice of the lyre is more sonorous; creative dreams are more vivid." The only conceivable art for him is "free art." He likes to banquet with his friends only when "freedom, my idol, rules the table." But Pushkin does not just sing the praises of elemental or individual creative freedom; he knows that it is inextricably linked to civil and political freedom. The latter is the true strength and glory of nations. Republican Rome aroused his respect ("I am a Roman at heart; freedom seethes within my breast!"). The glory and honor of monarchs also reside in civil and political freedom: he sings the praises of Alexander I "in free, simple words of truth" not because of the latter's imperialism, but because he brought liberation to the nations of Europe: "Are we really free? That terrible one [Napoleon], has he fallen?" Europe embraced "liberation from its servile bonds by the hand" of the tsar. Even Napoleon was great not because he was a despot, but because he "bequeathed eternal freedom to the world from the darkness of exile." The Russian poet awaits this freedom for himself, for Russia, for the whole world: "We await the moment of sacred freedom with hopeful longing" ("To Chaadaev"). The ode to "Liberty" expresses the highest social, legal, and political ideal of the poet: "The liberty and repose of nations." So he wrote in his youth, and here is how he expressed the highest value of personal, individual life at the end of his days: "There is no happiness in this world, only repose and freedom."

Liberty and repose, repose and freedom — these are the alpha and omega of his poetry. He could say, truly, of his lyre: "What does she sing? She sings of freedom, faithful to herself to the end." This is what he regards as the theme of his mature creativity in contrast to the poetry of his youth, which sang the praises of love, friends, feasting, "Bacchus and Aphrodite" — and liberty too, but another kind of liberty, one of arbitrary license. From now on, he resolves differently: "Smash the fastidious lyre — I want to sing forth freedom to the world, to strike down vice enthroned."

*　　*　　*

Is it possible for a human being to renounce freedom completely, to lose the very feeling, the very instinct of freedom? Pavlov's reflexology would require an answer in the negative, since freedom exists as an unconditioned reflex, common to every living thing. An animal, an insect, even a plant makes every possible effort to free itself when caught; and the human being, of course, does the same. Everything that lives wants to "breathe freely," that is, any impediment to its vital functions comes up against the unconditioned reflex of liberation. Since this is so, where then do the loss of freedom, domination, and submission come from? The problem is that another reflex exists, just as unconditioned, just as fundamental for every living thing, but antithetical to the first: the unconditioned reflex of power, of conquest, of appropriation, of mastery. The child seizes every object within reach and puts it into his mouth; the animal strives to run down and seize its prey; the human being strives to grab, appropriate, and subjugate everything that he can — and first of all his neighbor. The lust for domination is one of the most powerful passions. These two antithetical reflexes, or two innate instincts (for Pavlov a reflex and an instinct are synonymous) are unconditioned, in the sense that they are given by nature, from birth; they do not need to be learned; they are not created by culture; they are elementary and elemental like life itself. But culture can foster them, ennoble them, transform them from elemental forces into cultural values. They are opposites, and therefore they can contradict each other: the conflict of power and freedom is a constant theme in personal life and in the life of nations. But they can also be reconciled with each other; they can complement and serve each other (e.g., the power of law and justice that can preserve and protect freedom). Here is the entire nexus of problems from which the complex dialectic of freedom unfolds. This dialectic turns up in all of Pushkin's creative work. His major works are devoted to the inherent tragedy of power and freedom: *Boris Godunov, The Captain's Daughter, The History of Pugachev's Revolt,* "The Covetous Knight," *Poltava,* "André Chénier," the ode to "Liberty." Pushkin had a profound understanding of the nature of this inherent tragedy; he also knew what its resolution would be. Power is tragic because it may ally itself to crime; the tragedy is resolved by the justification of power, by power's ability to give to both persons and nations "liberty and repose."

Tragic conflict is the source of wisdom, for it awakens and purifies the spirit and demands resolution. But the wisdom of poets, Pushkin's wisdom, expresses itself differently from the wisdom of philosophers, scientists, and political experts: not in concepts and proofs, not in systems and doctrines, not in ideologies — but in living images, in symbols, in the varied incarnations of the beautiful word.

Pushkin portrays the will to power, like the will to revolt and liberation, as a series of living people. With the deepest insight he penetrated into the psychology of people whose nature was poles apart from his own: people thirsting for power and demanding submission, who live for nothing but "worldly sensations, greed, and battles." At the opposite extreme are people with a sense of a genuine and higher freedom, the kind of people who neither seek power nor accept subjugation to it. They are truly "conceived by freedom" and live "for inspiration, sweet sounds, and prayers." These words make clear just who these people are: they are the poets, artists, scholars, thinkers, prophets, apostles — people who partake of the creative spirit, "inspired" people ("poets" in the Greek sense of the word, i.e., "creators/makers"). As long as they are faithful to their calling, they desire "neither to rule nor to hold sway."[1] Pushkin indicates their high destiny: the "divine word" calls them through beauty, truth, wisdom, and the prophetic word ("burn human hearts with your word") to a freely accepted service. Such people "do not rely on princes, on the sons of man." "They do not bow their proud head at the feet of the popular idol." Pushkin himself is one of these "inspired" people, as is Pavlov. Here we should not forget that the reflex of freedom is innate to every human being, although not many can attain that higher spiritual freedom which Pushkin opposes to "worldly excitement."

But it does not thereby follow that the only ones who can understand and value freedom are certain aristocrats of the spirit. Discovery and revelation are the lot of some, but the good use of discoveries is the lot of all — and for this freedom is also necessary. Freedom of speech and thought is necessary in equal measure both for those who have something to say and for those who need to hear something. The ability to apprehend someone else's creative work, to be nurtured by it, to admire it, is also an activity of the free spirit. If Pushkin has value for all of us, this means that Pushkin's liberty — "sacred liberty" — still resounds in every soul.

What is astonishing is that Pushkin, in portraying those types of people which are antithetical to him, is able to recognize and delineate their subconscious essence, their basic instinctual patterns, in a way that is quite analogous to the methods of Pavlov's reflexology or contemporary psychoanalysis. Pushkin defines these types in terms of "greed and battles," but these are two manifestations of the same instinct: the instinct of predation, conquest, subjugation, appropriation. War is the source of both slavery and plunder. "Greed and battles," "gold and the sword" — these are two forms of the seizure of power, two forms of the lust for domination: "All is mine, said gold; all is mine, said damask steel."

Wealth through power, or power through wealth — but always power in the end. Materialism with its psychology of "interests" understands nothing of this. The covetous knight says: "Everything is subject to me, I

---

1. Socrates kept this faith — Plato did not.

5

to nothing; I know my own power, and the consciousness of it is enough for me. . . . And the Muses will bring me their tribute, and free genius and virtue and humble labor will be my slaves." Precisely the same thing could be said, with greater right and warrant, by the contemporary ruler of any totalitarian state. But wealth through power is much more dependable than power through wealth: the latter can always be seized by power.

Despite his raptures over power, the covetous knight is wretched, just as wretched as Boris Godunov, who was in fact a sovereign and tsar: "I have attained the highest power; for the sixth year now I have ruled in peace, but there is no happiness in my tormented soul." Why is there no happiness, no tranquillity? Because "that man is wretched whose conscience is not pure"; because "I see before my eyes the little boys, stained with blood"; because power has joined up with crime, and yet there still exists the "sharp-clawed beast that mangles the heart: conscience, the unexpected guest, the tiresome visitor." Power is not justified in every case — far from it; and far too often it is allied to crime (the covetous knight says: "I whistle — and villainy, covered with blood, crawls up to me obedient and timid, and licks my hand, and gazes into my eyes, reading there the sign of my will").

This holds true, surprisingly enough, for a whole variety of power-holders: for Ivan the Terrible, whose greatness was not negligible but who was criminally insane; for Boris Godunov, who was sober-minded, intelligent, in no way a cruel man. Even the best of our monarchs — Catherine the Great, Peter the Great, Alexander the "Blessed" — are tainted with crime (the murder of husband, son, father). Acquiescence in crime is the Achilles' heel of power. It is hard to figure out whether conscience can be completely eradicated in the human being (e.g., by means of atheism or a materialistic worldview), but one thing is beyond all doubt: the anxiety and fear of tyrants cannot be allayed, nor is there any way to get rid of the eternal threat that their power will be overthrown. To protect themselves from this fear, they resort to intimidation, that is, terror. Hence the ever-increasing vigilance and anxiety of power: for the unconditioned reflex of freedom is indestructible. Such is the tragic contradiction of power. It would seem that its resolution in modern law and the state had been found long ago, but this is not the case: we are still faced with this full-blown contradiction even now, and it demands a solution once again. This is why the higher freedom of the spirit spurns that demonic element, inherent in power, which constitutes power's permanent temptation, and which was rejected by the Divine Human: the urge to bow down before the spirit of evil. "I will give thee power over all the kingdoms of the world, if thou wilt fall down and worship me . . . for [this power] is delivered unto me; and to whomsoever I will, I give it" (cf. Matt. 4:9; Luke 4:6). This is why it is useless to pin one's hopes on the power of force as the sole means of salvation: "Do ye not rely on princes . . . for there is no salvation in them." But even less can you rely on the Pugachevs, the pretenders, the usurpers, the revolutionary tyrants, "chiefs" of any kind; still less is it possible to call them "geniuses." Here the severe word of the poet should ring forth: "genius and villainy are two incompatible things!" Genius and liberty are two inseparable things! There is no place for a free genius among tyrants and slaves.

*   *   *

The free genius of Russia is the free genius of Pushkin, which never submitted to anyone or anything: not to Alexander, or Nicholas, or Pugachev, or the Decembrists, or the Jacobins, not to "public opinion," or the dictates of society, or general utility. It is obedient to only one call — the "divine Word" — once that word "touches its keen hearing."

But Pushkin portrays not just the tragedy of power but the tragedy of freedom as well. These two tragedies are closely intertwined. Freedom may lapse into arbitrariness, into the self-will of the passions, into thievish "outlawry," into senseless and ruthless popular revolt, and finally into tyranny. The tyrant deprives everyone of any freedom whatsoever, and appropriates it exclusively for himself. But such a tyrant's "freedom" is criminal arbitrariness, which destroys genuine freedom. "You only want freedom for yourself," says the old gypsy to the tyrannical Aleko. The tyranny of jealousy turns Aleko into a murderer, and what a true "liberty" says to him is this: "We [the gypsies] are wild; we have no laws; we do not torture people or execute them; we do not need blood and groans; but — to live with a murderer: that we will not do." In the history of monarchs and peoples, things have not been resolved with such wise simplicity.

The tragedy of power is that it awakens the protest of revolutionary freedom; the tragedy of revolutionary freedom is that it awakens the innate instinct for power in the very liberators themselves. The overthrowing of power degenerates into the misappropriation of power — and of the very worst sort. The tragedy of power and freedom comes down to the same theme: tyranny and its overthrow: "Nurslings of capricious Fortune, tyrants of the world, tremble! But take courage, hearken and rise up, you fallen slaves!"

The ode of 1817 on "Liberty" provides the beginning of this tragedy.

7

It portrays legal tyranny and its overthrow. "André Chénier" (1825) develops it further: another tyranny — revolutionary tyranny — appears, casting down the first. But the eternal protest of liberty against bondage is expressed here in words that apply to any tyranny, for they express its archetypal essence: "Alas! Wherever I cast my glance, everywhere there are scourges, everywhere chains, the fatal dishonoring of the laws, the impotent tears of bondage; unrighteous power everywhere . . . has claimed a throne — the terrible Genius of Slavery and Glory's fateful passion."

Pushkin's words of prophetic anger can be applied to every tyranny on earth, past and future: "The nations read on your forehead the seal of a curse; you are the world's horror, nature's shame; you are a reproach to God on earth." Pushkin understood, as did Tolstoy and Dostoevsky, that evil power, tyranny, is the culmination of evil on earth, the kingdom of the "Grand Inquisitor." The first tragic conflict of power and revolutionary freedom, the first uprising of freedom in history, is launched against a legal, patriarchal tyranny.

Pushkin gives a striking description of how the horrifying picture of the emperor Paul's murder rises up before him in that horrifying and phantasmal city [St. Petersburg]: "When the midnight star gleams on the darkening Neva . . . the pensive singer gazes on the tyrant's deserted monument sleeping ominously in the mist, the palace abandoned to oblivion — and hears the dreadful voice of Clio behind those dreadful walls; he sees vividly before his eyes the last hour of Caligula."

But here comes the surprising part: despite all his revulsion toward and hatred of tyranny, the poet sees with his unerring moral instinct and free moral judgment all the repulsiveness of the clandestine and treacherous regicide: "He sees — the clandestine murderers are on their way, decorated in ribbons and stars, intoxicated with wine and malice, insolence on their faces, fear in their hearts. The faithless guard is silent, the drawbridge silently lowered, the gates opened in the dark of night by the hired hand of treachery. . . . O shame! O horror of our times! Like brutes, the janissaries burst in! The infamous blows fall. . . . The crowned villain has perished."

Of course he is a villain, but even so, his murder is still underhanded, treacherous, bestial, inglorious. If one calls to mind all the details and sees everything as it really was, then one will feel not joy, but "shame and horror." Pushkin, even with his free spirit — this man who was a Christian, who could say that he "awakened kindly feeling with his lyre" — could not feel otherwise. But now another scene of regicide arises in the poet's imagination: the execution of Louis XVI. In no way can we label this man — a kindhearted family man, weak-willed and a little slow on the uptake — as a tyrant and a villain; it would be difficult to find truer words to describe him than the following: "O martyr to notorious blunders, who in the blast of recent storms laid down his royal head for his forebears."

If you mull over these words, another shade will rise before you of another "martyr to the blunders" inherited from his forebears: the shade of the last Russian emperor, whose temperament so closely resembled that of the last prerevolutionary French king. But now the poet's revulsion against regicide becomes even deeper and more substantial: this is no simple revulsion against regicide or execution; it is a condemnation of a crime and an iniquity committed by the people and their chosen tyrants — the murderer and his executioners: "Louis ascends to his death under the gaze of acquiescent posterity. He presses his de-crowned head to perfidy's bloody scaffold. The law is silent, the people — silent, the criminal blade falls. . . . And behold — a villainous royal purple is cast over, transferred onto the Gauls." Such is Pushkin's angry condemnation of Louis' execution. Here is what genuine freedom of moral judgment means, a freedom that pays no heed to the catchwords of the crowd, or to the tyranny of some revolutionary complex, common to revolutionary power and its leaders, that regards any king, any emperor, as a "despot, feasting in a luxurious palace."

I know of no one in Russia with a freer mind than Pushkin. Here is another example: he sympathizes in a certain sense with the Decembrists as fighters for freedom; he commiserates with and consoles them after their conviction; he writes the poem "In the depths of the Siberian mines . . ."; but his keen mocking intellect, his unerring artist's instinct, cannot help but see the incoherence of this first putsch, carried out by the nobility in the manner of the later "intelligentsia," for "Constantine and a constitution."

Pushkin knew no fear. He was noble-hearted and brave enough to tell Nicholas I: "I would have been with them [the Decembrists]," but he was also wise enough to realize that nothing could have come of their revolt. Pushkin could even discuss all this with Nicholas and speak in such a way that Nicholas called him "the most intelligent man in Russia."

The conflict between power and freedom constitutes the central theme of Pushkin's mature dramatic work. The tragedy of freedom is the eternal fate of humanity and the eternal theme of the great tragedians and poets from Aeschylus to Shakespeare and from Shakespeare to Goethe, Schiller, and our own Pushkin.[2]

2. *Prometheus Bound, Julius Caesar, Coriolanus, Egmont, William Tell, Don Carlos.*

The first act of this tragedy is the patriarchal tyranny of a legal despotism. The second act is the overthrowing of this tyranny in the name of revolutionary freedom. The third act will be the revolutionary terror and the beginnings of revolutionary tyranny. The fourth act: the overthrow of revolutionary tyranny and the triumph of lawful freedom.

Pushkin takes the French Revolution as the symbol or prototype for his portrayal of this constantly recurring historical rhythm. This revolution has remained the prototype — a terrifying symbol and a moral problem — for philosophers, poets, and politicians. Of course, Pushkin is not merely portraying the history of the French Revolution, but the fate of many revolutions to come. He himself identifies with "André Chénier," addressing the same goddess of freedom: "Reveal to me the noble trace of that sublime Gaul, whose daring hymns you yourself inspired in the midst of those renowned adversities."

Patriarchal monarchy is the childhood of nations. The power of the "papa-tsar" is a continuation of the power of the biological father. But the clash of the son's freedom with paternal despotism is inevitable, unless of course the father liberates his son voluntarily.[3] The conflict between power and freedom, obedience and rebellion, is inevitable in both personal and social life. Albert rebels against the evil will of his father ("The Covetous Knight"). But even a loving authority can be experienced as tyranny. "There is no tyranny stronger than the tyranny of parental love," as Schiller said. This is why no patriarchal idyll, no "enlightened absolutism" (though very seldom enlightened in actual fact) can crush the awakening of freedom. Ordinarily this freedom comes dressed in an aureole of heroism and idealism, and embodies a noble protest against the crimes and errors of the old regime. The revolution is experienced as a creative act, as the joy of liberation. This is its romantic, "Girondist" phase. Thus the second act of this historical drama begins: "The chains fell off. The law, founded on liberty, proclaimed equality, and we cried out: What bliss!"

But this bliss lasts only for a single moment. The romance and rhetoric of revolutionary freedom is supplanted by a loathsome reality: sacred freedom disappears "in fits of unruly blindness, in the despicable rage of the crowd"; it conceals itself under a "bloody shroud," in the midst of a "senseless and ruthless" revolt. Pushkin and Schiller — both of them poets of revolutionary freedom — portrayed this "despicable rage" (cf. Schiller's "Song of the Bell"). Neither Dostoevsky nor Tolstoy doubted that some

---

3. "Shall I ever see a people finally liberated, and slavery struck down by the will of a tsar?" [Pushkin].

kind of "demonic possession" was showing its face here. And how many times has it appeared and will it appear in all sorts of "liberations"?

But the revolt and chaos of arbitrariness pass quickly, like natural disasters. A new act of the drama begins, even more dismal, and seemingly hopeless. "The impotent rebels cannot endure their own freedom, and search for someone to bow down to" (Dostoevsky). This is the origin of the "Council of People's Deputies" and the "Revolutionary Tribunal" (terms used in the French Revolution): "the Council of infamous leaders, those despotic executioners. . . ."

But these councils rarely take counsel with anybody. There can be no class or party dictatorship — every dictatorship ends up in the hands of a single individual. Any kind of freedom, even within the ruling party, is abolished: "Over the corpse of headless freedom looms the misshapen executioner — odious, dismal and bloody, the Apostle of death, he destines his victims to weary Hades with the flick of a finger." The victims here are the members of their own Jacobin party.

Now the tragedy of freedom reaches its point of highest tension: any kind of "liberty" dies; free will and resistance are beheaded. Here is how the "free genius" of our Pushkin describes the horror and misery of this second tyranny: "O misery! O thoughtless dream! Where are liberty and the law? An axe alone holds sway over us. We've overthrown the kings, and chosen a murderer and his executioners to be our king. O horror! O infamy!" This is the extraordinary dialectic of revolutions; this is its recurrent rhythm. A revolution destroys the very freedom for the sake of which it arose in the first place, and gives birth to tyranny, that is, to "conservatism" and reaction once again — a tyranny that struggles to preserve itself and fears above all a new revolution and a new uprising of freedom. The mass of sins and errors heaped up by a legal power are avenged by the mass of crimes piled up by a lawless tyranny.

And yet the ideal of freedom cannot be destroyed. Never does Pushkin's "liberty" enter onto the path of pure reaction, the path of the "Grand Inquisitor," of Pobedonostsev; Pushkin will never gloat maliciously and say: So that's where you end up with your glorious freedom! On the contrary: now, more than ever, freedom remains sacred to him, and he has faith in its eventual victory: "But you, sacred freedom, pure goddess — no, you are not to blame for the riots of unruly blindness, the despicable rage of the crowd, you hid yourself from us: your healing chalice covered with a bloody shroud. But you will come again with vengeance and glory — and once again your enemies will fall."

The poet does indeed believe that no one will ever be able to subdue, enslave, or completely suppress this primal element of liberty. Every tyranny is condemned to fall, both morally and by nature. That this is so is confirmed by the scientist, Doctor Pavlov: the reflex of freedom is an unconditioned reflex, or an innate instinct. The poet has good reason to believe in the fall of this second [revolutionary] despotism, as he believed in the fall of the first: "And the hour will come . . . and it is very near: You will fall, tyrant! Indignation will finally leap up. The cries of the fatherland will awaken weary fate."

However, times and terms are unknown here. The rhythm of history is not an astronomical one, and exact predictions are impossible: "the historian is not an astronomer and providence is not algebra" (this striking aphorism is also Pushkin's). "Thermidor" may linger on for years, for centuries even, and come to an end only with the demise of the state itself. Rome never restored its republican liberties and perished when the empire lost its legitimate foundation. In a certain sense, Pushkin has it right: "Freedom gave rise to Rome, and slavery destroyed her." The tragedy of freedom lies precisely in this incertitude: what if this is the place where history comes to a stop? The triumph of absolute evil may seem complete: tyranny knows how to preserve itself; nations and peoples may accommodate themselves and submit. It is this circumstance that gives rise to hopelessness and resignation and contempt for humanity: "Graze on, complacent nations! Honor's call will not awaken you. Why are freedoms given to herds: they're fit only for slaughter or shearing."

This is only a passing moment, however; the genius of freedom cannot "abandon hope forever." The third act is not the last. Evil, just like a disease, is not eternal: it comes to an end either through death or through recovery and redemption. As long as there is life, the reflex of freedom will continue to function as well. "Honor's call" still resounds in the soul. Against the second tyranny, which gave rise to and then shackled the mighty current of freedom, the poet appeals for a second revolution, more powerful and wildly elemental than the first: "Who has stopped you, waves? Who has fettered your mighty course? Who has diverted the turbulent flood into a quiet and overgrown pond? You, winds, storms, stir up the waters; bring ruin on the fatal stronghold — Where are you, thunderstorm, symbol of freedom! Come rushing over the waters of slavery."

History's fourth act is the inevitable liquidation of the second tyranny and the second despotism ("those autocratic executioners"). But how can this be done without turning the process into an eternal recurrence, an eternal succession of revolution and reaction? Neither the one nor the other provides true freedom. Genuine freedom is the freedom of creativity, but creativity requires a certain order and tranquillity. Permanent revolution is just as inimical to creativity as tyranny. This is why Pushkin expresses his social ideal as "the liberty and repose of nations."

They are attainable only where powerful laws are firmly conjoined with sacred freedom. In other words, freedom is secured and realized only in the form of law and justice. If we express ourselves in modern juridical language, we could say that Pushkin's wisdom — his prophetic wisdom — consists in his upholding, in the "cruel age" in which he lived, the value of a liberal, law-abiding state, for which humanity is nonetheless obliged to struggle. It was Pushkin himself who called himself a liberal. In every situation, he always was and will always be on the side of those who choose freedom rather than a totalitarian submission to power, even if that power were to guarantee everyone a full pot of porridge, dearest of all things to the "day laborer, the slave of necessity and cares." But what exactly is "totalitarian power," what is despotism and whom may we call a despot? There is a simple and precise answer: he who puts his own power and force of might above right and the law.[4] The masses along with their leaders — the nation itself in its "contemptible rage" or its rulers and monarchs — may all be tyrants. "And woe, woe to the tribes . . . where either people or monarchs control the law."

Only a free and law-abiding state justifies power and gives it the right to exist (otherwise power is "from the devil"). Pushkin says to rulers and tsars: "Bow your head first beneath the law's trustworthy canopy, and the liberty and repose of nations will stand as the eternal guardian of your throne." Otherwise we will never be done with the investing and dethroning of power. Byzantine and Russian despotism knows all about the succession of patricides and filicides. Someone has called such a state structure a "monarchy limited by regicide." "And learn today, O tsars: neither punishments nor rewards nor the shelter of dungeons and altars are reliable protection for you."

But Pushkin's wisdom goes deeper. The law that determines the structure of life in the state, the law established by legislative authority and to which that authority adheres, is not thereby the most absolute and eternal law. Until this law is revoked, it must be adhered to, as "positive right," "positive law" or decree; but it is subject to appraisal from the standpoint of a higher truth and justice, which may require its alteration or abolition. For example, the right to hold serfs is a violation of human

---

4. Lenin, absolutely correctly, defines dictatorship as power based on force, not law.

rights from this higher standpoint, and a law that establishes slavery is lawless from the standpoint of the higher law of truth and justice.

Just what is this "higher law," which stands above the legal system, the state, the nation, and the powers that be? From a religious point of view, it is the higher divine law of truth and justice; from the viewpoint of legal philosophy, it is the higher idea of natural law or the just law. This idea posits for the law-abiding state the eternal task of perfection, the never-ending quest for greater harmony and justice. Pushkin formulates this higher truth with striking brevity and concision: "Rulers! . . . You stand higher than the nation, but higher than you is the eternal law!" No kind of positive law or code of laws is eternal; therefore, the "eternal law" that stands over nations and power can only mean the eternal idea, the eternal task of the just law.

Pushkin is one of those people who wants neither to rule nor to be ruled, who are free from both the lust for domination and the lust for servility. Pushkin's "liberty" is our "liberty," which is universal. The poet along with the novelist sets forth the tragic problems, but he does not resolve them in the scientific or philosophical sense. It is not the poet's business to formulate political doctrines. But he does possess an intuition of higher principles; he hears the "divine word"; he has a feeling for what is sacred and what is despicable, and conveys his feeling with elemental force — he "burns human hearts with his word." Therefore it is not only professional Pushkin scholars who should remember, think, and talk about Pushkin. The Pushkinists do historical research on Pushkin: they study his temperament, his life, his environment, the pots and pans of his poetical trade. All this is endlessly valuable, but it is all oriented toward the past, whereas Pushkin himself gazed into the future and even into the eternal. If it is true that "poets are teachers of wisdom," as Plato said, then prophetic wisdom is the poet's highest gift — one which Pushkin possessed, and valued above all else: "The poet punishes, the poet crowns; he strikes evildoers with the thunder of everlasting arrows far into distant posterity."

CHAPTER 2

Pushkin's Liberty (Individual Freedom)

Revolutionary freedom, political freedom, civil and legal freedom — all these do not exhaust nor do they convey the genuine essence of freedom, but serve merely as the condition of its possibility, the means by which it may be achieved and defended. The true depth and height of freedom are revealed only in the concrete life of a person, an individual person or the person of the nation as a whole. Law and the state are only the organizational framework for this freedom. Pushkin had a lively feeling for and creatively expressed all the multiple meanings and degrees of freedom; he understood its depth and height. The lower, deep-lying, irrational freedom modulates into the willfulness of the passions ("so ravishing is the language of mad and turbulent passions"), or, if we probe even more deeply, into the unconscious, elemental might of the soul. We must turn to the following astonishing lines by Pushkin if we want to grasp immediately just what this kind of freedom involves:

> Why does the wind twist round in a gully, stirring up the earth, blowing the dust around, while the ship on a stagnant sea eagerly awaits its breezes? Why does the terrible and gloomy eagle fly away from the mountains, past the towers, to light on a rotten stump? Ask him! Why does young Desdemona love her blackamoor? Because — for the wind, the eagle, a maiden's heart — there is no law! Be proud — you, poet, are like them. For you likewise there is no law! [*Egyptian Nights*]

What is depicted here is the cosmic, natural, animal element, incomprehensible and not subordinate to human law. It is dangerous and some-

15

times destructive, but beautiful all the same in its mysterious force. Gershenzon picked up on this element in Pushkin.[1] Citing these amazing and insufficiently remarked-upon verses, he says: Over the boundless Russian plain, from the Arctic circle to the warm seas in the south, the twisting whirlwind rushes, impetuously and aimlessly; and the impetuous Russian soul rushes along with it. Gogol knew this Russian element early on, and portrayed it in the Russian troika that rushes freely and impetuously . . . whither and why — no one knows. Tyutchev knew it well ("the poet is all-powerful, like the elements"). Dostoevsky portrayed it constantly; Tolstoy knew it and bore it within himself. We cannot understand Pushkin if we do not take into account the insanely elemental nature of his soul. So much has been said, mistakenly, about his "sobriety and harmoniousness" — but his early years, his marriage, his violent demise all contradict this view. Can a sober good sense declare: "All, all that threatens perdition harbors inexplicable delights for a mortal heart"? [Nikolay] Karamzin said of Pushkin: "A splendid talent indeed: a pity that there's no peace in his soul and not the least bit of prudence in his head." "The Feast in the Time of the Plague" is the negation of any kind of sobriety and tranquil harmoniousness. The chairman's song is described as a "free, boisterous, bacchic song," and what it hymns is the antithesis of sobriety, that is, intoxication, the antithesis of reason, that is, madness. [Fyodor] Tyutchev understood the meaning of songs like these: "O, sing not those terrible songs of ancient, native chaos."

Here we must admit that poetry is impossible without a certain madness and intoxication. The artist creates in a kind of divine frenzy — so says Plato. Poetry creates "as if in a dream," unconsciously, like the Pythia [the priestess of Apollo]. The "fever of rhymes," the "sacred delirium of poetry" are liberated from any of the dictates of reason. However, it is impossible to construct poetry, or art in general, on the basis of madness alone: mind is also necessary. And Pushkin surely had one — a mind that was both sober and insightful; and if there was insufficient prudence in his life, there was wisdom enough in his poetry. Art is not chaos, but it is a cosmos, that is, beauty; and this beauty is created out of chaos, from the elemental play of forces. Art harbors both of these elements: consciousness and the unconscious, Apollo and Dionysus, harmony and dissonance, sacred madness and holy wisdom; and the only harmony worth having is one that allows for dissonance. Dostoevsky says, "Beauty will

---

1. Vysheslavtsev is paraphrasing here from the famous essay by M. O. Gershenzon, *Pushkin's Wisdom* (Petrograd, 1919). Trans.

save the world." Saint Seraphim of Sarov and Father Sergei Bulgakov talk about immediately intuited [*umnyi*] beauty, uncreated beauty. Not without reason and not in vain has the epithet "divinely beautiful" been applied so often to high art. The Russian people have been endowed with a sensitivity to the beautiful; and our music, our poetry, and, above all, Pushkin bear witness to it. But service to beauty, the adulation of beauty, even the perception of beauty are freedom, the liberation of the spirit, and it cannot tolerate any kind of violence, any kind of constraint. You can order people to lie, to flatter, to grovel, but you cannot force people to like what they do not like. Genuine art is always "free art."

Of course, Pushkin provides a poetry, not a philosophy, of freedom. But his poetry contains wisdom, and this wisdom, clothed in beauty, is readily discernible to the philosopher. Here is the content of that wisdom: freedom is precious at all levels, from the lowest to the highest. It is false to say that the elemental quality of natural forces and passions is evil in itself. On the contrary, this elemental quality is the condition for creation, since the cosmos has been created out of chaos: and this is as true for absolute divine creation as it is for the human "arts." In response to Job's demand for lawful justice and a rationally comprehensible Providence, God reveals to him the irrationality of the mysterious, elemental, divine energies. Afterward Job bows down before this mystery: "Then the Lord answered Job out of the whirlwind: . . . 'Where were you when I laid the foundation of the earth? Tell me, if you have understanding. . . . Have the gates of death been revealed to you? . . . Can you bind the chains of the Pleiades, or loose the cords of Orion?'" The stupid ostrich, the bold horse, the terrible, invulnerable Behemoth — have you any idea why such creatures exist? (Job 38–41).

These natural cosmic forces exist in the human being as well. The unconscious freedom of arbitrariness has been given to me by God, who "called me forth out of nothingness, filled my soul with passion, disturbed my mind with doubt." Such is the irrational profundity of freedom at its most elemental level, the level of elemental arbitrariness (the "lesser freedom" according to Augustine). But freedom extends not only into the depths but also up to the heights. Below it is the "abyss," but above it is the "Spirit of the Lord." Pushkin attained this higher level of freedom (the "greater freedom" according to Augustine) through his creative work. Genuine art is free art — the genius always a "free genius." But its liberty is twofold: it requires the lower, elemental, natural, cosmic freedom — as well as the higher, spiritual, mystic, divine freedom, that freedom about which it is written: "Where the Spirit of the Lord is, there is freedom"

[2 Cor. 3:17]. In the human soul this higher freedom is a response to the divine call, which summons him to a creative mission, a "holy sacrifice." But this sacrifice, this mission, is not slavery; it is not even the "yoke of the law," but just the opposite: it is a voluntary calling, which is the spirit's freedom, the same about which it is said: "you were called to freedom, brethren!" [Gal. 5:13]. The free genius interprets his calling as a mission to serve beauty and truth, as a poetic and prophetic mission. He hears the "divine word," he fulfills the divine will: "behold and attend!" From this will, he receives the higher freedom of spiritual insight and comprehension: "And I heard the shuddering of heaven and the flight of the angels on high and the movement of the sea creatures under the water and the growing of the vine down below." And yet another freedom was granted to him: the freedom of the prophetic word, which fears neither kingdom nor priesthood, the freedom to "burn human hearts with his word" ["The Prophet"].

Such is the higher and lower freedom. There are gradations between them, sometimes an upward leap: from the willfulness of the passions to the acceptance of a higher will ("Thy will be done"), from elemental natural forces to the creativity of culture, to the veneration of the higher values sacred to humanity. Free creativity — but in essence the whole of human existence as well — oscillates between these two poles: between depth and height ("Out of the depths have I called unto thee, O Lord!" Ps. 130), between the depth of the natural elements and the height of the divine spirit. Natural forces, natural drives and passions, are necessary for creative work, even for life itself; but at the same time their free arbitrariness can "threaten perdition." Creative freedom is the overcoming of chaos, contradiction, chance. The harmony of the cosmos is created out of opposing natural forces. This is the principle of any creativity — whether artistic or moral. Creativity is the transition from the freedom of arbitrariness to the freedom of self-control. Freedom means autonomy, self-determination, independence: "I myself make decisions, act, choose, evaluate." But what exactly is it that "I myself" have in myself? Answer: all the energies of body and soul. Dostoevsky constantly talks about this self-control, this self-mastery. The Russian's task is to master the unconscious, elemental force — the Russian element — that he feels in his soul. This is his moral task, the condition of his morality. Pushkin was perfectly conscious of this; his moral judgment is distinguished by a rare probity and sensitivity. He never confused good and evil; he never stationed himself beyond good and evil; he had a profound sense of sin and repentance: "in vain do I strive toward the heights of Zion: sin is pursuing me, dogging my heels": and further, "reading over my life with revulsion, I tremble and curse." The ascent to a higher freedom is accomplished through an autonomous, free moral judgment. In Pushkin's case, nothing distorted this freedom of moral judgment — neither outside influence, nor coercion, nor personal ambition, nor the pressure of public opinion, nor any dictate from society.

CHAPTER 3

The Problem of Freedom and Necessity

The Significance of This Problem in Life:
The Russian Materialists and Marx

The significance of the antinomy[1] of freedom and necessity is apparent not only in philosophy but also in life. To demand its resolution is in no way a piece of philosophical pedantry, for the philosophical contradiction harbors a vital sociopsychological one.

To proceed from the idea of absolute freedom and arrive at absolute slavery is not nowadays just a philosophical contradiction (as it was for Shigalyov in Dostoevsky's *Demons*). We are confronted here with a certain inherent tragedy in the personal and sociopsychic setup. It constitutes an independent problem.

The Russian materialists, positivists, and atheists (à la Bazarov [the hero of Turgenev's *Fathers and Sons*]) were still decent people, well-meaning "idealists" who burned with love for humanity. It was about these types that Vladimir Solovyov remarked: "Man has descended from the apes, ergo, let us love man!" They did not notice any contradiction in this. But then love for humanity began to undergo a transformation into hatred for living people; the humane Belinsky called for a universal guillotine. The

---

1. An antinomy is a logical contradiction harboring a system of contraries that is actually harmonious. Kant resolves antinomies in such a way that despite their apparent incompatibility both thesis and antithesis remain true, albeit in different senses. They help to unfold the actual system of being, as a harmony of differing and opposing senses and significances: for concrete reality does not have one single, unambiguous meaning, but many — it is pregnant with meaning.

20

worldview of materialism and atheism did not hinder this development in the least, for it recognized no absolute "mystical" interdictions. Dostoevsky's Grand Inquisitor still talked about love for people, but what flowed out of this love was a complete contempt for the living person and an extravagantly organized inquisition.

Finally Marx decisively cast aside and came to loathe the jargon of humanity and love; faithful to his materialism and atheism, he did not talk about morality and justice. He did not remain faithful, however, but embarked on a path of moralizing immoralism — one of the most repulsive psychological mind-sets. Marx ceaselessly moralized, exposing and condemning his enemies, while at the same time he himself intrigued, lied, and slandered (the Bakunin affair), exhibiting a consistent immoralism.

Marxism moralizes in its exposure of "exploitation," while simultaneously being immoral in its social and political practice. Moral protest makes an appearance in order to provide a basis for and justify hatred, only to vanish once again so as not to interfere with the workings of that hatred.

Why didn't Marx deepen his concept of "exploitation" and realize that it is based on an admission of the value of the person as an end in himself?[2] Because the idea of the person is essentially Christian in origin and bound up with an ethic of love. Marx found all that repulsive and antipathetic. What he needed was an ethic of hate. Positive values were unnecessary and dangerous for him. They could lead him to the "sacred" and force him to bow down before it. He needed a negative value to underpin hatred and negation, and he found it in exploitation.

Negative moralizing is by no means an expression of love; it is a function of hatred. Mephistopheles was the greatest master of tracking down negative values; his solemn mission, as he saw it, was the infallible detection of evil; and in this sense he was the greatest moralist, in no way inferior to any puritan.

An extraordinarily keen eye for evil and a valiant attempt at reducing everything to unworthy motives constitutes the essence of some temperaments. The method of reduction to the lowest is equally typical of Marx and Freud, whether it is a reduction to "class interests" or to the sexual drive. (This has been correctly pointed out by S. L. Frank.) Scheler has labeled such a method "speculating on debasement." In no way does this method result in the "sublimation" discussed by Freud, but rather in a profanation of the sublime, a destruction of the feeling of reverence. Freud's

---

2. Cf. my *Philosophical Poverty of Marxism* (Frankfurt am Main, 1952), §28.

psychoanalysis can degenerate into the mental illness of erotomania (which is not to deny his scientific discoveries, of course). Marx's materialism degenerates into his contempt for people. After all, is there any good reason to pay reverence to the descendants of apes? Marx hates and despises the bourgeoisie and his socialist comrades (e.g., Bakunin, Lassalle) in equal measure. If everything around him was depreciated, he himself grew in value. Herein lies the secret of "speculating on debasement."

Why did Marx cling to his materialism, atheism, and determinism, and take pains not to notice the clear incompatibility of such a worldview with any kind of moralizing, and specifically with his condemnation of "exploitation"? Because atheistic materialism bestows a total freedom from any qualms about the means when the end is the seizure of power and dictatorship over the proletariat, both of which are imperative for a revolutionary "chief." Atheistic materialism furnishes a perfect opportunity for positioning oneself "beyond good and evil" — a great advantage for the "professional revolutionary and politician."

These are the psychological reasons why Marx was unable to recognize the ethical principle underlying his concept of "exploitation," why he was unable to recognize the well-known antinomy of freedom and necessity or to appraise correctly the significance of the antithesis. All of that was shoved down into the unconscious and suppressed. Moral judgments make their appearance in consciousness only to serve as condemnations. To acknowledge them any further would be unnecessary and dangerous. Positive values — love, class cooperation, solidarity, the law — were unnecessary and even harmful in his eyes: they weakened class hatred.

Positing the Problem of Freedom and Necessity

The antinomy of freedom and necessity appears under differing aspects:

> "Existence determines consciousness" — no, "consciousness determines existence."
>
> "Everything is nature, everything is matter" (it is impossible to escape from natural necessity) — no, "everything is not nature or matter, and a leap from the kingdom of necessity to the kingdom of freedom is possible."
>
> "Everything is determined by causal necessity" — no, "not everything is determined by causal necessity, a free purposiveness still exists."
>
> "It is impossible to begin a causal sequence, because the chain of

causality stretches back to infinity" — no, "it is possible to begin a causal sequence, because there is a causality by way of freedom."

Kant was the first to formulate this antinomy in his "dialectic." One could say that without his dialectic of freedom and necessity, Fichte, Schelling, and Hegel would have been impossible. They altered and deepened Kant's solution in many ways, but all of nineteenth- and twentieth-century philosophy constantly returned to this problem: every great philosopher, even those who were by no means Kantians, has carried on this dialogue with Kant. It was Kant who introduced genuine dialectic into modern philosophy, and he did so by means of his antinomies. They persist, although other solutions have been given for them that deviate quite far from Kant's. Kant's third antinomy, the antinomy of freedom and necessity, is present in any kind of philosophizing, even in the Marxist system.

During the "renaissance" of the late nineteenth and early twentieth century, Russian philosophy undertook a critical study of Kant, Fichte, Hegel, and the neo-Kantians, absorbed the finest achievements of the classical dialectic preserved through the ages, and outlined a solution to this antinomy that then received confirmation in Western philosophy.

There is no way to show here all the achievements of science and philosophy over the last hundred years, citing scholars from every nation, or to go over the whole dialectical path that leads to this solution at the pinnacle of philosophical culture. I do consider it necessary, however, to indicate the positive way out of the contradictions, to outline the results of the age-old work of thought. Here are those results.

The antinomy of freedom and necessity by itself is not bound up with any specific system of philosophy, or with any specific "metaphysics." It is present in all systems. The greatness of Kant is that he posed it most sharply, leading finally to the dialectic of thesis and antithesis. The problems of Kant are immortal, but not his solutions.

A genuine resolution of the antinomy should be free from all "isms" — free from materialism as well as from subjective idealism. It should not even be based on the Kantian dichotomy of the "phenomenon" and the "thing-in-itself."

It should be rooted in the very dialectical nature of existence (the "ontological") so that it participates in the best traditions of Hellenic and Russian philosophy. For dialectic must be learned first of all from the Greeks (as the Greek word itself indicates), and only after that from Kant, Fichte, and Hegel.

The thesis derives from the universal causal necessity encompassing the whole of nature. It allows for no exceptions. Even man is not an exception: he is created by nature and belongs to the kingdom of nature. In this sense he is not free: there is no freedom from the causal nexus. Causal conditionality (determination) does not allow for a break in causality. Such a break would be an absolute chance event, but freedom is not a "matter of chance." On the contrary, it is a struggle against blind chance.

Freedom is a consciously purposive activity, and such activity is in no way chance, arbitrariness, or indeterminacy; on the contrary, it is strictly conditioned, but conditioned otherwise than motion in nature. Man cannot evade natural determination, but he can stand under the power of another determination, another pattern of regularity, constituting another degree of being. Man contains within himself many levels of existence: he is mechanical nature (physicochemical nature), biological nature: but could it be that he is not only "nature," but something even greater and higher: civilization and culture?

Here a new level is revealed, a new sphere of being, the sphere of consciously purposive activity, in short, what I have called the sphere of freedom. It must have its own kind of conditionality: autonomous, but in no way violating the other, lower determinations of natural necessity. In this way the antinomy could be resolved.

The trouble is that a consciously free conditionality in pursuit of goals seems incompatible with natural conditionality: it claims to begin causal sequences; it does not admit of a passive subjugation to natural necessity; it even wants, as it were, to rule over the latter — in a word, it excludes the sovereignty of nature from its kingdom of freedom. Here is the sticking point of the antinomy, but here also is the key to its solution. What if conscious purposiveness does not exclude causality but, on the contrary, includes it within itself?

The Resolution of the Antinomy of Freedom and Necessity

What is "free action"? What is its ontological essence? It is primarily:

1. a goal, proposed by consciousness, and consequently:
2. a search for and invention of means that are capable of reaching that goal, and, finally:
3. the setting in motion of the sequence of means which would realize that goal.

24

Now it is immediately clear, from the very beginning, that the choice of means is a choice of causes that are capable of producing the desired effect. The conscious striving toward a goal is nothing other than a sequence of causes that will produce the desired effect. Conscious purposiveness does not exclude causal necessity; on the contrary, it presupposes and contains it.

What is especially remarkable is this: causal necessity not only does not contradict or cancel out free purposiveness: on the contrary, it is the necessary condition of its possibility. Only under circumstances where the laws of causal necessity remain inviolate is man able to reach his goals through a sequence of means, for a sequence of means is in fact a sequence of causes.

If nature sometimes upheld and at other times violated the laws of mechanical causality, for example, the laws of gravity, then one could not build a house, for the house could all of a sudden topple down on one's head. If nature functioned in a free and arbitrary way, one would incontrovertibly lose all freedom of action: one would become a slave to chance or perhaps a slave to those freely acting spirits that populate nature.

The result is clear: a free will acting in pursuit of goals is possible only in the kind of world that is causally determined throughout. "Indeterminism" would destroy freedom of action (a paradoxical result of the dialectic of freedom).

Trying to salvage freedom of action by eliminating, limiting, or weakening causal necessity would clearly be insupportable. On the contrary, the firmer and more absolute this natural necessity that man has succeeded in discovering and ascertaining, the more secure for him the sphere of purposiveness, the sphere of free creativity.

Free purposiveness presupposes and contains natural necessity, but not vice versa. Natural necessity is impartial to any of man's goals and desires: it is an "indifferent nature"; it can serve in equal measure goals that are diametrically opposed; it can kill and save; it can just as well not serve any goals whatsoever, functioning in relation to them like blind chance. But free purposiveness is not indifferent in relation to natural necessity; it is ceaselessly cognizing it, weighing it up, and coming to terms with it. After all, this purposiveness reaches its goals by means of causal sequences, combining those sequences and constructing a new form of being out of the matter, as it were, of natural elements.

A statue preserves in itself all the properties of matter (marble or bronze), making use of all the laws of physicochemical existence; but the statue itself is a new and higher form of existence that emerges from the matter. A house preserves and contains the bricks with all their physicochemical properties, but the bricks do not contain the house: they do not predetermine its architecture. This is why a house is a new and higher level of being, a higher form, created out of lower matter. A brick, in its turn, is also a form created out of matter, that is, from clay: a brick is a form in relation to the clay, but it is matter or material in relation to the building.

Thus Aristotle depicted the interrelation of levels of being through the opposition between form and matter. Being is not homogeneous; it is made up of a multitude of levels. Moreover, every higher level of being presupposes and contains the lower, but not vice versa; and this is why every higher level is a new form of being, for which the previous level serves as its "matter."

Free purposiveness is just such a new and higher level of being, just such a new form of being, which presupposes and contains, as its matter/material, the lower level of natural necessity. The antinomy of freedom and necessity cannot be resolved if you picture these two forms — the sphere of nature and the sphere of freedom — as standing toe to toe and battling over territory with each other. Freedom and necessity are antitheses, but they are not mutually exclusive. Rather, the one is contained within the other.

This separate, extremely subtle dialectical opposition has been expressed by Aristotle in terms of the interrelation of form and matter, and by Hegel, who follows him here in principle, with his basic dialectical concept (an essentially untranslatable one). Here is what Hegel's concept means: all the regularities of the lower level of being are "raised" to a higher level and are preserved in it, as matter is preserved in a new form; and at the same time these lower regularities are, as it were, dissolved in the higher; they lose their significance, while remaining self-evident; they are "eliminated," or, more precisely, they are transformed beyond recognition. Thus marble is transformed into a spiritualized beauty, a physical sound wave into a symphony; and in just such a way natural necessity is transformed into creative freedom.

This special interrelation of the levels of being pervades all of being and creates a special hierarchy of being: the biological includes and contains the physicochemical — but not vice versa: the psychic presupposes and in a certain sense contains the biological (the organism); finally, the spiritual being of a free person, one who cognizes and acts, presupposes and contains its psyche and bodily organism. Spirit is not at all indifferent to the life of the body, although the functions of bodily life are indifferent to the spirit. "Spirit" is not at all that being which the materialists fear so much, nor is it the spirit of psychics and spiritualists. There may be no such thing as a bodiless spirit roaming freely about, but what unquestionably does exist is embodied spirit, or spiritualized flesh. "Spirit" denotes a special level of being that no species of materialism can deny. This level has its own determination, its own set of patterns, expressed in separate categories that are not found in nature or in the science of nature.

We designate as "spiritual" being the being of a freely acting and cognizing person in order to distinguish this level from the lower, material levels of being. If materialism prefers to call this level "spiritual matter," then we can only point to the ugliness of such a term. But the main quarrel is not about terminology, but lies in the dialectical necessity of acknowledging a new level, a new form of being, possessing new categories.

Thus free purposiveness is a new determination of being, which presupposes and contains the determination of causal necessity. Could it be that dialectical materialism might find such a resolution of the antinomy appealing? Especially since any "means of production," any machine, provides an illustration of it. A machine is a sequence of means by which a freely posited goal is realized; and, at the same time, a machine is the purest model of mechanical causality. One more difficulty can be resolved in a satisfactory manner: "socialism is, and is not, a science." This antinomy can be resolved in the following way: Socialism is not a science, but an ethics, insofar as it proposes goals and ideals; but socialism is a science, or becomes "scientific," insofar as it seeks out the means for realizing its goals scientifically, that is, through the mastery of the causal nexus and the "iron laws" of economics (provided that such things really exist).

The Basic Categories of Freedom: The System of Values

At first glance, it seems that Marxism would have no trouble accepting this resolution of the antinomy of freedom and necessity, a resolution that has the added advantage of not being bound up with any kind of dogmatic metaphysics. However, things are not that simple. Insofar as "diamat" [*dia*lectical *mat*erialism] is dialectical, it can and even should accept this resolution; but insofar as it is materialist, it cannot do so.

To demonstrate this, we need to lay out the whole semantic content of this new determination of being, which I have called, in brief, "free purposiveness." Purposiveness first proposes a goal and then deliberates over and searches for the means to accomplish it. The goal is that which does not exist in the real world, which is foreseen and anticipated in the future. The goal is that which does not really exist, but should exist. So where exactly is this "goal"? It exists only in consciousness, in the subject; it does not exist in "objective reality." Deliberating over and devising the means to accomplish the goal also take place only in consciousness, in the cognizing subject. Only when a goal has been proposed and the means found — when the subject has completed these two spiritual acts — does the third act begin, the act of realization. We might call this act the "embodiment of the idea," its materialization (the ideal project of the house gets embodied in actual matter).

It is perfectly apparent that here, when it comes to the understanding of real activity, one cannot do without the opposition between ideal and real, spiritual and material being. The being of consciousness in this case determines material being, and not vice versa.

In this way purposive activity presupposes a "dramatis persona," the subject of the action, who transforms and alters objective reality. There simply is no category of the subject, or dramatis persona, if one assumes that being determines consciousness. This category cannot exist in a consistent materialism, which is, in fact, a monistic determinism.

Thus conscious purposiveness requires a category of the person as well as a category of the goal pursued by various means. But this is not enough: we want to know what determines the goal. The choice of a goal is not accidental or absolutely indeterminate, although it is a free choice. But freedom follows its own rules, which differ from those of nature. Necessary goals do exist, but the necessity in this case is qualitatively different from natural necessity. This is the necessity of the "should," and not of the "is":[3] the necessity of appealing to freedom, for the "should" can only be addressed to a free subject. No one says that fire "should not" have burned down the house, but anyone will tell you that the person who set fire to the house "should not" have done so.

The free person, acting in the pursuit of goals, comes under the category of the "should." But the determination does not stop here. What kinds of goals are defined as those that should be pursued? Those that are deemed valuable. The judgment of value lies (consciously or unconsciously) at the foundation of every positing of a goal, every action, every decision. As with any judgment, it can be mistaken and subjective, neither can it be true and objective. Truth and objectivity reside in the values themselves.

---

3. The necessity of that which does not exist but should exist.

No philosophy can deny this, for the various systems quarrel only about what exactly it is that is truly valuable, and not about whether something valuable exists — this is always taken for granted. Science is an objective value, social organization is an objective value, the economy and technology are objective values, the person is an objective value, and finally life is an objective value (what is more, life itself is the ceaseless — conscious or unconscious — assessment of value).

The manifold activities that fill up a person's life do not present an unsystematic chaos, but form some system (always imperfect), some "form of activity." This system or "form" is defined by a system of values, which the person in question recognizes and incorporates into his life (this is what the person ultimately loves and values).

The free person, the dramatis persona of history and of personal life, is a separate category. It is not only consciousness of the goal and deliberation about the means to achieve it (and therefore the cognition of causes); it is first and foremost the cognition of the system of values and the energy of will directed toward the realization of those values. Without this there is no free person. The person is the highest unity of the subject that cognizes, evaluates, and acts.

The person, individual and conciliar [*sobornyi*], the people, the nation (but not the class), are themselves the most precious phenomena of culture. Every nation and every culture has its own system of values, which it "cultivates," and its own highest value and sense of the "sacred," which it honors religiously.

CHAPTER 4

The Metaphysics of Freedom

Law and the Kingdom of God

Every great religion contains and reveals some system of values; in other words, it proposes some ethical doctrine. It would be an enormous mistake to assume that all religions reveal exactly the same values and coincide in their ethical doctrines.

Christ revealed and announced to the world a totally new system of values, expressed in a single symbol, the "kingdom of God." This is his "revelation," his "good news," and his "New Testament." "The gospel of the kingdom of God" — this is the primary and simplest definition of the teaching of Jesus Christ: "the kingdom of God is at hand" (Mark 1:14, 15; Matt. 3:2; 4:17, 23). This kingdom of God, or heavenly kingdom, is absolutely valuable and absolutely desired; it is what we believe in and hope for: "Thy kingdom come." The parables describe the "kingdom" as the highest value, for the sake of which it is worth giving up everything else; as a pearl beyond price, as a treasure buried in the earth. It is the ultimate goal of human strivings.

This new system of values, the New Testament, stands in the strongest opposition to the old. The whole Sermon on the Mount is built on this constantly repeated opposition: "You have heard that it was said to the men of old . . . but I say to you . . ." (Matt. 5:27-44, passim). The righteousness of the scribes and Pharisees is contrasted to another, higher righteousness without which one cannot enter the kingdom of heaven (Matt. 5:20). In this contrast, the old system of values is most often understood as the concept of law (Torah): "The law and the prophets were until John: since then the good news of the kingdom of God is preached" (Luke

16:16; Matt. 11:12, 13). Or, as Paul says, "the old has passed away, now everything is new" [2 Cor. 5:17]. Indeed, the righteousness of the "scribes and Pharisees," that is, the Jewish scholars and spiritual leaders, consists precisely in the most stringent and punctilious fulfillment of the letter of the law. Law is the highest value of Old Testament religious ethics, and quite probably of pre-Christian ethics in general.

Law and Grace

What stands opposed to the law is not a "yoke," a "burden" (the "heavy burdens" of Matt. 23:4), a command (an imperative) or intimidation, but rather the alleviation of burdens, liberation, the invitation to a feast, joy, and bliss. The kingdom of God is the bliss proclaimed in the Beatitudes: it is the joy granted to human beings, salvation, sublime beauty and "enchantment," or grace.

It would be totally incorrect to assume that the opposition between law and grace was laid down only by Paul, and that Paul's Christianity is some separate kind of Christianity. Paul is the first Christian philosopher, the one who contributed the most to the Christian understanding of the revelation, and yet he is in every way faithful to that revelation. The opposition between law and grace, law and love, law and the kingdom of God, runs through all the Gospels, and is precisely formulated as the basic principle of Christianity in the prologue of John's Gospel: "the law was given through Moses; grace and truth came through Jesus Christ" (John 1:17).

Christ proclaims that we cannot be saved by the law: righteousness through the law, the righteousness of the "scribes and Pharisees," shuts up the entrance to the kingdom of God (Matt. 23:13). After all, if the law could save us, the Savior would have been unnecessary! The most righteous man who preached the religion of the law and the prophets — John the Baptist — is less than the least in the kingdom of God (11:11-13). Therefore, woe to the lawmakers who lay on people's shoulders heavy burdens, hard to bear (23:4). Here, then, is the threshold of this absolute opposition: the kingdom of God is something new, altogether and qualitatively different. The conversation with the Samaritan woman offers the most profound and perhaps most radical contrast between the religion of the law and a different interrelation of "spirit and truth." The religion of the law divides people into the pure and the impure according to their observance of external forms, the norms of time and place — norms that delimit where and when and in what ways God should be worshiped. But there is another kind of worship: the worship of God in spirit and truth; and it directly opposes the first: "neither on this mountain nor in Jerusalem . . ." (John 4:21), but in spirit and truth.

The philosophy of Paul with its dialectical opposition of law and grace is only striving to disclose the plenitude of that showing — that "revelation" — inherited from the Teacher.

The Resistance of the Flesh and the Resistance of the Spirit

The ethic of grace is opposed to the ethic of law. It is born from the critique of law, the critique of "moralism." The essence of this critique is that "law" does not sublimate, that is, it does not raise up or transform the subconscious; it does not sublimate because it arouses the irrational resistance of subconscious impulses, that is, it excites the unconscious resistance of the human will. Every grand scheme of the ethic of sublimation (which bases itself on the subconscious, the imagination, suggestion) is nothing other than a brilliant attempt to evade the law of the resistance of subconscious impulses; in the language of Paul, it is the attempt to evade the resistance of the "flesh" by transforming and enlightening the flesh. The whole success of this enterprise depends totally on how profoundly the law of irrational antagonism has been understood and how exhaustively the mysterious sphere of its activity has been explored.

We must declare right now that this sphere has not been exhaustively explored: irrational resistance is more deeply rooted than we thought. There is another aspect to this resistance, altogether different and much less noticeable, that some people refuse to acknowledge. The resistance of the "flesh" is very noticeable and quite familiar to ancient ethics, but ancient ethics knows nothing of the resistance of the "spirit." Contemporary psychology has thoroughly investigated the resistance of the subconscious, but the question of the resistance of consciousness has not been raised. The resistance of affects (impulses) is thrown in our faces, but the resistance of arbitrary freedom remains invisible. What we see here is a different dimension of and a different source for the spirit of irrational antagonism (i.e., a different form of evil).

In the psychological analysis of the resistance of the flesh that we find in Paul (Rom. 7:14ff.), it is quite easy to show where this phenomenon — rarely understood and laden with meaning — is to be found and how likely it is to occur. This common, widespread phenomenon of human resistance consists in this: that "I serve God's law with my mind, and the law of sin with my flesh." In other words, the human being still desires the good; one agrees in one's spirit ("according to the inward man") with the law, recognizes it as valuable; but one sees in one's members another law, antagonistic to the law of the mind, that makes one a captive of the sinful law dwelling in one's members (Rom. 7:23). In other words, we have here the resistance of the flesh along with the complete subjugation of the mind, the spirit, the inward, higher "I." But is it really true that the mind always serves God's law? Do people always *au fond*, in the depth of their hearts, desire only the good? Is there really no such thing as a consciously evil will? The spirit, the mind, the inner person, the higher innermost "I," is just as capable of desiring evil and transgression as the resisting flesh. The blame for evil in this form can no longer be shifted onto the weakness of the flesh, nor really onto any kind of weakness whatsoever. On the contrary, this is the force of spiritual resistance, the force of the proud arbitrariness of the evil will.

Freedom as the Root of Satanic Evil and Freedom as the Image and Likeness of God

What has been depicted here is not that ordinary form of evil caused by a mistaken evaluative judgment, the only kind recognized by Socrates ("they know not what they do"); nor is it that other form of evil — the resistance of the flesh, described by Paul. We are not dealing here with a desire for the good coupled with an inability to achieve it: "What I would, that I do not." Here it is a force — arrogant self-will — directed against the good: "I will do what I want!" At the basis of such a form is the principle of autonomous resistance, the principle of revolt: I consciously refuse to serve God's law with my mind; I refuse to serve everything higher, anything sacred; I refuse to "serve" altogether! What is being denied here is the axiom of dependence that is the foundation of religion: the principle of reverence, of bowing down before what is highest and most sacred, before the divine hierarchy of values.

Images of this "noetic" [*umnyi*] antagonism, the antagonism of the spirit, not the flesh, of hubris, not "sinful weakness," have been limned with immortal power by Dostoevsky. People are no longer people, but "demons," or people possessed by a demon, for they can all say along with the Grand Inquisitor: we are not with Thee, but with him![1]

---

1. The first stage of autonomous antagonism is crime (transgression of the law out of the sheer spirit of insubordination, the spirit of contradiction). The second stage

33

In a concrete human personality, the law of irrational antagonism can be present and function in one or the other form: the resistance of the spirit or the resistance of the "flesh." The astonishing myth of the Fall depicts both these aspects: on the one hand, the diabolical spirit of resistance: do not submit to the least prohibition, proclaim that "everything is permitted," and you shall be as gods; on the other hand, purely human cravings, instinctively unconscious urges: "the woman saw that the tree was good for food, and that it was a delight to the eyes, and . . . to be desired" (Gen. 3:6).

The law, prohibitions, and imperatives are clearly impotent to struggle against such a form of evil because they immediately call it up. The very commandment is the direct pretext for sin; the desire for evil arises because the law says, "Do not desire." For such a will, sin revives when the commandment comes (Rom. 7:11).

This form of evil was known not only to Dostoevsky, but as early as the Russian bylina [epic tale]. Here is the description of the strange demise of Vasily Buslaev, who paid no heed to dreams or sneezes. Once Buslaev was strolling along with his companions and saw on the path a black stone with an inscription on it: it is forbidden to jump across this stone and whoever jumps will break his neck. Buslaev immediately set off at a run, jumped, and — perished.

The extreme cases of such an audacious challenge hurled at the higher sacred things (the "Holy Sacraments") have been noted by Dostoevsky: "Who will dare the most?"[2] Dostoevsky portrayed a number of times this absolute superhuman freedom of arbitrariness, this "everything is permitted." Here is where it makes contact with the eternal root of satanic evil: "Ye are gods," and therefore "everything is permitted"; "Ye are

---

of resistance is the abolition of any law standing over me (pure mutiny, revolution). I am god and there is nothing above me ("You shall be as gods" [John 10:34, quoting Ps. 82:6]). The third stage: tyranny, dictatorship — the self-appointed elevation of one's own criminal will into a law for others, the "Grand Inquisitor." This is the ultimate incarnation of evil on earth — the "prince of this world." All these moments of the dialectic are displayed in the living images of Raskolnikov, Peter Verkhovensky, Ivan Karamazov, and, finally, the Grand Inquisitor. Obviously, there can be no question here of any "sinful weakness." On the contrary, this is a sinful power, basing itself on a higher source of power, on the freedom of the spirit. It is sufficient to recall the figure of Stavrogin — that incarnation of the might of free arbitrariness.

2. Raskolnikov — *Crime and Punishment,* trans. Pevear and Volokhonsky, p. 418. Trans.

gods" and therefore neither commandments nor prohibitions apply to you; there is no other God above you.[3]

The force of this "superhuman" temptation rests on the fact that we really and truly are gods, and everything really is permitted to us. The Divine Human and his apostle confirm it. We really are "superhuman," for the image and likeness of God subsists in us. It has been given to humankind as a gift — this absolute and arbitrary freedom, this ability to say "yes" or "no," "let this be so," "let this not be so." The astounding gift of freedom, which wrenches man out of the whole kingdom of nature and raises him up to dizzying heights, unbearable for many[4] — precisely this gift provides the grounds for saying: "Ye are gods; and all of you are children of the Most High" (Ps. 82:6; John 10:34); humanity's likeness to God lies in maximum freedom, as Descartes has indicated with great perspicacity.[5]

Ultimate freedom is a fulcrum for temptation (which exists for every free spirit, including the Divine Human), but it may also serve the lever of salvation.

Law, authority, power do not operate in the uttermost depths, in the irrational "abyss" of the primordially choosing act: any law must first be freely acknowledged, any authority must be freely accepted, any power or right must be freely established (cf. "statute," deriving from the same root). Arbitrary freedom can respond to any imperative with "transgression," or with a prideful resistance to the very form of law (anarchism). In response to the "shouldness" that proceeds from a system of values, one can always answer: there is nothing that I should do — I do what I want.

The Divine Invitation to Freedom

The lever of salvation can only be applied to the true center of selfhood, from which contradictory possibilities emanate. One can appeal to freedom only with a call, an invitation ("many are called, . . ." Matt. 20:16), with a "kind offer," a loving summons. God can call man, as man in turn can call on God. The divine call is not law but grace, and grace appeals to

---

3. In *The Single One and His Property* [the English translation is titled *The Ego and His Own*], Max Stirner has expressed in systematic form the idea of such an absolute "ontological lack of principles" (anarchism), which acknowledges its own "I" as the only value, the only sacred thing, while rejecting all other values and forms of the sacred before which one is obliged to bow down.

4. "They cannot endure their own freedom" — the Grand Inquisitor.

5. *Meditations* IV.

35

the primary free human act: to give grace fully, it must be gracefully received. Grace can always be turned down.

Only the divine call of love, only the grace of the Holy Spirit, can transform and sublimate both arbitrary and creative freedom. "You have been called to freedom, brethren!" (Gal. 5:13). Only a call will work: we cannot be dragged to freedom. We are talking here, of course, about the higher, creative, true freedom, about which it is said: "I will teach you the truth, and the truth will make you free" (John 8:32). Such freedom creates life, it brings us to life, and it is impossible without the grace received from him who is the "giver of life."

The free creativity of humans is always a cocreativity; we are always the "fellow workers" of God, and without his creativity there is nothing that we can create. We are always building, and we cannot help but build, but only with the help of gifts granted to us gratis; we build things out of the values given by the Master — out of "gold, silver, precious stones, wood, hay, straw" (1 Cor. 3:12-13); we are freely in charge, but only of the "talents" received from the Master. Since this is so, we can build wisely only "according to the grace of God which is given to us" (1 Cor. 3:10).

When the apostle says that we are "called to freedom" this means "called" to creativity, to deeds, to the conciliar [*sobornyi*], "common task" (Fyodorov), to the full plenitude of historical creativity, to the stewardship of God's mysteries (1 Cor. 4:1). In this stewardship, it is our freedom that acts, but God's grace acts in it as well; it is the "stewardship of God's grace" (Eph. 3:2), and grace acts on our freedom in the only way it can: our godlike freedom can be influenced only by a call: "God calls me by his grace!" (Gal. 1:15). Paul signifies by this word his own mystical experience, that call which resounded for him with special force and to which he responded with all the force of a free resoluteness. He is the apostle who was "called" (Rom. 1:1), but after all, all Christians (Rom. 1:6-7) and all pagans are also "called" in the end by Jesus Christ. There is no one who has not heard those divine calls at some point in life: Socrates already spoke of them. But we need to be responsive and attentive: as Christ says, we need ears to hear.

The "call" is a meeting of two freedoms, two wills — the divine and the human. The "call" is not an "order." It is not power and submission. Directly contrary to this is the mystical experience, whereby Paul heard his call: "Saul, Saul, why persecutest thou me?" (Acts 9:4). This is the invitation to freedom, to the depths of the heart, the invitation to love . . . the unexpected wafting of the Holy Spirit into the hardened soul — and "where the Spirit of the Lord is, there is freedom" (2 Cor. 3:17). Love is free volition, election, partiality; and therefore, if grace is instilled by love, then it can address itself only to freedom.

Thus the spirit of contradiction, the satanic spirit of absolute resistance, is conquered: not by law, not by command, not by threat. A command arouses the revolt of the slave; law arouses the resistance of arbitrary freedom. But the call, the "kind offer," addressed to freedom, cannot call forth revolt, rebellion, prideful opposition. Rather may it call forth an answering movement of love.

The rational norm of the law appeals to the middle sphere of the reasoning consciousness and the resistance of both subconscious affects and supraconscious freedom is set against it.

The mysterious call of grace is perceived as a certain image, vision, voice, endowed with the capacity to seize the attention instinctually, to awaken the subconscious work of the imagination and at the same time to call forth an answering yes (let it be so!) from the depth of the free godlike "I."[6] Only the call of grace has the power to penetrate into the "heart and reins" (Jer. 11:20), into the uttermost depth of the innermost "I": and from there to transform, to sublimate, to deify the whole microcosm, the whole human being — flesh, soul, and spirit. The whole of human nature — everything given to our spirit as material — is sublimated.

Sublimation, "the elevation of the reasoning creature above nature," has various aspects and levels:

1. The subconscious "libido," sexuality, with its search for happiness and "bliss"[7] is transformed and sublimated into divine Eros.
2. The arrogance of the supra-conscious godlike "I" is transformed and sublimated into the honor and glory of our status as God's children, into the kingdom with Christ.
3. Arbitrary freedom is sublimated into the freedom of creativity, into creative service,[8] for every work of creation is a sacrificial service.

In the writings of Paul such expressions as "to put on the arms of light," "to put on Jesus Christ" (Rom. 13:12, 14) refer to a sublimation that has been realized.

6. And this is why "like seeks after like" (Plato). The call of grace is interpreted as a "recollection" of something that is native to us, that is our own, but that we have forgotten, a "recollection" of our lost heavenly home.

7. "What the mob calls bliss" (Plato).

8. "Apollo summons the poet (i.e., the creator/maker) to a holy sacrifice" (Pushkin, "The Poet").

The Problem of the Ethic of Grace as the Ethic of Freedom in Contemporary Philosophy

The problem of sublimation brings us to the question of the sublimation of arbitrariness, or, in theological terms, to the question of the mutual relationship of freedom and grace. It is extremely important, however, to show that the central problem of the ethic of grace is not just a theological problem; and its examination here is by no means addressed exclusively to believers, let alone Christian believers. It is aimed at people who desire and are able to think philosophically, even though they might not accept any kind of orthodox theology. I am claiming that the problem of the new ethic, as an "ethic of grace," confronts them as well: and precisely as the problem of an "ethic of joy and beauty (physical grace)," an ethic of joyful freedom, or free joy. For the Christian philosopher, of course, this is just a translation of the term "grace" — an incomplete translation, but one that makes its viewpoint relevant and comprehensible to contemporary thought outside religion, to Jung, to Charles Baudouin, to all those who understand the meaning of sublimation.

The sublimation of freedom can be expressed in the terminology of the contemporary philosophical problematic, in the language of that philosophical school which has done the most in the sphere of ethics. I am referring to Max Scheler and Nicolai Hartmann, whose ethical investigations are intimately interconnected and mutually complement each other. Scheler examines the correlation of emotions and affects on the one hand and systems of values on the other. He feels an affinity for the idea of sublimation, but he knows only one kind: the sublimation of Eros through ideas, that is, the sublimation of the real material of emotions, drives, and affects by the ideal being of values. But Scheler conducts his inquiries as if there were no such thing as freedom. His ethics do not take freedom into account. Therefore, the problem of the sublimation of freedom, the second moment of sublimation, does not exist for him.

Hartmann's case is different. The problem of freedom is the most original, most precious part of his ethics. The problem of the sublimation of arbitrariness (although he does not use the term) turns up unconsciously in his work. But the problem of the first sublimation, the sublimation of Eros, is absent. Therefore, it seems as if Hartmann has no need for the theory of the unconscious or for the discoveries of contemporary analytical psychology in the field of emotions, affects, and drives, whereas Scheler's worldview finds a place for them.

Scheler proceeds as if human beings knew only affects and values, and phenomena such as "freedom" or "decision making" simply did not exist. With Hartmann, on the contrary, the only things that do exist are values and freedom, as if human beings did not have affects, drives, emotions growing out of the unconscious, or as if this sphere were ethically neutral. One might suppose that the former philosopher enjoyed a rich emotional life and contemplated intellectually sublime things, but had absolutely no experience of the will, decision, free choice; conversely, that the latter philosopher had the deepest experience of freedom, arbitrariness, choice, decisions of the will, and, needless to say, reached the heights of intellectual contemplation (a quality both men share: otherwise they would hardly be great philosophers) — but had absolutely no experience of a rich emotional life.

However, ethics requires both the sublimation of drives and the sublimation of freedom. Only the second completes and in the final analysis provides grounds for the whole process of sublimation. Indeed, the problem of freedom pops up constantly when we are investigating the sublimation of the unconscious. Freedom determines whether we embark on the path of the sublimation or the profanation of Eros, the path of the creative or the depraved imagination. Freedom makes and accepts suggestions, because any suggestion is founded on autosuggestion. Freedom accompanies us at every step: suggestions, sublimations, whether they are successful or not — the human being is liable for all of them.

We have to say that, ultimately, it is freedom and only freedom that sublimates. Freedom hovers over all the material of emotions, drives, and affects, directing and amending the involuntary-unconscious sublimations, successful and unsuccessful; it searches for ways of penetrating into the subconscious and it finds those ways so that it can affirm one thing and reject another even there. Freedom is responsible for the entire content of both consciousness and the subconscious.

Two Freedoms: Negative and Positive — Freedom within Arbitrariness and Freedom within the Good

Freedom is first of all arbitrariness of choice, freedom of the will. This is unsublimated freedom. The phenomena of spiritual resistance, the revolts against the hierarchy of values that are bound up with this freedom, display the depth, might, and untamability of free arbitrariness. There is also a sublimated freedom, however, that is, the kind that steers the helm toward values, that voluntarily "chooses" and takes upon itself the realization of the ideal "should."

So there are two freedoms, or two stages of freedom: the freedom of arbitrariness and the freedom of creativity. The transition from the first to the second constitutes the sublimation of freedom. In Russian philosophy it is N. Berdyaev who developed with special power and persuasiveness the correlation between these two freedoms: "freedom within nothingness," freedom grounded on nothing, and freedom grounded on truth and the good (according to the words: "I will teach you the truth, and the truth shall make you free"). Berdyaev is correct in pointing to a philosophical tradition of ignoring the first kind of freedom. Both ancient philosophy (including Plato) and Thomism (the doctrines of Thomas Aquinas) are defective in this regard. The problem of freedom is consequently posed in a superficial way. By ignoring the first freedom (of arbitrariness) one is bound, first of all, to fall into a misunderstanding of evil and a certain optimistic naivete, since one thereby ignores the difficult transition from the first freedom to the second — in other words, the central ethical problem of the sublimation of freedom. Furthermore, discounting the freedom of arbitrariness can lead to an underestimation of this freedom in comparison to the second: its denial and suppression in practice, in the name of freedom within the good. Then we get the despotism of the Grand Inquisitor, that is, the complete elimination of any kind of freedom whatsoever in the name of the elimination of subjective arbitrariness. It is this which is now threatening the world.

The distinction between the two levels of freedom is very important indeed. Kant early on distinguished between negative and positive freedom. But it was only the second that he considered to be ethically and theoretically valuable. Ethically, it denotes the "good will," the will that voluntarily submits to the principle of the moral law, and only such a will is valuable. Theoretically, it denotes the new lawfulness of practical reason, founded on and subjugating the lawfulness of nature, causal lawfulness. And according to Kant, only such a positive interpretation of freedom can solve the celebrated antinomy of freedom and necessity. Negative freedom cannot do so, since it would be a freedom from any kind of lawfulness whatsoever. Kant's solution, on the contrary, affirms the efficacy of two lawfulnesses: the natural-causal and the moral, while showing their compatibility. Kant plugs in the principle of lawfulness everywhere, and therefore he is incapable of valuing a freedom that is outside the pattern of lawfulness. When it comes to his philosophy of law, however, even Kant is forced to allow a certain value to negative freedom, since subjective law protects the freedom of arbitrariness within certain limits.

In all of modern and contemporary philosophy, negative freedom has a nasty reputation. In contrast to the situation in medieval philosophy, it has become customary to dispute it theoretically and deny it ethically. Fichte — that philosopher of freedom — in his second philosophical phase ended up by requiring the complete self-annihilation of freedom on the highest level of the good. Only the imperfect will is free; the perfect will has sacrificed its freedom, has made its choice once and for all, and the choice between good and evil is no longer open to it.

Despite Fichte's beautiful ethical design, which correctly upholds the necessity of a higher ethical level rising above free arbitrariness, we get a paradox: freedom within the good is no longer freedom. This is a profound mistake. Positive freedom preserves, transforms, and sublimates freedom of choice, arbitrary freedom, the lower freedom. Truth makes us free, and in no way requires the murder and suicide of freedom. Otherwise it would be impossible to say: Brethren, you have been called to freedom! What Fichte wants to say is perfectly clear: freedom within truth and the good is no longer arbitrary freedom; that is, the second freedom is not the first; positive freedom is not negative; and this is absolutely true. But it is not true that positive freedom is not freedom; on the contrary, it is true freedom (where the Spirit of the Lord is, there is freedom). Preserving and transforming but not destroying the sublimated material is precisely what sublimation does. Here is the fundamental law: the higher concept contains the lower;[9] arbitrariness is a necessary moment of freedom, and it is preserved in the higher concept of creative freedom, freedom that acts to limit itself by acknowledging the moral principle.

Arbitrariness cannot be the ultimate definition of freedom. Arbitrariness is only a categorial (and consequently a dialectical) moment in the full meaning of genuine freedom. But where do we look for this principle? Obviously, not in the sphere of natural necessity, not in the sphere of causal sequences. In this sphere nothing can be arbitrarily changed: there is no freedom of choice. Things are otherwise in the ideal sphere of values: here one can arbitrarily choose one value to be realized in life and reject another; one can choose the lower and reject the higher; one can keep to the hierarchy of values, but one can just as well reject the value system as a whole. True enough, values postulate the realization of values, their embodiment in existence; but this postulate is only an ideal "should." Here the will is free in relation to this "shouldness" that pro-

---

9. This law is expressed (imperfectly) by Aristotle in the interrelation of form and matter; Hegel's concept of *aufheben* shows the dialectic of this law. In contemporary philosophy Nicolai Hartmann gives the clearest formulation of it.

ceeds from values. The will is not delimited by the ethical "should"; here and only here is the sphere of action in which arbitrariness can operate, the sphere of choice.

A legitimate objection immediately arises, however: How can one say that? The ethical "should" is precisely what delimits the will! The will may be free in relation to the causal nexus, but it is not free precisely in relation to the "should." It is precisely here that no kind of arbitrariness can operate, for values are given as immutable. The tension between contradictory affirmations becomes ever more acute: the will is delimited and not delimited by the "should." At this point contemporary ethics sets up a second antinomy of freedom, one that Kant, having established the first antinomy of freedom and necessity, did not suspect. This new antinomy might appropriately be called the "antinomy of shouldness," for it lays bare an antagonism in the very sphere of value and the "should."

We must come to an understanding of all the novelty and paradoxicality of this new antinomy, this new logical contradiction: "the will is delimited (determined) and not delimited (determined) by the 'should.'" This antinomy will not be understood by anyone who immediately conjures up the customary Kantian solution: the will should — but is not forced to — submit to the "should"; in other words, on the basis of the "should," the will is subordinate to values — but in empirical fact it often violates them.

If one clings to such an interpretation, this situation — that the will is not forced to submit to the "should" and can violate it in real life — is just a melancholy fact of reality, something that should not happen. This solution reduces the antinomy to a clash between the "is" and the "should." But the antinomy of shouldness refers to something totally different: it reveals a contradiction on the plane of the "should" itself; it reveals the clash of two "shoulds."

Indeed, this situation — that the will is not forced to submit to the "should" and can freely violate it — is understood in this case as a value, as a "should." Arbitrary freedom is a value and it should exist. It is the condition that makes it possible for us to receive praise and blame for what we do; it makes a good will possible. A robot of the good, exclusively and teleologically determined by the Deity, has no ethical value. Only a free will that has the power to say yes or no has ethical value, because it is held liable for what it does.

Only now do we arrive at the real antinomy: complete submission to the "should" is something that should not be; nonsubmission to the "should" is something that should be. The shouldness of the values addressed to the human being ought to be absolute and inviolable; and at the same time this shouldness dares not and should not be absolute and inviolable. Values demand unconditional supremacy in the life of the bearer of values, the human being. At the same time this supremacy of values should not be unconditional — and it is the values themselves that make this demand. Values lay claim to the complete determination of the very person who has value only if he is not fully determined by them. In religious terms this contradiction might be expressed thus: God wants humanity to be his slave — God does not want humanity to be his slave. These two positions cancel each other out; both of them are necessary and at the same time incompatible. With this interpretation, we arrive at the second antinomy of freedom, as the "antinomy of shouldness," where both thesis and antithesis pertain to the sphere of the "should." The significance of this antinomy lies in the clash of negative freedom with positive freedom; freedom within arbitrariness clashes with freedom within the good. We can put it this way: arbitrary freedom has value and arbitrary freedom does not have value; freedom within the good is the sole thing of value — and is not the sole thing of value. Two sovereign instances come into conflict here: on the one side, the sovereignty of values, the sovereignty of the principle; and on the other side, the sovereignty of the "I," the sovereignty of the free person.

But the resolution of this contradiction is so easy to conceive, so feasible! Ethics formulates it in the following manner: positive freedom (freedom within the good), which is the highest and ultimate definition of freedom (for the indefiniteness of arbitrariness cannot be the highest definition), contains not one but two defining principles: the autonomy of the person and the autonomy of the principle; and the relationship between them is not antinomic but complementary. This is because values (the principle) cannot actually limit or determine anything on their own: they only express an ideal postulate. An actual will is required, a will that wants to take responsibility for the realization of the values. On the other hand, an actual will, freedom of choice, arbitrariness cannot ideally determine or realize anything, cannot make good into evil or vice versa. The free will, in order to choose, to make decisions, to orient itself, must be able to refer to an order of values that has been given to it and in which it can alter nothing. The intuition of the "heart" (the "organ" for the apperception of values) discovers and observes values as they are given in the ideal world.

Personal autonomy requires the autonomy of the principle and vice versa. Real conditionality requires ideal conditionality and ideal conditionality requires real. . . . A freely chosen act requires the "logic of the heart" (Pascal), the logic of values, the contemplation of the ideal tendencies of what should and should not be. Otherwise it will be blind, devoid of meaning, that is, in the final analysis it will not be a consciously free choice and decision. The ideal conditionality or determination of the "should" will in its turn be powerless and therefore meaningless if there is no really free will to make it into a reality. An imperative, an order, loses any meaning if there is no autonomous person who can fulfill or violate it.

The antinomy is resolved and all the variations of the basic contradiction are eliminated with the help of a distinction between actual and ideal conditionality. "The will is determined and not determined by the 'should'" — there is no contradiction here, because the will is conditioned ideally, but not conditioned really.

"Arbitrary freedom has and does not have value" — it has value insofar as the value of a real determination, proceeding from a free will, is affirmed in it; it does not have value insofar as one can interpret it as the arbitrary rejection of an ideal determination, an unwillingness to come to terms with it. "The shouldness of values should be absolute and inviolable" — insofar as we are referring to an ideal determination, which appeals with its postulates to all the acts and decisions of the will, which preserves its ideal sovereignty, its own ideal resonance, both when those postulates are adhered to and when they are violated (and as the voice of condemnation in the latter case). "The shouldness of values dares not and should not be absolute and inviolable" — insofar as it cannot and should not really determine the will, for if it were determined in this way, then the will would turn into a robot of the good. Values are inviolable in their ideal being; and values are very much violated in real acts of the will.

"Freedom encounters the 'should' as nonfreedom" — but this is an illusion fabricated out of a confusion between ideal determination and real determination. "The 'should' encounters freedom as what should not be": — this is the same confusion, because real self-determination (freedom) is something valuable, something that should be, even if its action be judged, in an ideal definition, as what should not be. Shouldness does not destroy freedom: the anxiety and revolt of freedom are mistaken. The only thing that proceeds from the "should" is an invitation — freely to elect value.

We expressed the same thought in religious terms as an "appeal," an "invitation," coming from the Deity, from the highest value and perfection. The Kantian conception of the "should" was inadequate, because the "should" was identified with the form of law, with duty, with an imperative. Such an interpretation is legal drivel, moralism, Pharisaism; it

arouses the revolt of freedom, it does not sublimate, and therefor
without grace.

Freedom of the Will and Creative Arbitrariness

Free will is assessed in quite a special manner when we turn to the sphere of
creativity. Creativity is always something arbitrary, both in the positing of
goals and in the pursuit of means. It is true that the arbitrary interacts with
the necessary (it interacts with the law of causality in the pursuit of means
and with the fixity of values in the positing of goals), but in such a way that
no creativity is possible without it. If the human being and the world were
exclusively conditioned by causality and teleology, then creativity would be
unnecessary and impossible. Creativity is the "art of combination," the
play of possibilities and alternatives; hence the value of crisis and arbitrariness in the sphere of creativity. This value exists side by side with the opposing value of pure mediumship, Pythianism [referring to the priestess of
Apollo, the conduit for the god], the pure passivity of illumination.

Creativity is sublimated whim (a "successful neurosis") and sublimated arbitrariness. The sublimating principles have nothing arbitrary
about them; nonetheless, in any creative, that is, "poetic," sublimation,
"arbitrariness" is marvelously preserved and immediately experienced as
playful freedom and the freedom of play. You can verify harmony by algebra, but you cannot use algebra to create harmony.[10] Pushkin's Mozart is
whimsically arbitrary as well as mediumistic (he overhears "the songs of
paradise"); Salieri is rationally grounded, and this is precisely why his creative work is not "poetic."

At this point a totally new light is cast on the freedom of arbitrariness, the freedom of absolute choice: negative freedom gets a positive
meaning. This is because negative freedom is not exhausted by the choice
between yes and no, between the affirmation and denial of the hierarchy
of values given from above, between good and evil. There is freedom of
choice between different and contradictory yeses, between different combinations of values, between different solutions to conflicts in values, between different combinations of means — in a word, between different creative possibilities.

10. Vysheslavtsev refers here to "Mozart and Salieri," one of Pushkin's *Little Tragedies*. In his opening monologue, Salieri takes pride in having learned to "dissect music
like a corpse" and to "regulate harmony with algebra." Trans.

The Sublimation of Freedom as a Resolution
of Its Antinomic Nature

The transition from the first level of freedom to the second is the sublimation of freedom. What must be surmounted is the autonomous antagonism that could resist this transition, that could resist sublimation — being lifted upward. Where does this resistance come from? It springs from the fact that the person is afraid of losing his autonomy: he does not see and does not believe that he will be preserved as an "end in himself" in the "kingdom of ends." The person assumes that he will be turned into a means; he does not see and does not believe that arbitrariness and freedom of choice can be preserved in the higher conditionality of the "should," in the ethic of grace. And the age-old ethic of the law, which really denies the value of arbitrariness (all of ethics in antiquity), the age-old moralism, and, finally, the modern tradition of Kantian ethics all confirm the person in his lack of faith.

If we can radically overcome the autonomous resistance of the person and the sheer revolt of arbitrariness, then we can solve the antinomy of the "should": we can show the compatibility of personal autonomy and the autonomy of values. The key to this solution is grace. Grace means that the conditionality or determination proceeding from the kingdom of values does not by nature destroy but preserves freedom of choice, arbitrariness, personal autonomy, individual self-determination in a new form. Thus the antinomy of shouldness is resolved through the sublimation of arbitrariness: "freedom within the truth" contains arbitrary freedom in a transformed state: otherwise, if freedom were destroyed and extinguished within the truth, what sense would there be in the words: "the truth shall make you free," "brethren, you have been called to freedom"?

In negative freedom the positive does not yet exist, but positive freedom contains and preserves the negative. Despotic arbitrariness does not contain the determination proceeding from the kingdom of values, and can go against it. But the kingdom of values, embodied in reality and determining it, necessarily contains arbitrary freedom, for the simple reason that arbitrary freedom makes ethical values possible and consequently is itself an ethical value.[11] The person as an end in himself can ignore the kingdom of ends and refuse to be determined by it, but the kingdom of

---

11. Any damage inflicted on the lower freedom makes the attainment of the higher freedom impossible, makes sublimation impossible. Instead of sublimation one gets a "fall" into slavery, the grand inquisition, against which any revolt seems just.

ends cannot ignore the value of the person and necessarily contains the person as an end in himself.

Such an interpretation of sublimation provides the classic solution to the antinomy: thesis and antithesis do not exclude each other, as it seems at first; rather, the antithesis contains the thesis, as form contains matter. Kant and Fichte resolve the antinomy of freedom and necessity in this way: freedom and causality are compatible, because freedom contains causality in the new form of purposiveness.[12]

The Christian Solution to the Problem of Freedom

Contemporary Christianity cannot help but nurture and protect both personal autonomy and arbitrary freedom in their full measure. The Christian solution goes beyond thesis and antithesis, but in such a way that the thesis of personal freedom suffers no damage.

If the religious antagonists of freedom try to drag in the phrase: "Thy will be done" in defense of a humble "obedience," as a denial of freedom, as freedom's eradication by a higher will — then we must point out to them that freedom of choice and personal autonomy are preserved in all their inviolability, as plain as day, precisely in that "let it be done." For "let it be done" is the most valuable expression of free will, which can also say "let it not be done." "Let it be done" resounds from the depths of autonomous selfhood, as a free response to the invitation of the divine will. "Let it be done" — it is I myself who say it, making up my mind and choosing my path, and this is the only kind of response that God needs. The words "Thy will be done" incorporate the combination of two wills, not just one;[13] and this combination is the sublimation of the lower human will by the higher, divine one.

From our point of view, the antinomies of freedom and the inherent tragedies of freedom are resolved through sublimation. As indicated above, the antinomy of shouldness might be expressed as follows: God wants — and does not want us to be his slaves; we should — and should not be his slaves. The solution of the antinomy goes like this: God wants us to fulfill his will (and in this sense he wants obedience), though not as slaves, not as mercenaries, but as friends and children (and in this sense he does

---

12. The solution is examined in detail in my book, *The Ethics of Fichte* (Moscow, 1914).

13. Maximus the Confessor fought for this position.

not want obedience pure and simple). God wants love, and any love is freely elected, any love is a combination of two wills and two freedoms. "Thy will be done" is an expression of love for the Father, for the highest and most valuable, for the one who stands above me and can therefore sublimate my will. If there is nothing and no one above me, then sublimation is impossible. If what is above me is absolute power, an imperative, the law — then sublimation is likewise impossible, because freedom does not submit to the dictatorship of the "categorical imperative." The relationship of God-Sonhood is the sole adequate symbol of sublimation: "from above," from the Father, from the hierarchically higher, comes an invitation. The son answers this "invitation" with freely given love. But his answer to a tyrant's order would be refusal, even if he outwardly obeyed it.

The True Meaning of Sublimation

Sublimation is the elevation of the lower to the higher, to the sublime; to understand this elevation there must be a system of categories of being and a hierarchy of values. Sublimation presupposes a certain categorial, hierarchical law, noted and formulated by Aristotle as the relationship between form and matter: the lower category of being serves as material for the higher, which appears as its form. Form is something newer and higher (e.g., a statue), although it presupposes the lower as the condition of its possibility, as its material (e.g., marble). This material is not destroyed, but preserved and transformed into the higher "form" of beauty. The higher form is something absolutely new, a new and higher category, in which the lower is in some sense "destroyed," in some sense "preserved," but chiefly "lifted" to a higher level — in other words, sublimated, transfigured, transubstantiated. But it is precisely this preservation of the lower in the higher that deludes so many people into missing out on the higher altogether. Mechanical and chemical processes, for example, are preserved in the organism in all their inviolability; causal sequences are preserved in purposive and free creativity.[14] Thus we are tempted to assume that the organism is only a complicated mechanism, that freedom is only a combination of causes.

 If we say that a statue is only sublimated marble, that love and religion are only sublimated sexuality, that science, art, and culture are only

---

14. The solution to the celebrated antinomy of freedom and necessity depends on this. Cf. my *Ethics of Fichte*, pp. 267-395.

sublimated economics (Marxism), then we are repeating this classical reductionist mistake. The mistake is encapsulated in the word "only." It is precisely not "only" so! Genuine sublimation is creativity, that is, the creation of an altogether new level of being, one that did not exist before. This creative moment of sublimation is splendidly expressed in Plato's concept of Eros. Plato's Eros raises sublimation to a new level of being, it reveals new categories of life: (1) As libido, as carnal striving, Eros is the continuation of the race, the birth of generations; (2) as poetry (making/creativity), Eros is the birth of the "children of Homer and Hesiod" and the "royal art," politics, which creates the state. The second level of Eros presupposes the first, for poetry, culture, and the state presuppose the continuation of the race and the succession of generations; but the second level is a new level — a new category of life. Even here Eros does not come to a halt, but mounts even further upward and reveals yet another new stage: (3) as philosophy, the contemplation of ideas — and this level also presupposes the first two, for in order to philosophize one needs to live and to live in a culture, to have an economy and a state (as Plato shows in his *Republic*). But philosophy is an absolutely new being, a new category in comparison with economics and politics. Its ultimate ascent is the ecstasy or trance leading into the Absolute. Here it encounters something completely new, incommensurable with anything lower.

What is Eros then, if its nature remains the same on all the levels of its ascent, its sublimation? Obviously it cannot be identified with the sensual drive, for this is its function only on the first level.

The genuine essence of Eros is revealed as a striving. Eros expresses the striving and impetuous drive of our being, our deepest core, our "heart" that "beats on the threshold, as it were, of a dual being." Hence the duality and dialectical nature of Eros. Striving is dialectical: it moves from thesis to antithesis; it forever encounters boundaries and forever goes beyond limits, it forever transcends. Plato symbolically portrayed the wandering, capricious, seeking, longing nature of Eros; it remains the same in love, in the succession of generations, in poetry, in politics, in philosophy. Eros cannot endure any "immanentism": immanence is residence in a cave. But Eros is a trance and constantly "is in a trance." It calms down only when it transcends the whole hierarchy of levels of being and values (the many mansions), when it encounters the open expanse, the infinite expanse of the Absolute.

But if Eros ranges over so many meanings, how can it preserve the original sexual meaning implied in the notion, as Plato makes it do? The transcending nature of striving provides a clear and conclusive answer.

The "libido" is striving, and consequently a trance, the first and most natural going out of the self, a way out beyond the limits of any kind of "autoerotism," the point of departure for any self-affirmation, any quest for plenitude and infinity.[15] But this is only the first level of striving. It gets left behind. The essence of Eros is revealed in the startling fact that any genuine experience of "being in love" goes beyond the limits of sexuality, and that any reminder of sexuality is then interpreted as a profanation of love. Furthermore, genuine love goes beyond the limits of the immediate object of love: it embraces the moon, the sun, the stars, the entire cosmos. . . .

"You gaze at the stars, my radiant star" ("Plato" — Vladimir Solovyov). If it is true that genuine love makes people into poets, then it makes them into creators and, consequently, lifts them up to new levels of being, where new ideas, meanings, and values take on shape and form.

Hierarchically lower striving can enter as a constituent factor into some higher complex: it is uniquely transformed and ennobled in this higher complex without, however, ceasing to be itself. This is the meaning of genuine sublimation, outlined by Plato in his dialogue, *Symposium*. It is this *Symposium* that offers the best symbol of such a sublimation — a symphonic unity of manifold emotions and aspirations: friendly, aesthetic, erotic, dialectical, philosophical, mystical. Here, in this integral unity, we cannot deny the presence of the lower drives — the gastronomical. Otherwise, the *Symposium* would not be a symposium [i.e., a banquet]. Bread and wine can serve as the foundation of the most sublime human communion. The first requirement of the most spiritual love is to feed the hungry.

In this breathtaking symphony that we call the *Symposium* of Plato, the voices of the lowliest vital drives are heard, but they are transformed beyond recognition, borne upward to an unapproachable height. The wine is still wine, and yet it seems like wine no longer — that stuff which intoxicates Socrates.

Plato's *Symposium* does have an "economic basis." But to say that it is only sublimated appetite and sublimated drunkenness is the real profanation.

---

15. Infinity in the succession of generations, the completeness of the androgynous bond, self-sacrifice in parental and conjugal love — these are the values of the first level of Eros, discovered by Plato.

CHAPTER 5

The Problem of Power

Alexander I and Leo Tolstoy

Power is something of a problem and an enigma. It is enigmatic in its essence, in its social and psychological nature, and problematic in its value. Power is what most attracts and repels people — those "rebels searching for someone to bow down to" — what they worship and at the same time hate. Power has something divine and something demonic about it.

There is a mystique of power, and it is the terrifying mystique of a two-faced demon. Here is why sovereigns are two-faced: "That potentate [Tsar Alexander I] was such a type, accustomed to contraffections, a harlequin in his soul and in his life" (Pushkin). What was said of the "blessed Alexander" could also be said shrewdly and perceptively and truly of the Russo-Byzantine temperament of all the tsars. But this would not be entirely fair. Alexander bore in his soul the living tragedy of power, the living antinomy of power, the affirmation and negation of it; he knew that power was bound up with tyranny and tyrannicide, with liberation and enslavement, and he could never get used to these "contraffections" right up to the end of his life. How did he resolve the antinomy of power, the antinomy of good and evil locked within it? (This is the very same tragedy that Pushkin put into the heart of Boris Godunov.) The inherent tragedy is the aporia, the trap from which there is no way out; and yet Alexander found a way out in his great departure, reminiscent of the great departure of the Buddha. There is a certain Hindu flavor to this renunciation and repudiation of power, might, splendor, greatness. It is repeated in the fate of Leo Tolstoy with his little departure — which would have been comic had it not ended in death.

51

However, Alexander's renunciation of power and Tolstoy's denial of power have not only a Hindu element of renunciation and nonresistance, but also a purely Christian element of genuine anarchism — an element that runs through the entire Bible from the anointing of the kings to the Apocalypse and that sounds most clearly in the words of Christ: "the princes of the earth exercise dominion over them, and they that are great exercise authority upon them. But it shall not be so among you" (Matt. 20:25-26). These are the words that Alexander heard and fulfilled. And at the moment when he became Fyodor Kuzmich[1] and did not fear the lash, he was not less but more of a Christian, perhaps, than at the time of his coronation or his victory over Napoleon. The Russian monarchists, who think that the anointment of tsars gives an exhaustive account of the Christian view of power and the kingdom, usually forget about the Muscovite tsars' ancient custom of taking strict monastic vows before their death, that is, renouncing power in the name of Christ. But one can renounce in the name of Christ only what is lower, not higher, only what is transient, not eternal. Power thus confesses that it is a lower and transient principle: "it shall not be so among you." If this custom of renunciation and withdrawal from power and the world is left to the last moment and is not, so to speak, taken seriously, if it is just a symbolic ceremony undergone by a dying ruler, then Alexander acted contrary to custom, for he realized this custom in all the fullness and depth of its meaning. And this meaning is the affirmation of the intrinsic sinfulness of power.

The Sinfulness of Power in the Bible

The idea of the sinfulness of power runs through the whole Bible from the first book of kings [i.e., 1 Samuel] down to the Apocalypse. Samuel knows that to "set up a king" means to "repudiate God" (1 Sam. 10:19). He knows that the people are doing a "great evil, by asking for a king to rule over them," and however strange it may seem, the people themselves are forced to admit it (1 Sam. 12:17-19). Samuel warns the people that power means tyranny, and finally utters the following prophecy: you yourselves will be slaves to the king that shall reign over you and "in that day you will cry out because of your king whom you have chosen for yourselves; but the Lord will not answer you in that day" (1 Sam. 8:10-18). All of history is

---

1. Legend has it that Alexander I did not die in 1825, but abandoned the throne to become a saintly hermit under the name of Fyodor Kuzmich. Trans.

a never-ending confirmation of this prophecy. This is the ancient Hebrew view of power. We find it in the prophets, for whom the ultimate evil on earth was incarnated in the great tyrants (e.g., Nebuchadnezzar).

The Gospels develop this thought more fully and profoundly: Christ says in answer to the disciples who ask him to grant them power and place above the others: "Kings and rulers of the people exercise lordship over them and their great ones exercise authority upon them" — the so-called benefactors of the people — "it shall not be so among you: but whoever would be great among you must be your servant; and whoever would be first among you must be your slave" (Matt. 20:25-28; Luke 22:24-27; Mark 10:42-45). These words are reproduced with striking insistence and exactness in all three Synoptic Gospels and part of them in great detail in Mark, who is so chary with words; and the Fourth Gospel embodies their meaning in the symbolic washing of feet.[2]

Perhaps this is the place to bring up the "sovereign ministry of Christ." But this is not a ministry dressed in the forms of power. This is not the kind of ministry which proclaimed that "the monarch is the first servant of the state." The path of Christian ministry is opposed to earthly greatness and power, for the servant is opposed to the master, and slavery is opposed to the exercise of power. Christ refuses the power to rule, which is offered to him twice, once in the desert and once in Jerusalem, as a temptation of the devil. And he was betrayed by Judas, repudiated by the high priests, and abandoned by the people essentially because he was not a messiah who exercised power, and he did not come down from the cross.

There is something demonic about power: in its essence it is "from the devil": "And the devil said unto him, All this power will I give thee, and the glory of them [the kingdoms of the world]: for that is delivered unto me; and to whomsoever I will I give it." The condition for obtaining power is to fall down and worship the devil (cf. Luke 4:5-8; Matt. 4:8-9). This is perhaps the most forceful thing ever said against the very principle of power, against etatism; at times the condemnation even seems too forceful. But the Apocalypse confirms and reinforces it: the demonism of power will grow throughout history. Great power over all the nations of the earth will be given to the "beast" and Antichrist, and they will receive this power from the dragon (the devil) precisely because the condition for obtaining power has been fulfilled: all the earth will fall down and worship the devil.[3]

---

2. Here we get a synthetic translation of all three texts together.

3. Therefore what the devil says in the desert cannot be regarded as an exaggeration or a lie.

Perhaps there is no book more ruthless toward kings and rulers than the Apocalypse, in which the corpses of kings, the corpses of mighty men, the corpses of the chieftains of a thousand men, are tossed out to birds of prey in order to prepare the way for the second coming of the Logos.

The Divinity of Power

This theme of anarchism runs through the whole Bible, just as it runs through the course of human history and thought. However, it would be premature to derive a "Christian anarchism" from this fact. There is a naive anarchism that has no notion of the antinomy of power. Power is essentially antinomic; it is a positive and a negative value; it is "from the devil" — and it is also "from God." "There is no power but of God: the powers that be are ordained of God. Whosoever therefore resisteth the power, resisteth the ordinance of God" (Rom. 13:1-2). Who has not cited these remarkable verses of Paul? History is in turn now ravished, now revolted by these words. Sometimes these words provoke astonishment and seemingly go a bit overboard, just as the claim that all power belongs to the devil seems to be overdoing it. But the Bible asserts all of its themes with the utmost force.

"There is no power but of God" — this is absolutely not Paul's invention, as those who are offended by it sometimes claim. No indeed: every thesis of the apostle, the first philosopher of Christianity, can be supported by citing the words of Christ himself. "You could have no power at all against me unless it had been given you from above" — so he tells Pilate (John 19:11). "Render . . . to Caesar the things that are Caesar's, and to God the things that are God's" (Matt. 22:21): thus he requires us to carry out the legitimate demands of power, and reminds us that he came not to destroy the law but to fulfill it. Throughout the Bible, in history and in human thought, the theme of the value, sanctity, and divinity of power resounds with the greatest force — a theme counter to anarchism.[4] Power is a real "blessing" for nations and peoples; kings like David and Solomon do exist. The Old Testament and the New Testament church sanction the anointing of kings. There have been kings and princes who were pious, devout, even saints, who have baptized whole nations. In the future, power may accomplish great things. The Apocalypse foretells the

---

4. Peter says the same thing about power as Paul does (1 Pet. 2:13-18), although he refers to it more rarely.

"thousand-year kingdom of the saints" who will reign with Christ (Rev. 20:4).

But the most important and most convincing point that apparently indicates the divinity of power is that in the Bible God is always called the heavenly and earthly King, the "ruler over all" *(Pantokrator);* Christ is called King, to whom "all power on heaven and earth is given" (Matt. 28:18); and the transfiguration and deification of the world is always designated as the kingdom of God. After all, it is the kingdom of God that is the core symbol of the Old and New Testaments.

The Antinomy of Power

This then is the amazing antinomy of power: power is from God and power is from the devil. Do we reproach Christianity and the Bible because they contain the "most profound internal contradiction"? But, after all, the world and humanity and all creation are made up of the most profound internal contradictions: the world is finite and infinite, beautiful and "everything lies in evil" (cf. 1 John 5:19); humans are mortal and immortal; they are "king and slave, worm and God." The contradictions actually go very deep; thus the only one to see them is the one who can see into the mysterious depths of being. The insights of philosophy and mysticism are just as antinomic as the inherent tragedies of life and history. The meaning of Christianity, the meaning of a great religion, is that it bears up under and resolves the deepest contradictions, the deepest tragedies of being. The presence of the "deepest internal contradiction," the positing of an antinomy, is the sign of a genuine revelation, of genuine philosophy; and this is because God is a unity of opposites.

All the higher principles of genuine religion are antinomic: Divine Humanity, marriage and virginity, providence and freedom. Of course, religion promises to resolve these antinomies, though not here and not now, but only "in the end," that is, in God. Some antinomies even seem totally irresolvable for human beings (after Job has been reproached by his friends, God answers him in this vein) — this says nothing against their genuineness, rather the contrary. But there are also antinomies whose resolution we "see through a glass darkly, and in riddles" (cf. 1 Cor. 13:12): we can guess which way to turn in order to solve them. The antinomy of power falls precisely into this group. It seems to me that the solution to this antinomy is best given or (to be more precise) most clearly posited in Christian philosophy of history and eschatology.

Mistaken Solutions to the Antinomy of Power

First, however, the solution to this antinomy must not be too easy. An easy solution would be a false one. Such is the solution of Origen, in his gloss on the text "there is no power but of God": powers are from God insofar as they conform to the divine laws; they become the devil's insofar as they violate those laws. Any power is given by God in the same way that hands, feet, and tongue are given — and they are all given for good use. But it is possible to use them for evil as well, to make them into an instrument of evil, an instrument of the devil.[5] Origen's solution ends up by turning power into a neutral instrument, or organ, which can serve good and evil in equal measure. Power can be completely in the hands of the devil, and the very same power can pass completely into the hands of God.

But if power is just a neutral instrument, then there is no antinomy of power — it is simply an illusion. After all, there is no antimony of the hand or tongue based on the fact that they can serve good and evil equally well. This is why Origen's solution does not comprehend the depth of power. An antinomy exists only if power is not in fact a neutral instrument, if it contains a certain intrinsic evil. And this is indeed the case: after all, the symbol of power is the sword ("the ruler does not bear the sword in vain"; cf. Rom. 13:4) and Christ says: "Put your sword in its place, for all who take the sword will perish by the sword" (Matt. 26:52). These words set up the internal contradiction of the sword; there is no place for such an instrument in the kingdom of God — and yet the kingdom is based on the sword. If any power is coercion, then it is clear that there is no place for coercion in the kingdom of God — and yet any "kingdom" is power and therefore coercion.

A second solution suggests itself here, and it is also an illusory solution. It is fabricated out of a semantic confusion in the word "power." The power of God and the power of Christ are not identical to the ordinary power of kings; and the kingdom of God is in no way an earthly kingdom. This intrinsic difference appears most forcefully when Christ is standing before Pilate: he is a king, but in a very special sense of the term. His kingdom is not of this world; he has no servitors, no defenders, no army; his kingdom is the kingdom of truth. His power is not like Pilate's power; his power is the power of truth (John 18:36-38). When Pilate hears this, he understands that the man he sees before him is the teacher of truth, not a claimant to power at all.

The antinomy is not illusory, however, and this becomes compellingly apparent precisely when we get rid of the second, metaphorical,

---

5. Origen, in Migne, *Patrologia graeca,* 14:1226-27.

symbolic meaning of power, leaving just the first, precise, and narrow meaning of power. Thus we need, first, to eliminate from the antinomy the ultimate and otherworldly concepts of the "kingdom of God" and the power of the Divine Human, which are metajuridical and go beyond the boundaries of the law. The "kingdom of God" can never prop up the thesis of power; it can neither be inserted into this thesis nor can it be introduced into the antinomy. It is the power of this world that is antinomic and split into thesis and antithesis, into affirmation and denial. The kingdom of God is not antinomic: on the contrary, it resolves the antinomy, and we want to see how exactly it does so.

We would be committing a great error if we tried to prove the thesis of power by introducing into it the kind of power signified by the power of truth and the "kingdom of God." This would be to stray beyond the bounds of the question, for the question concerns the prince of this world, the power of Pilate ("I have power to crucify you, and power to release you," John 19:10), the power of the ruler who "does not bear the sword in vain" — power in the strict and literal sense of the word. Such and only such power is essentially antinomic, for the Logos himself both affirms and denies it, as I showed earlier. It is "from the devil," for it crucifies — and it is "from God," for it is "given . . . from on high."

This error is quite instructive and influential — it has had an enormous influence on the course of history, and people keep on making it up to the present day. People try to prove the sacredness of power, the sacredness of monarchy from the fact that God is a king and an autocrat and an absolute monarch. This was Ivan the Terrible's theory of power. The proverb puts it in a nutshell: "What God is in heaven, the king is on earth." Ivan the Terrible did not see, had no inkling of, any antinomy of power; he was completely ignorant of biblical, prophetic, Christian, and apocalyptic antistatism and anarchism. All he knew was the thesis of power, and so he conflated the divine and the earthly king: they have the same power to pardon and to punish, a power that is merely transferred from the hands of God into the hands of the king. The earthly king is, so to speak, the earthly representative of God. And therefore earthly tyranny is a reflection of the heavenly tyranny. This theory — blatantly anti-Christian and antibiblical — rests on a confusion between "kingdom" in the strict sense and "kingdom" in the figurative, symbolic sense, on a total incomprehension of "my kingdom is not of this world" (John 18:36).[6] All attempts to

---

6. This is splendidly shown in three articles by N. N. Alekseev, "The Idea of the Earthly City in Christian Dogma," "Christianity and the Idea of Monarchy," and "The

sanction and justify earthly power because God is called the heavenly King should be abandoned forever. Rather does the radiance of that kingdom, as it were, burn to ashes any earthly power. The earthly kingdom in the Bible is seen as a falling away from the heavenly King, a betrayal of him — and the restoration of the kingdom of God in heaven and on earth is seen as the abolition of earthly powers: "After that will come the end, when he will hand over the kingdom to God the Father, having abolished every principality, every ruling force and power" (1 Cor. 15:23).

The Solution to the Antinomy of Power

Only now do we arrive at the antinomy of power in its pure form. In the earthly power that arose after the Fall there is something morally intolerable and at the same time morally necessary.

In the chapter on democracy in *The Crisis of Industrial Culture,* I give a detailed sociopsychological analysis of power, which I do not want to repeat here. In summary, that chapter says that power is often used in a figurative sense, for example, the "power of ideas," "the power of beauty," but that we only get the genuine phenomenon of power where we have command and submission. Only this constitutes the social phenomenon of power. This power also has a special feature, in that the command requires unquestioning obedience whether those who are subject to that command agree with it or not. This absolutism of power can be absolutely minor and strictly limited, but it is always present in any power. Examples might be the power of traffic officers or soccer referees. This power is also "unquestionable," although no one finds it burdensome.

I have set forth the religious problem of power from the ancient

---

Russian People and the State." Cf. *The Way,* nos. 5, 6, 8. Alekseev correctly points out that L. Tikhomirov and all the Russian theoreticians of absolute monarchy are reproducing the theory of Ivan the Terrible, and that the absolutism of power is a pagan theory, in total opposition to the ancient Hebrew and Christian worldview, which can only give birth to the struggle against absolutism. For the Christian, says Alekseev, the following dilemma inevitably arises: either (1) to accept the biblical, prophetic, and apocalyptic view of the state, and in that case to acknowledge that Christianity has more in common with democracy than monarchy; or (2) to be forced on the whole to doubt the binding force of the Old Testament canon and that portion of the New Testament idea which is directly connected to it (*The Way,* no. 5 [October 1926] p. 39). There has never been a clearer or more daring formulation of the problem in Russian philosophy.

prophets to the Apocalypse in such detail because nowhere else has the antinomy of power been expressed so forcefully and so profoundly as in the Christian religion. Therefore we have to start from here, from this posing of the problem in order to arrive at the philosophical solution of this extraordinary contradiction that comprises power and that has been the source of the tragedy of history.

First, we must note the extraordinary feature that the greatest evil necessarily assumes the form of power, while the greatest good never does so. This amazing assertion should enable us to approach a resolution of the antinomy. As with all resolutions of deep contradictions, matters start to get resolved when we realize that power has taken on two different meanings. Petrazhitsky at some point found terms that successfully convey these two meanings: "power for use" and "power for power's sake." The power that comes "from God" and is religiously and morally justified is power for use — power in the service of truth and justice. Right after his famous text, Paul goes on to tell us just what kind of power can be called power from God: only that power which serves truth and justice — those higher divine values that are stationed above power. In this sense it now becomes clear that the ruler is God's servant, and he bears the sword not in vain but precisely for the defense of the good and the struggle against those who are evil. In this case, power is clearly taken to refer to the normative state based on law, even such a one as Rome with its Roman law.

What else does power refer to, if the Gospels come right out and say that it is from the devil? The other meaning of power should be called power for power's sake (or the "lust for mastery" in Augustine's phrase), because it serves no higher principles: it serves no one and nothing. On the contrary, this kind of power forces everyone to serve it. Such a power and the ruler who serves such a power bear the sword not at all for the struggle with evil, but, on the contrary, for the perpetration of evil and the intimidation of the good, the free, and the independent — those who have no desire to fall down and worship them. And what does this requirement to "fall down and worship" mean? It means accepting from the hands of the devil three basic forms of evil: murder, lying, and tyranny; for the power obtained by these methods does belong to the devil and becomes totalitarian. The devil is not exaggerating here (as the more naive of the church fathers supposed), for he could not deceive Christ.

We see what an extraordinarily rich philosophical content can be developed out of these symbols; and it becomes understandable why the two most original works of Russian philosophy take the form of an eloquent meditation on this text about the "temptation of power." I am referring to

Dostoevsky's "Grand Inquisitor" and Vladimir Solovyov's story about the Antichrist. Today they have assumed an absolutely authentic prophetic meaning. Yet the mystique of evil and the perfection of its organization turn out to be even more terrible in real life. Tyranny takes on fantastic forms.[7]

The Ideal of an Anarchical System and the Hierarchy of Values

"Thou shalt worship the Lord thy God, and him only shalt thou serve" (Matt. 4:10): what exactly do these words of Christ mean? They eliminate the temptations of tyranny by reminding us of power's will to serve the divine principles of truth and justice. Only under these conditions does power receive its mission "from above," as power was granted even to Pilate as long as he defended the law and justice: "I find no fault in this righteous man" (cf. John 19:4). And he would have defended justice to the end if he had not been scared by the threat of a political denunciation in Rome ("thou art not Caesar's friend," John 19:12). I have always been amazed by the Gospel narratives' presentation of Pilate. Many Christian legends have been based on this figure and his subsequent fate, and even in the credo it does not say "crucified by Pontius Pilate," but "crucified under Pontius Pilate."

Perhaps this is why Paul had a relatively high esteem for Roman law, the Roman courts, and Roman citizenship. But no text in history has been so badly misused as these words: "There is no power but of God." Moreover, nobody reads the chapter all the way through to the end, where we are told what kind of power receives divine sanction and in what sense. That any power is divine under any conditions whatsoever is something that Christians have never claimed. This claim is directly refuted in all the Gospels and in the Bible as a whole, as I have already shown. On the contrary, the religion at the basis of our Christian culture decisively affirms an organizational ideal that is based not on power but on mutual service through the fulfillment of gifts, on an ideal of human interaction in love and solidarity. There is no denying that this ideal of free human interac-

---

7. The Catholic Church, organized today as a fighter for freedom, should not take offense at Dostoevsky. His "Inquisitor" was in no way directed against it: what he had in mind was the creation of a new antireligion, directed against God and Christ ("we are not with You but with him").

tion played an enormous role in the working out of the contemporary liberal democratic state, and that it can be developed and realized only in a liberal state based on law.

On the other hand, Christianity has never asserted that power is always "from the devil" or that power is in itself an absolute evil; it has never supported an instantaneous utopian "anarchism." This idea is promoted only by sectarians like the Doukhobors or Tolstoy, who have no notion at all of the regulative, ethical, and legal value of power. Here we have an example of the nondialectical, rationalistic thinking that Hegel used to mock, in which any contradiction gets resolved by eliminating the thesis and preserving the antithesis, or vice versa. Thus Tolstoy simply erases the thesis of power from his Gospels and proclaims the antithesis of anarchism and nonresistance. Conversely, Ivan the Terrible's theory of absolute power in heaven and on earth does it the other way round.

The Christian solution consists in the establishment of a hierarchy of values: power has value when it serves truth and justice. Justice and the law have value when they serve and make possible the fellowship of love. Under these conditions, power does receive sanction from above. Conversely, power truly belongs to the devil whenever the whole hierarchy of values is perverted: when power serves no one and nothing except itself; even worse, it uses all the means of evil, recognizing nothing higher than itself.

At this point it is clear why ultimate evil takes on the form of power. Even the pre-Christian world had no doubts on this score and regarded tyranny as the greatest evil. Medieval moral theology raised the question of tyrannicide — under what conditions is it permissible? The whole question, of course, revolves around who should be called a tyrant.[8]

At this point we need to ask: if ultimate evil necessarily takes the form of power, then why does the highest good not concur in doing so? ("But among you it shall not be so!") The answer is contained in the analysis of command and submission that I have already given: submission always involves a replacement of my will and freedom by the will and freedom of another, a replacement of my "I" by the "I" of another; it always

8. There is no doubt that Caligula or Nero was a genuine tyrant. Julius Caesar cannot be called a tyrant because of his extraordinary talent and relative nobility of purpose, but the claim that Alexander II, the great Russian tsar-liberator, was a tyrant is absolutely monstrous. The enormous contribution of Aldanov is his reconstruction of this historical tragedy in his novel *Roots.* The roots of genuine Russian freedom were at that time in the hands of Alexander II; and what was in the hands of his assassins, who took themselves to be "liberators," were the roots of a genuine Russian and perhaps even world tyranny.

involves an obedience due to "fear, not conscience." The situation becomes oppressive when my own conscience does not acknowledge the command to be reasonable or just. Not only religion but also the rational philosophy of law has noted this unavoidable imperfection in legitimate coercion. I have already shown in detail how Fichte formulated this "antinomy of the law" (in my chapter on democracy in *The Crisis of Industrial Culture*). Essentially the same thing is confirmed here as in the religious antinomy: the defense of legal freedom requires power and coercion — and yet genuine freedom repudiates any coercion in principle. The struggle against the violation of laws is ethically necessary: the resolution of the antinomy has to start here, but it cannot stop here. We have to move on to the education of the person for independence, the education of one's "selfhood."

Here we have the most ancient prototype of the father, which contemporary psychology has discovered in the collective unconscious. The principle of a normative upbringing follows the same trajectory in the patriarchal family, in the patriarchal monarchy, and in the development of the liberal state based on law: first, the power of the father who prohibits and gives orders; next, the education of the youth toward independence and the ability to judge for himself what should and should not be; and, finally, respect for the authority of the father and friendship with him on the part of the grown-up son. The same pattern is repeated in the development from patriarchal autocracy to a liberal democracy based on law, when the individual person and the people as a whole can say for the first time "I myself" and "we ourselves." In *The Crisis of Industrial Culture* I showed in detail what a fragile juridical mechanism contemporary democracy employs so that the danger of arbitrary power, or the "lust for mastery," is reduced to an absolute minimum. This ensures that power, within these limits, receives the full and voluntary acknowledgment of those who are subject to it, and that they see power as functioning to provide the service and organizational framework that makes life easier for them. One need only recall the English police, who are really nannies to the population. Nevertheless, power always retains a certain temptation for humans, and we can observe this struggle for power in any parliament. But it can be transformed into a method of selecting the best and the freest. We can meet up with remnants of the "lust for mastery," not devoid at times of a certain comic element, even in the legal bureaucracy; and here it is not hard to observe groveling to those higher up, and capricious arbitrariness toward those who are lower and subordinate.

All these defects in purely hierarchical relations serve to bring out more clearly the higher stage of interaction between people, a stage that transcends power, law, and the state, but on the foundation of the latter. This stage of higher human interaction is not the utopia of anarchism at all: it is familiar to everyone and we come across it all the time in the spiritual dialogue among people in the spheres of science, art, religion, friendship, love. Christ was referring to this stage of fellowship when he said: you are no longer slaves of God the Father, but friends and sons. This is what Paul meant in his teaching about harmonious fellowship as the fulfillment of gifts and the knowledge of all the mysteries of wisdom and authority by hearts knit together in love (Col. 2:1-3). In the light of Christianity, it seems indubitable that "the way, the truth, and the life" (John 14:6) are set forth here for the whole of humankind, not only for the particular branch of society in the world that we call the "church," even if the leading and didactic role in this vein has been granted to the Christian churches as they have developed over the course of time.

These are the general principles revealed in the religious as well as the philosophical, ethical, and legal meaning of power. These principles on the whole coincide with each other because philosophy is confronted with Christian culture. After all, Christian culture, like any culture, was formed in the first place under the influence of religion.

CHAPTER 6

The Inherent Tragedy of the Sublime

Materialism and Spirituality, Russian Thought and Marxism

Nowadays baseness of heart has afflicted the people of every nation. This is something worse than falling into sin. The fallen one has not reached ultimate baseness: he still knows what's up and what's down. But ultimate baseness claims that there is no "up," and that what gets labeled as "base" is the most genuine, useful, valuable, and invincible thing, which is rightly supposed to have dominion in this world.

The clearest form of such clouding over of the mind was manifested in the parliamentary declarations of the communists, who tried to argue that they had nothing to do with murder in the streets, because their doctrine allows only mass, but not individual, terror. This means: murder is justified when it is committed in large numbers — not only justified, but held up as a praiseworthy service, elevated into a principle.

About these morally beclouded types, who suffer from a distortion of their faculty of judgment, it has been said: "They know not what they do." With these words Christ prayed not for those whom it is easy to forgive, but for those whom it is hardest to forgive: he prayed for his crucifiers, who committed the most grievous crime the world has ever seen. Vastly better are those who "know what they do": ordinary robbers, who know what the good is and where it is, but who choose evil out of weakness or passion or greed. The problem of Socrates rears its head once more: isn't virtue first and foremost knowledge? Of course, it is a specific knowledge, the knowledge of good and evil, the ability to evaluate them accurately. But it is not something that is self-evident. There have been ages when humans had a sound knowledge of the good, even if they did not have the strength to do it! Such was the classical Middle Ages. But there are other times when this higher knowledge of the heart has been lost — and such is the present age.

The remedy for this deafness and blindness can be found only in Christianity, for it broadens and deepens the ethical judgment. Russian thought and Russian literature have contributed much to such deepening. Dostoevsky and Tolstoy — they are the deepened dialectic of the heart. Their main problem is whether crime is admissible in the name of progressive, rational, social goals. There is something prophetic in their way of posing the problem, when Tolstoy foresees that what is terrible for humanity is not the crimes of individual evildoers, but the crimes of collectives and states, so-cially "justified" crimes; when Dostoevsky sees that the "achievements of progress" will be built on and paid for by the tears of the tormented.

Some judgments about Soviet Russia seem strange — judgments coming from people who acknowledge the principle of Christian culture, who read the Bible. They say: There have been great technical achievements; unfortunately, however, there is no freedom, and personhood has been oppressed. But the entire Bible does nothing but expose and condemn such construction, which is founded on sin and transgression, on the denial of the value of personhood, on oppression.

Marxism is perfectly aware of its primordial and implacable opposition to Christianity, and continually emphasizes it (it says: Christianity builds on love; we build on hate!). To promote this opposition, it preserves the concept of materialism, which by now has gone completely stale and flat philosophically, and means almost nothing. Yet this concept still means opposition to spirituality, opposition to Christianity. If God is spirit, then Marxism stands for enmity toward God and spirit.

What we need is a philosophical understanding of the essence of both materialism and spirituality. They are two mind-sets, two dispositions of consciousness. This has nothing to do with old-fashioned materialism and spiritualism, which want to discover the substance of all things and quarrel about whether the world consists of material atoms or spiritual monads! Contemporary materialism is a mind-set, a method of action and a method of interpretation, elevated into a principle. Marx elevated into a principle that mind-set which everyone in the nineteenth century had tacitly begun to acknowledge, although everyone hypocritically denied it in words. Any bourgeois was an "economic materialist" in practice and has continued to be one. This down-to-earth practical materialism is also a specific kind of religion — what is more, the basest religion that has ever existed. It is said about this religion: "their god is their belly!" (Phil. 3:19). Marx denounced the bourgeoisie not because it set such store on the "economic substructure" and steadfastly believed in it — Marx himself believed in nothing else — but because it hypocritically preached about the "spirit" and "spirituality" in order to soothe its soul. We have had enough of hypocrisy, says Marx, let's admit what everyone has been thinking for a long time now: everything is built on an economic substructure, on the satisfaction of needs, on interests, exactly as the classical bourgeois economists taught. What is important is just that the "economic substructure" should not be occupied exclusively by the capitalists; what is important is that the proletariat should get a piece of the pie. Or is there some chance that the proletariat is not materialistic? Could it possibly believe in something other than needs and interests? Marx did not see such a proletariat: that it might exist never even occurred to him. Henrik De Man assures us that any modern proletarian dreams of only one thing: the satisfaction of his bourgeois needs. He wants to live like the bourgeoisie. This is a bourgeois-philistine ideal. If one starts talking about a spiritualizing proletariat, it means that one repudiates Marxism and crosses into religious territory.

Marxism is the apotheosis of philistinism and the bourgeois ideal, for it infects everyone and everything with the bourgeois ideal and philistinism: it makes philistinism collective and international. The real opposition to these monstrosities is spirituality, not collectivism or communism. A spiritual communism is possible and we see it in the communism of the first Christian community — a communism of love, good deeds, and sacrifice; it was alien to any kind of philistinism, any kind of "economic materialism." "Economic materialism" is first and foremost a quenching of the spirit: Christianity, in contrast, says: "Quench not the spirit!" (1 Thess. 5:19).

We might call Marx's philosophy "speculation on debasement." This is not mere irony, but a philosophical characterization of its essence.

Levels of Being

Genuine philosophy sets out a system of categories of being, a system of levels of being. Moreover, every level reveals a new quality of being. Simplifying and schematizing, we can observe the following levels:

1. Categories of physicomathematical being (material-spatial processes).

2. Categories of organic being (plant and animal processes).
3. Categories of psychic being (consciousness and the unconscious). This is the kingdom of nature: above it rises the kingdom of spirit and freedom. Spirit and freedom are one.
4. Categories of spiritual being, which also has several levels: science, technology, economics, law, morals, art, religion.

The kingdom of spirit and freedom introduces us into the sphere of creative values: technology, the economy, science, art are values; there is no creativity without valuation. This whole ladder of levels can be evaluated; and at that point we can correlate the higher and lower levels of being. Thus the organism is richer and more complex than a simple machine — and therefore more valuable; psychic being is richer and more valuable than the merely physical; the spiritual is richer and more valuable than the psychic.

If we take a good look at this hierarchy in spiritual being, we can easily discern one startling law: it was formulated early on by Aristotle and later by Hegel. Any higher level of being and value presupposes and contains all the mechanical and chemical processes; psychic life presupposes and contains the processes of organic life. Spiritual life presupposes and contains the psychic processes of the subconscious and consciousness. In this sense, humans in all their plenitude are mechanisms, "chemisms," organisms: they are inanimate plants and animate animals, and, finally, creatively free spirits. Aristotle expressed this correlative law of the levels of being in the concepts of form and matter; any lower level of being is matter for the higher one, which is its new form; thus the organism is a particular form of the physicochemical processes; the psyche is a particular form of organic life. Spirit and freedom are a particular form of the psychic processes. Clearly, any new and higher form presupposes and contains the previous and lower one as its matter, and gives it a new form.

The Error of Materialism — Speculation on Debasement

Such a correlation of form and matter shows clearly what makes materialism possible and where its error lies. Materialism is the reduction of any higher form to its lower matter. Materialism tells us that organic life can be reduced to physicochemical processes, that humans are in essence only animals, that consciousness is only a neural network. Materialism tells us that the statue is only marble, that music is only a sound wave. But materialism will also tell us, in exactly the same way, that culture is only a particular form of the economy ("economic materialism"), that spirit is only a particular form of the basic sexual psychic energy, as Freud has done.[1] This reduction of higher forms to lower ones can get fixated at any convenient level one chooses: different materialists have their favored species of "matter": for Timiriazev, "matter" is physicochemical processes; for Marx, "matter" is the economy (production and distribution); for Freud, "matter" is sexuality, which is not a spatiomaterial object at all.

What do all these various sorts of materialism have in common? Clearly, there is nothing in common in what they take to be "matter." What *is* common to them all, however, is the method of reducing higher forms to lower ones; and this is what I have labeled "speculation on debasement."

The fundamental error of this method, which has spread over time throughout all of science, philosophy, and the psychic realm of humanity, rests on the following claims: "culture is only the economy," "the spirit is only sexuality," "the human being is only a living organism," "the organism is only a mechanism." Herein lies the whole falsehood. Precisely not "only" — but "also!" A downward movement through the levels explains nothing: the movement must go upward. But as soon as we say: "not only, but also," we can immediately run through the hierarchy of levels from bottom to top: "not only marble, but also a form of beauty," "not only a sound wave but also harmony," "not only nature but also freedom," "not only the processes of consciousness but also the creative spirit," and, finally, "not only relative but also absolute." Here is the ascent that Marxism cannot accept, for it leads to the Absolute Spirit, it ascends to the absolute summit, to the sublime God himself.

The opposite path leaves us only with speculation on debasement: always to say "only," always to reduce every form to lower matter — but then not to come to a halt and to keep going down to the primary material, as atomic materialism does. Soviet philosophy cannot make up its mind to do one thing or the other; it comes to a halt on Marx's "matter," on the economic process. On the one hand, to say that this is "only the mechanics of atoms" means losing the revolutionary impulse, the Promethean spirit, titanism: it means plunging into a mechanistic fatalism. On the other hand, to say: "not only the mechanics of atoms, but also creative invention, also the Promethean spirit" (for every means of production is

---

1. This analogy has been correctly pointed out by S. Frank, "Psychoanalysis as a Worldview," *The Way*, no. 25.

68

an invention, a creative Promethean act) means opening up the categories of spiritual freedom, that is, making a break with materialism and the game of speculating on debasement. Soviet philosophy does not have enough dialectics; it does not have the courage to lay it all on the line, to think things through to the end. For dialectics is also the art of thinking things through: "The wise differ from the foolish: they think things through to the end" (A. Maikov).

The Pathos of Profanation

Speculation on debasement dialectically requires delving into primary matter. Buechner and Maleschott might regard this as a clear and simple thing to do. Even Timiriazev could think that we would find a solid foundation for materialism in atomistic mechanics and chemistry. But science now lacks any such foundation. Primary matter has become totally problematic and threatens to turn into nothing at all. Determinism and the "iron" law of causality are tottering on the brink. Leibnizism can almost celebrate a victory: quanta look just like monads!

This is the strange position in which Soviet Marxism finds itself today. Does its "materialism" mean anything at all? There is no real matter to which its "matter" can refer, and it has never dared to ask what exactly matter is. But its "materialism" does refer to the method of speculating on debasement. Here it stands firmly. The expression "speculation on debasement" contains an amusing ambiguity. It refers to a method of explanation, a philosophical speculating with concepts, while referring at the same time to a method of action, a particular kind of speculation on values, a game with debasement in the sense of a wager on the lowest values. Materialism has a meaning both in theory and in worldly practice.

The point is that the reduction of everything to any kind of lower matter, which then serves as the ultimate foundation and universal substructure (like Marx's economic substructure), takes this substructure as the essential reality on the one hand, but on the other hand also takes it as the main value: in other words, as a fulcrum in both the theoretical and practical sense. If the economy is the most essential thing in social life, then it also has the highest value in social life. In this sense economic materialism is a value judgment that gives rise to practical behavior. The same thing goes for any other speculation on debasement: if humans are in essence "only animals," then mere animal life has the most value; if the essence of psychic energy is sexuality (the libido), then sexuality has the most value, and so on. In all these cases, there is a postulate (assumption) that out of necessity admits a true reality with a true value behind it. A theoretical philosophical "speculation" turns into a practical norm for behavior, into a wager on the lower values, on the soundness of the economic substructure.

Speculation on debasement distorts (1) the law of the correlation of categories, which states that the higher category is a new and independent kind of being, irreducible to the lower; and (2) the law of the hierarchy of values, which states that one should not prefer the lower to the higher. But it is precisely the lower values that everyone finds so convincing and attractive; when it comes to preferring the value of the "economic substructure," Chichikov [the acquisitive protagonist of Gogol's *Dead Souls*] would agree completely with Marx, and the French bourgeois with the Russian communist.

It is worthy of note that this wager on debasement will always be the most attractive one to the populace in both theory and practice. The easy accessibility of Marxism and any kind of materialism accounts for their attractiveness. It is always easier to go down than to go up — this is the law of inertia in human nature, the path of least resistance.

With what rapture do we learn that we are descended from apes, that we are only animals, only matter, that sacred love is only sexuality, and so on! Any "only" seems to afford us profound relief, while any "not only" makes us uneasy and spurs us on to action. With what enthusiasm and ingenuity do people expose all sorts of "unvarnished truths," discovering a universal greed and lust. No man is a hero to his valet; to the lout, anyone of a higher rank is a "despot, feasting in a luxurious palace." Whence comes the pathos, the inner source, that animates this strange thirst for debasement?[2] It is the pathos of profanation, which is diametrically opposed to the pathos of sublimation, the pathos of the sublime.

The pathos of profanation gives life and breath to Mephistopheles and Peter Verkhovensky (in Dostoevsky's *Demons*). But it is this same mind-set that we encounter in Marx and Freud. What unites them all is the conviction that everything sacred and sublime is only an illusion (cf. the title of Freud's book [on religion], *The Future of an Illusion*).

In this intrinsically philosophical sense, not just in the colloquial sense, the pathos of Marx and Freud is a pathos of profanation. Hence the aesthetic and ethical loathsomeness of Marxism, hence the absolute fail-

---

2. Cf. Dostoevsky's *Demons:* "We will pluck down the high mountains; we will stifle any genius in his cradle" (Shigalyov).

ure of any Marxist art, the uncouth style of its press ("the kulak and leftist deviations and excesses," "the general line," "womanization"); art and ethics are sublimation, and Marxism is profanation. The essence of profanation consists in reducing everything to the lowest motives: religion is "fear" and "priestly greed"; love is "sexuality." As a result, nothing is sacred, and so the ultimate step is taken: acquiescence in crime. In contrast, the essence of sublimation is the transition to the higher forms and levels of being, the feeling for the sublime, reverence. Sublimation presupposes height and perfection, it presupposes the sublime God himself. This explains why Marxism and any kind of speculation on debasement show such enmity toward God and such aversion toward any kind of reverence.

Profanation and the Exposing of Evils

Someone might retort, however, that even if profanation is repulsive, still the exposing of evils has a value, and even its own kind of grandeur. Isn't the pathos of Marx and Marxism first and foremost a pathos of exposing evils? Doesn't Marx ceaselessly expose the sins of the bourgeoisie?

This objection is legitimate and dialectically necessary. The exposing of evils must be distinguished from profanation. The exposing of evils is the business of prophets, and it is possible only before God; only the one who has turned his face toward God can do it. Profanation is the business of Mephistopheles, and it is possible only for the one who has turned his back on God, the one who finds heaven repulsive ("we will leave heaven to the sparrows and the priests" — Heine).

The exposing of evils aims to turn humanity toward God. Profanation aims to turn humanity away from God. It would be ridiculous to think that Mephistopheles wanted to "expose" Faust. This is not his role at all. A prophetic pathos would be ridiculous in Mephistopheles, just as it would be in Marx. A godless prophet, or a prophet who has renounced God, is pitiful and ridiculous.

The exposing of evils aims to show up false sublimation, false elevation, so as to restore true sublimation, true elevation. But true sublimation is possible only for the one who knows the category of "the sublime," "the sacred," who knows the sublime God, who knows the hierarchy of being and the hierarchy of values. True sublimation is impossible for Marx and Freud, because they regard "the sacred and the sublime" as illusions. It would be ridiculous for Freud to expose his patients' sexuality. Likewise it would be ridiculous for Marx to expose the bourgeois ideal of the bourgeoisie, for this would mean to call for spirituality. It would be ridiculous to expose the class egoism of the bourgeoisie and its struggle against the interests of the proletariat, for this is precisely what the class nature of humanity amounts to. But exposing exploitation would be the height of folly. The word "exploitation" is just as devoid of meaning in Marxism as it is in Darwinism, or any other causal-naturalistic worldview. When it comes to exploitation, the words of Spinoza should be hammered home to the Marxist: "Greater states swallow up the lesser ones by the same law that big fish swallow up little ones" — and we might add, kulaks swallow up the poor! In such a worldview, problems of law and justice do not arise; there is no room for absolute value or the idea of freedom, any notion of sin is nonexistent. The only people who have the right to talk about exploitation are the ancient Hebrew prophets and Christ, not Marx. To pose as a prophet exposing evils is indecent for someone who regards prophecy as the "opium of the people." To "expose" means to expose the "base," but the "base" exists only for one who has a sense of the "sublime." Whoever denies the sublime and the sacred has no notion of either the base or the sublime. How could a person like that expose anybody?

The Value of the Skyscraper and the Value of the Sublime

Spinoza understood that naturalism and determinism do not give us the right to either "mourn or mock." Marx could never get this through his head. Due to his complete inability to recognize his philosophical premises, he did not even see the dilemma: either the right to evaluate and expose — or the worldview of Marxism! The one excludes the other. Marx evaluated, he "mourned and mocked" at every turn; but with no understanding of evaluation and no knowledge of the hierarchy of values, he evaluated falsely.

Subconsciously, values are admitted even here; but they are the values of bulk, not greatness; the values of the vertically high (the skyscraper), not of the sublime; the values of the insolently strong, not of the generous and noble.

We get a religion of power and force, a religion of the earth, of the belly, of the prince of this world, of the beast. Biblical symbols from the tower of Babel and Nebuchadnezzar to the beast of the Apocalypse perfectly give the exact measure of such a mind-set. The ideal of a despotically regulated and universally dominant collective is the contemporary expression of such a mind-set.

It may seem that a certain peculiar sublimation is operating here too. But this is an illusion: here we have no transition to the higher, spiritual levels of being. There is only an intensification and expansion of that same lower level; there is self-praise and self-inflation ("We will liberate ourselves by our own hand" — the Russian version of the socialist "Internationale") that merely produces height and bulk, not genuine greatness.

Christianity's standpoint is the opposite. It affirms the value of the sublime and not of the vertically high; the sacred, not the strong; it affirms the value of greatness, not of bulk (i.e., it affirms the value of the kingdom that is not of this world, the power wielded by meekness, the visage of the slave, the cross). Obviously humanity finds this standpoint much harder to accept than the opposing wager on bulk and strength. Sublimation is not easy; it requires risk taking, sacrifice, heroic efforts. The lower values of power and the economy seem so much more steady and reliable, while heroism and sainthood seem risky and ephemeral, perpetually leading to death and destruction.

The Correlation between Categories of Being and Stages of Value

A certain natural inertia in humankind, a constant aspiration to "sink," a constant preference for the lower values of Mammon — all these are deeply rooted in a special correlative law between categories of being and levels of value. This law was formulated in all its philosophical rigor and inexorability by Nicolai Hartmann in his "Categorial Laws." The law runs as follows: The height of a category is inversely proportional to its robustness. Higher forms of being are the most complex, circumscribed, and dependent, and therefore the weakest and most fragile; while the lower forms are the least circumscribed, and therefore most stable and unconditioned. Human life on earth requires an infinitely complex network of cosmic conditions governing the temperature of the sun, the structure of the earth, the availability of air and water; in other words, a complex network of conditions that is extremely rare and that some astronomers think may be unique in the universe. If even one of these conditions is disturbed, then all the higher forms and stages of life would immediately break down, culture would cease to exist, humankind and all of organic life would disappear. Like the moon, however, the earth would still have stones and rocks, since these are more robust and require far fewer conditions for their existence. The mechanics of atoms and chemical processes would be unaffected by a world catastrophe, by the earth's destruction, for the lower level of physicochemical being is the most robust. Another example: a human being dies and turns into a corpse, which then decomposes; the higher forms of psychic and organic life disappear, but the physicochemical processes in the corpse are unaffected. They are indifferent to life or death. Nothing scares them; they keep on doing their inviolable work. A skeleton is infinitely more robust in its ghastly simplicity than the fragile and ingeniously articulated living organism. The pyramids are more robust and reliable than the pharaoh. This is a sad law, a kind of universal entropy. If we think about it seriously, then the law of the general tragedy of existence is revealed to us — an existence that is threatened by general debasement, a retrograde descent to the lowest levels, back to the primordial soup. The plenitude of the higher stages of life, their flourishing prime, must be saved, and this requires a miracle — the Savior!

What is revealed here is an astonishing insight into the cosmic tragedy known to the great religions of humankind, Hinduism as well as Christianity. Everything that is sublime, noble, precious is simultaneously the most fragile and vulnerable. A human being is more vulnerable than a plant; a plant is more vulnerable than a stone; "noble" plants like the rose and the grape are much less hardy than weeds and ivy; the lower and lethal bacteria possess incredible tenacity and power of resistance. It is precisely the highest that can suffer and die, not the very lowest. Thus it is easier to kill Socrates than the tyrant of Syracuse, easier to kill Christ than Pilate. Therefore why not prostrate oneself before the prefect and the tyrant whom it is impossible to kill and who themselves have the power to kill everyone? This is how the crowd always reckons; the fact of force, power, bulk always appeals to it. The crowd always wagers on what is lower, but more robust and sure. Hence its respect for dictatorships, and especially the dictatorship of the proletariat: the proletariat arranges matters so that no one can offend it, and it can in turn offend anyone. This also accounts for the respect shown to the household tyrant in Ostrovsky's comedy: "Who can offend you, my dear fellow? You yourself can offend anyone."

The history of heroes, martyrs, prophets, and saints positively confirms the law of tragedy, the law of the weakness and fragility of the higher forms of life. But what is really astonishing is that it is just when they die that they reach their greatest height. The sublime is like that — it dies without a struggle; it does not defend itself; it even, as it were, seeks out its own perdition by sacrificing itself. Hence, if there were no destruction, there would be no sacrifice either, and thus no greatness of sanctity. The very weakness of the higher stages attests to their genuine height.

74

A certain greatness of soul is needed to understand the beauty of risk, sacrifice, perdition. Risk is a "noble business" only for the noble person. Some people understand this right away, but others never do, like the eternal and universal Chichikov. For him the stability of the lower forms of being always has more value than the ephemerality and fragility of the higher ones: a titmouse in the hand is worth more than a crane in the sky. He always refuses to be the hero and argues convincingly, like the soldier in the joke: "Better a coward for half an hour than a corpse for the rest of your life." The vast majority of people always consider safety, force, power, and wealth to be more reliable than sainthood, heroism, beauty, greatness. But what if power and wealth come to be associated with crime? At this point people begin to waver: crime is not so easy to accept. But the wavering does not last long: when crimes, particularly collective crimes, are successful, they are easy to forget. No one judges the victors — and woe betide the losers! There is no adage that is more immoral, more anti-Christian.

But it is precisely this saying, "No one judges the victors," this involuntary worship of fact, this worship of strength and grossness, that lies at the basis of all bolshevizing [majority] judgments — judgments acceptable to any morality whatsoever, but not to the Christian one. It says: True enough, there is no freedom — but look at all that marvelous construction! This means: the spirit is quenched but matter flourishes; personhood is killed off, but the machine lives on. Can one have any doubts about the evaluation of this way of life from the Christian point of view? "No one judges the victors" — here we have a classic instance of the perversion of moral judgment.

The Tragedy of Existence and Its Relative Overcoming

This strange law, that the highest, the most noble, is the most fragile and destructible, expresses the tragedy of existence. It meets us at every turn we take in ordinary life. Right now I am listening attentively to the ticking of my grandfather's watch, and the precise rhythm of its steely heart amazes me. It will keep on resounding long after the living hearts of its owners have fallen silent. There is a deep tragedy in the very clothes of people now dead who have been close to us: the immortality of those insignificant rags is strange compared to the transitoriness and death of creatures who are full of infinite meaning. But any tragedy and any suffering that fall to our lot bring us closer in a mysterious way to the tragedy of Golgotha, precisely because the cross and Golgotha are the fullest expression of the essence and depth of tragedy. There is an extraordinary similarity to the fate of Christ in the fate of every person insofar as he approaches genuine tragedy; beginning with those remnants of clothing for which strangers "cast lots," and ending with the disciples' betrayal, the mockery of the crowd, and "God's forsaking" at the moment when the ascesis [*podvig*] reaches its greatest height. Christ says nothing to the person who knows nothing of tragedy.

There is tragedy in every "human tear," but the pinnacle and ultimate limit of tragedy is not illness, death, and suffering (as the Buddha thought), but the triumph of evil and the humiliation of the good. The Divine itself submits to being spat upon. The sublime itself (the Most High himself) is condemned to the basest fate. The God-Man is crucified. Here is genuine tragedy. If *this* is the last word, the eternal word of senseless "necessity," then there is an end to everything, then it is not worth living, striving, acting, then it is impossible to accept the world, as Dostoevsky thought; then it is impossible to accept God, as Job thought.

If this were indeed the case, then any tragedy (even communism) would kill the soul. But tragedy does not kill, but purifies and elevates, even delights. This is the miracle of tragedy: How can tragedy, that is, death and perdition, enrapture us and be beautiful? Why go to the theater and cry your heart out? The strange dialectic of tragedy transforms the perdition of heroes and martyrs into victory, transforms the end into the beginning of something else. It gives us a presentiment of a way out, even (or especially) when the dialectic gets stuck. The way out, the "trans-," is the great action of tragedy. Tragedy, as it were, tears us out of life, out of the plane of the ordinary and the everyday. This is its hidden joy and rapture: "All, all that threatens perdition harbors inexplicable delights for a mortal heart, the pledge, perhaps, of immortality" [Pushkin].

The joy comes from the fact that in tragedy (just as in humor) the spirit, that is, the genuine deep-lying "I," experiences and recognizes here for the first time its royal dignity, its absolute freedom from all the lower stages of being, from any kind of nature or necessity. But it is a special kind of dignity and a special kind of freedom: it belongs only to the one who is willing to endure the full brunt of tragedy, who has the absolute courage not to tremble for his life. Whoever does not fear the "threat of perdition" is granted the "pledge of immortality." And whoever "preserves his soul [life] will lose it" (John 12:25). In *The Vocation of Man*,[3] Fichte

---

3. The passage paraphrased here by Vysheslavtsev actually comes from *The Vocation of a Scholar*. Trans.

evokes this freedom of spirit that rises above all the categories of nature. He apostrophizes natural necessity: You can destroy my body, you can dash me onto the high mountains and wipe me off the face of the earth, but you can never do away with my free will, my free yes or no, which keeps on resounding forever in my very perdition! Here we have tragedy's Promethean consciousness of spirit. But it is granted only to the one who shares the fate of the suffering God.

Spirit reveals here the eternal, ideal kingdom of meanings — the kingdom to which spirit itself and its ideal valuations and affirmations belong. Let Romeo and Juliet perish: still the eternal meaning of their love and the eternal harmony of their individualities faithfully abide despite or, more precisely, because of their destruction. Let Socrates die: still the eternal meaning of his wisdom and the eternal theme of his fate are immortalized by the very fact of his death. All their strength abides in this: they found the "pledge of immortality" in the "threat of perdition"; they said their yes and no once and for all: yes to what they loved and held sacred, no to all the hostile forces and actions set in motion by the world and other people. This is the immortality of heroes, martyrs, and saints. It resides in the eternal significance of their meaning, in the perpetual victory of their ideal. Christianity itself is a mighty historical argument that shows that defeat (the cross) can signify victory ("in this sign you will conquer").

The Christian Faith That the Tragedy Can Be Absolutely Resolved

However majestic this ideal strength of spirit, this overcoming of tragedy through immortality, may be, it is still not Christianity's last word. After all, in the final analysis, it would be an immortality of eternal memory; it would mean that everything of value is saved and preserved only ideally, on another plane of existence, in "the other world," in Plato's kingdom of ideas, in Plotinus's seat of the mind [*umnoe mesto*]. "This world" — untransformed and unsaved — would still be given over to death and destruction. It would not be on earth as it is in the kingdom of heaven. Such an "ideal" victory is not enough for Christianity: it is the deincarnation of the Logos and contradicts the idea of incarnation and resurrection. The ideal triumph experienced in tragedy must be transformed into a real triumph. Death, perdition, suffering, the cross — these are not the last word for Christianity. The ideal victory of martyr and saint and their "eternal memory" — this also is not the last word. Only the real resurrection of Christ and the real transfiguration of the whole world is the last word. This means: what deserves life will live, what cannot die will not die.

The Christian religion cannot proclaim otherwise — this religion of the absolutely desired, which promises to fulfill all of humanity's cherished hopes, which promises that "every human tear will be wiped away." We can rejoice in the greatness of martyr and saint, we can pray for them, but we cannot desire that martyrs be tormented or the God-Man crucified forever. The desire for a full and potent victory of all values, of all that is sacred, and their incarnation here on earth and in the entire cosmos ("Thy kingdom come") cannot be banished from the human heart. We believe in the final victory of good and the inherent self-destruction of evil, and we cannot help but believe. There is nothing at all arbitrary in this faith: after all, atheists believe in the realization of their ideal just as "believers" do, only they wager on the lower to make things more stable and reliable. The one who wagers on the higher must have the courage to take risks, but neither can one renounce one's faith in victory. Total lack of faith makes any kind of action impossible. The total unrealizability of our desires would be the basis for another religion: not the religion of the absolutely desired (Christianity), but the religion of the absolute renunciation of all desires (Buddhism).

Any creativity is spiritual — it is faith in the victory of the spirit, in the conquest of the lower categories by the higher ones, in freedom's conquest of nature. If the law of the weakness of the higher were the only law, then everything that is higher would have collapsed long ago and could, indeed, never have appeared in the first place. If there were only a law of entropy — the law of universal cooling off and the cosmic leveling out of heat — then life would simply be impossible. For life is based on the diametrically opposed law: on warming as opposed to cooling, on the creation of contrasts as opposed to the universal leveling of the temperature. Spiritual life too is based on a diametrically opposed law: not on debasement but on sublimation, on the potential strength, force, and victory of the sacred and the sublime, on the potential advent of the kingdom of God. If holiness and strength were forever disjoined in principle, then the life of the spirit, that is, sublimation, creativity, incarnation would be intrinsically impossible. Holinesss and strength are disjoined at every turn in life and in history — and this is their tragedy — but they are ultimately one and will be united. This is the essence of faith, for God is the Holy Mighty One, the Holy Immortal One. God is precisely what "in the end" exists and what should "in the end" exist, Alpha and Omega.

Christianity believes that God is the Holy Mighty One, and therefore the victory of the holy and the sublime is assured in the long run: it is guaranteed in the deepest essence of the spirit. But only "in the long run" — not at every turn, not instantly, not at some midpoint in life or history between the beginning and the end, between Alpha and Omega. The Russian people believe that "God sees the truth, but does not hasten to proclaim his judgment." Sometimes, though, he does proclaim it very quickly, even right away (Goethe thought that "every crime is avenged here on earth"), but sometimes "heaven is silent" for a while so that the word of heaven, when it does come, may be proclaimed more powerfully and terribly: "Vengeance is mine, I will repay!" Often people cannot or do not want to hear the destructive divine word resounding throughout history. Only the prophets can really hear it, and only they are bold enough to speak it to the people. This is precisely why they are stoned, for humankind often finds this word unbearable.

Christianity and ancient Judaism are great religions because they lift the human spirit up to the height of ethical judgment by revealing a unique dialectic of evaluation. Here are their two principles:

First, the ability to see and comprehend the insignificance of the ruling powers and their triumphs, the ability to see the lack of greatness in mere strength and bulk (in the colossal). This is the Old Testament dialectic of the prophets, who destroy the value of the tower of Babel and Nebuchadnezzar. This dialectic was taken over in full by Christ, who established, however, another, new principle.

Second, the ability to see the worth of the sublime, even if it be humiliated; the ability to recognize the King in "the visage of the slave"; the ability to behold God in the one who "hangs on a tree." This is the other dialectic, the dialectic of the New Testament, but it presupposes the first. The philistine ideal says: "no one judges the victors," but the prophets judge them all the time. The philistine ideal says: "no one judges the victors," but Christianity proclaims: the prince of this world has already been condemned [John 16:11].

But the dialectic of the Old and New Testaments goes even further: it binds together ideological condemnation with real condemnation, it binds together ideal approval and sanctification with real victory. The dialectic of the prophets proclaims that any false triumph, any false elevation and pride are necessarily destroyed from within. The dialectic of Christianity proclaims that any humiliation of the sublime, any destruction of the divine and sacred, grants them victory and resurrection. Both dialectical moments are secured by Christ: "he hath put down the mighty from their seats, and exalted those of low degree" [cited from the Magnificat].

The tragedy is just that what we see in history, in the temporal, transitory, intermediate plane of existence, is continual alienation and conflict, the antinomy of greatness and force, holiness and strength. The only one who can overcome this antinomy is the one who is aware of this separation (as Job and the prophets and Christ were aware of it), does not fear it, and at the same time believes that it will finally be overcome. The higher principle of life and creativity is antinomic and tragic. To be aware of the weakness and fragility of the holy and the sublime and, risking perdition, to seek out victory and strength; never to seek out strength and force by giving up the higher ground, but preserving every aspiration toward the higher sacred things and values, to seek to strengthen them and empower them, while knowing that any failure in sublimation is a success of sorts — all this is a heroic gesture, which points upward and anticipates the final accomplishment. Christianity has its dialectic of tragic victory: "In this sign [the cross] you will conquer"; "Unless it die, it will not live" (John 12:24); death trampled down by death ("the negation of the negation"); victory goes to the one who makes sacrifices. The antinomy of holiness and strength is resolved in God, for he alone is the unity of all opposites. He alone is the Holy Mighty One. Faith that the tragedy can be absolutely resolved (belief in the Paraclete, the "Comforter") is the essence of Christianity. Without this faith life is impossible. The "Comforter" is the "giver of life." But this absolute resolvability, or resolution in the Absolute, can imply a relative irresolvability, or lack of resolution, on the plane of relatively time-bound existence. "God sees the truth, but does not hasten to proclaim his judgment" — but he will ultimately proclaim it.

CHAPTER 7

Two Paths to Salvation

Wisdom and the Symbol of Salvation

The philosopher should realize first that he is one of those people who constantly searches for the stone of wisdom, the "philosopher's stone." Every scholar is faced with the temptation of trying to find this stone in his own field of knowledge — in chemistry, mathematics, mechanics, biology, and, finally, in our own time, in psychology. But this can never be done, for wisdom, Sophia, in her all-embracing unity, in her ultimate understanding and ultimate solutions, goes beyond the boundaries of every particular science. The "philosopher's stone" can only be found by a philosophy that is able to use all the discoveries of the particular sciences, with all of their technical inventions, to achieve its goals. A positive science, built on the law of causality — a "causal" science — is absolutely incapable of investigating the problem of our ultimate goals, or of giving people an answer to the question about the ultimate meaning of life.

Technical invention always presupposes a system of values (an axiology); it presupposes values that are silently taken for granted. The medical and psychoanalytic sciences have no axiology. They extract specific values, such as health or the "normal" condition of body and soul, from the common hierarchy of values. But nobody knows what it means to be "normal," because nobody knows what exactly the "norm" of a human being is. The answer depends on what humans want to be and what they should be. In any case, it is certainly not "normal" for humans to think only about their health. If we want to arrive at an ultimate resolution and understanding, then we must embrace the whole plenitude of meaning and posit — clearly or indistinctly, consciously or unconsciously — the whole system of values and all of being. After all, interpretation is an orientation toward the "whole," toward the all-embracing "symbol" of the Absolute, toward the sublime "coincidence of opposites."

Yet the ultimate question of the meaning of life rises up from the depths of self-consciousness just when the "I" is caught in a tragic contradiction, when it comes face to face with non-sense, un-happiness, in-justice.

The resolution of this tragic contradiction is not provided by logic, by some scientific theory or technique; it cannot be obtained through scientific thinking or rationalistic consciousness. What we need is a redemption (salvation) that proceeds from the beyond, from the transcendent, from the kingdom that is "not of this world." All great religions are religions of salvation, because the thirst for salvation has its source in the vale of this life, in suffering, in tragic conflict.

In itself this redemption or salvation from the tragic contradiction, from the inescapable trap (aporia) where no way out is visible, is experienced as something miraculous, as a kind of "revelation." The solution comes from the Absolute's ultimate hidden unity with us; it arises from the "hidden God" who exists "beyond the barrier of opposites" and miraculously unites the opposites so that they cannot destroy each other in spite of their conflict, so that even this conflict can be transformed unexpectedly into harmony, for "the most beautiful harmony is born from opposites" (Heraclitus).

Such a resolution is never rational: it is religious, for we find it through our bond (*re-ligiia* = bond) with the transcendent, through our sense of dependence on the Absolute. But this sense of dependence in its abundant meaningfulness — this sense of being rooted in the Absolute — cannot be expressed otherwise than through a multifaceted and mysterious symbol. Only thus can the supraconsciousness appeal to consciousness and the subconscious, and only thus can the otherworldly Father speak with his this-worldly Son. Yet the symbolic wisdom of the salvific word is not elucidated by any kind of rational knowledge, but is attained only through insight; it is made clear through philosophical prophecy; for the love of divine wisdom, philosophy itself, is a "mirror" in which salvific wisdom, even if "in riddles" and "in part," nevertheless appears [1 Cor. 13:12]. Intuition and dialectic are the methods of philosophy. The mysterious symbol of salvation is grasped intuitively in the infinite multiplicity of its possible appearances and is then unfolded dialectically in all the antinomic duality or even multiplicity of its meanings. Philosophy always deals with ultimate unity and antinomies, with the Absolute and the coincidence of opposites. Therefore Hegel is right when he says that the object of philosophy is the same as the object of religion.

Wisdom must be sought on the common ground of philosophy and religion. This is the domain of the infinite, the unconditioned, the Absolute, where contradictions are born and the dialectic begins. Dialectic in turn is the art of dealing with contradictions, of discovering and resolving antinomies. Anyone who talks about the "coincidence of opposites" enters into a domain that falls under the purview of philosophy, and one enters into it even when one encounters some problem that is specific to one's own field of knowledge.

Two Mind-sets: The Dialectic of Tragedy

All the great religions, as I said, are religions of salvation (redemption), that is, they provide a resolution of the tragic contradiction, the fundamental antinomy of life. If we intuitively grasp and experience their "credos" in all of their depth and plenitude, we immediately run into the most profound contrast between the European and Asiatic worlds, between the Hindu and the Christian-Hellenic idea of salvation. We can see a priori that there are two possible solutions to the tragic contradiction, two different mind-sets about it:

First, one can escape from the contradiction, free oneself from it, save oneself by fleeing from the full-blown contradiction of the world; and in so doing, one can transform the world of opposites into an "illusion."

Second, one can throw oneself into the real contradiction, the struggle of opposites, like a tragic hero who makes war on the forces opposing him, without fear of perdition, with the firm conviction that he can "overcome" any kind of defeat, and with the hope of fulfilling all his most cherished desires.

The second mind-set basically assumes that every really existing contradiction is resolvable in principle — if not here and not now, then in the "other world." This is the Christian-Hellenic mind-set. We find its antithesis in Hinduism: the contradictions of life in this world are in principle irresolvable. Unraveling and struggling with the oppositions means entangling oneself in contradictions and suffering from them. Hinduism says that the best thing to do is to disentangle and free oneself from them.

Now the fundamental experience of the tragic takes on different forms in the Hindu soul than in the Christian, Hebrew, and Hellenic soul, because there are various levels, various stages, of tragedy. Every tear in itself is tragic, and so is any grief and any suffering (therefore it is written in the Apocalypse that "God shall wipe away every tear from their eyes" [Rev. 7:17]). But there are various tears and various levels of sorrow. The Buddha presents the tragic as sickness, old age, and death. Among the Hindus, the inevitability of suffering and death is the fundamental experience of the tragic; they rise as far as this stage — which is not, however, the highest stage of tragedy. What is even more tragic is to suffer and die unjustly, like Prometheus, Socrates, Job, and Christ. Here the experience of the tragic goes even deeper. We long to live — and yet we cannot help but die; we want to be healthy and happy, and yet we are stuck with suffering. This is a tragic contradiction, but there is another one that is even deeper, one that Socrates formulated in his "Apology": a person deserving of the highest honor is condemned to death! As the level of injustice increases, we approach the summit of tragedy: and this is the suffering and prosecution of an innocent person, a person who is honored and holy — ultimately, the God-Man. Tragedy can go no further, no higher than this: the one who is most worthy, holy, and divine is trampled on, humiliated, and destroyed. The summit of the tragic is Golgotha. Here the Christian soul finds the archetype, the prototype of the suffering God, the archetype of the tragic situation. All the tragic experiences of humanity focus on this point as if through a lens: the injustice of the court, the meanness of the crowd, the inquisition of the hierarchy, the incomprehension of all that is sublime and divine in the "Son of Man," disloyalty and the disciples' betrayal, and, in the last instance, abandonment by God and the silence of heaven. The tragic contradiction in this ultimate case is something that humans cannot bear, and therefore it is here, right at this point, that resolution and "salvation" must be found.

To explain how this is possible, we must first bear in mind the deeply paradoxical nature of tragedy: instead of crushing the soul completely, tragedy gives rise to a feeling of "salvation," to a hard-to-define "catharsis" (purgation). In the depths of the soul, consolation is always present, elusive though it may be. The Spirit of the Paraclete (the Comforter) breathes gently over tragedy, but as something that is incomprehensible and unknowable. In tragedy courage is not lost, but only intensified and heightened, elevated to something unknowable, as it usually is during moments of deep insight — hence the feeling of the sublime. This particular phenomenon implies that in principle a resolution to the contradiction has been presupposed and foreseen. A new vehicle of understanding is born from the transcendent.

Thus one can discover the remarkable dialectic at work in tragedy:

the tragic hero, the holy martyr, the suffering God takes upon himself and bears the unbearableness of tragic fate. He does not submit and he does not turn and flee — he pits his own higher value against the lower values and nonvalues. Injustice is powerless to destroy the righteous will. The greater the injustice, the more sublime is the unjustly suffering, holy will. In the condemnation and death of Socrates, the greatest human shame is combined with the greatest human glory. On the heights of Golgotha humanity's deepest sin is united to its highest "justification" and glorification in the God-Man.

Right at the very moment when God could say that he repents of the creation of humanity, he could also say that there is no need for him to repent of it. This is what "salvation" is, in the sense of redemption and justification: the divine "let justice triumph!" should not mean: "let the world perish," "let humankind perish." There are indeed values that redeem everything that has a negative value.

This, then, is the first "purgational" meaning of the tragic: the essential and the inessential, the meaningful and the meaningless, the positively and the negatively valued, the greatness and insignificance of humanity, are all combined in the tragic.[1] We may derive a token consolation even from the fact that it is impossible to turn everything into nonsense and negative value, from the absence of grounds for utter despair and resignation, from the fact that the decisive condemnation of being ("let the world perish, let man perish") may hereby be averted, since the sublime, the holy, the otherworldly are always present in the tragic situation. Yet it is a sorry consolation, because the "ideal world" is always here, but only "to the extent that it is not" (Fichte). The true, the holy, the otherworldly — all this is "only an idea." And when the one to whom the contemplation of this idea is revealed, and who himself should rightfully be regarded as its incarnation, descends into the dark cave of our world to liberate the captives fettered here and to lead them out into the light of the sun, these very prisoners are the ones who hand him over to be put to death, as happened with Socrates. After all, the one who stands opposed to all the life conditions of the prisoners is in tragic conflict with everything that he finds in the cave. If God wants to come down into the world, all of which "lies in evil," then he himself must suffer and die. This is not the resolution of the contradiction, however, since a "suffering God," a mortal God, is a contradiction. God is blessed and immortal. This means that he must

---

1. And in principle in the comic as well, as Socrates and Aristophanes were aware in the *Symposium*.

85

rise from the dead and "supersede" the tragic contradiction of suffering, death, and sin; he must "supersede" the very "world that lies in evil," so that he may show forth the kingdom that is "not of this world."

Sublimation and Synthesis

The concept of "supersession" discovered by Hegel, with its lovely dialectical ambiguity,[2] points at once to both paths of salvation. Hindu salvation is the "supersession" of this tragic contradiction in the sense of its abolition, the conversion of the world into a phantom. The contradictory opposites are transformed into an illusion. Christian salvation is this "supersession" of the world in the sense of its preservation at the highest level, in the sense of its transfiguration and "deification." Salvation in this case is elevation, sublimation.

Sublimation (*anagoge* in Greek) is the fundamental philosophical category that found its first dazzling interpretation in the idea of the Platonic Eros and was given another, more sober expression in Aristotle's notion of form and matter. Both the Platonic and the Aristotelian tradition were preserved and put to good use throughout the Middle Ages. The celebrated maxim of Thomas Aquinas, "Grace does not abolish nature, but perfects it," already contains the principle of sublimation. Alexander of Hales used the same expression: "the elevation [sublimation] of the reasoning creature over nature." Aristotle's doctrine of the hierarchical ordering of forms and their uplifting was dialectically grounded and deepened by Hegel. His doctrine is preserved in principle in Hegel's doctrine of "supersession" in the sense of "lifting up" the lower categories and their transposition into higher ones. Nietzsche had an excellent understanding of the category of sublimation and valued it, especially in ethics; he used the word "sublimation" in his own writings. At present we find a continuation of this tradition in Nikolai Hartmann's doctrine of the hierarchical structure of the system of categories.

Freud is absolutely correct in applying the concept of "sublimation" to the theory and practice of psychoanalysis, especially in his references to the Platonic Eros. But in taking up this category, one is obliged to apply it in its deepest and most positive sense, as this has been established by the enormous dialectical labor of philosophy. But we see nothing of the kind

2. The German word *aufheben* means "to lift up," both "to preserve" and "to abolish."

in Freud's work. This is why the idea of "sublimation" has become such a popular catchword for a public intrigued by psychoanalysis, and why it can all too easily be interpreted philosophically by way of a crude positivism, which reduces all the higher movements of the human soul to sexual drives, and explains everything by declaring it to be "nothing other than . . ." (the speculation on debasement that we see in Marxism).

By this very ruse we arrive at the antithesis of philosophical sublimation. But the basic principle of the qualitative independence of every level logically prevents us from either reducing a higher categorial level to the lower ones or using the lower levels to explain the higher one. What then is the meaning of the "sublime"? What is the higher and what the lower form? What are we seeking and what do we find in the "lifting up" of the soul?

Freud provides no answer to any of these questions. The popular interpretation of "sublimation" obscures and hushes up important philosophical and psychological problems. This is why Jung has every reason in the world not to settle for the popular interpretation of "sublimation," but to push the analysis further, so that a precise and proper understanding of "sublimation" may be determined. Adhering to the sobriety of the Aristotelian interpretation, Jung says: one must seek a middle path, that is, a way out of the aporia, the "dead end," the contradictory situation. Finding such a way out is extremely difficult, since this amounts to the resolution of a contradiction where "tertium non datur." This "third" way, which is not given and the finding of which seems impossible, must nonetheless be found — and it will be a totally new synthesis of the opposing forces or contradictory tendencies. This is a special art, a discovery that transcends the stratum of dueling opposites, the surface of the contradiction, with the aim of finding in another dimension the synthesis that is impossible at the previous level. This new synthesis is like a new level: we call it higher only because all the positive forces and elements that were formerly in conflict are preserved in it and at the same time enter into a new combination — one that resolves the contradiction.[3] This is sublimation, or the discovery of a higher form. Without this "middle path" as a way out, without the unity of opposites, without the "dialectical approach," it would be impossible to grasp the meaning of sublimation or to evaluate it in practice.

Contemporary analytical psychology also wants to work a "change"

---

3. Here the spatial relation of "height" means only that the "higher" level encompasses and contains the "lower"; it presupposes the "lower," but not vice versa.

in the soul, that is, to overcome psychic conflicts. Thus it takes its stand on the ground of the "problem of salvation," since it is seeking a resolution to the tragic contradiction. The soul is the first to strive for salvation and "redemption," but other spheres of existence can also suffer from tragic contradictions. There are cosmic catastrophes, just as there are biological, sociological, juridical, ethical, and national conflicts. The soul has its own ways of moderating its dissonances, by apprehending them and transforming them into its own tragic experiences. Injustice is the same tragedy for the soul as it is for the state or the law.[4] The very same principle of tragic contradiction is a defining principle for both macrocosm and microcosm.

Opposition and contradiction are not psychological categories, but universal ontological principles that apply to all fields of being and knowledge (and thus to psychology as well). Whoever talks about opposition and contradiction enters into the dialectical process and the field of philosophy. Here we are also confronted with the problem of tragedy.

Three Kinds of Relationship between Opposites

It is impossible to grasp the meaning of the tragic contradiction or its resolution without unfolding the whole problem of opposites. This is the basic problem of both Hindu and Greco-European philosophy. Among the Hindus this problem is set forth in the philosophical myths of the Rig-Veda (X, 129) and in all of the Upanishads, and it is definitively formulated in the great philosophical systems of India. The most ancient prototype or archetype of the birth of opposites marks, in fact, the simultaneous birth of philosophy. The European dialectic begins with the separating out of objects from the "boundless" of Anaximander, and with the Pythagorean table of opposites. Jakob Boehme's principle of "division" or "separation," the "mediation" of Fichte, and everything designated by the Greek particle *dia* ("through") — all of this lies at the foundation of any kind of being and thinking. In logic, A is conceivable only "through" non-A. This most elementary of principles already contains all the complex problems of the dialectic as it develops from Heraclitus through Plato and Aristotle down to Boehme, Kant, Fichte, Schelling, and Hegel. The ultimate mysteries of being are always antinomic. Antithesis

---

4. Since it is the same idea of justice, in Plato's words, which is written with capital letters in the state and with small letters in the soul.

and synthesis constitute the eternal theme of philosophy, and nothing since the time of Aristotle or Hegel has ever been conclusively resolved. The "coincidence of opposites" contains a number of wonders and revelations. In the realm of opposition, in the realm of polarity and contradiction, the philosophical dialectic enables us to make new discoveries. For our purposes, it will be sufficient to single out three kinds (aspects) of relationship between opposites.

1. The indifferent coincidence of opposites. All opposites are "linked by their ends," as Plato says, but this link is a variable one: on the one hand it can be irresolvably stable and eternal: it can have an ontologically given character. On the other hand it can be resolvable, mobile, posited. The first [stable] kind of link includes such opposites as part and whole, north and south, cause and effect, substance and accident, positive and negative. The spatiotemporal opposites, such as "here and there," "now and then," also belong to this group of oppositional relationships. I have labeled it the "indifferent coincidence of opposites," since the opposites here invariably coincide: a "part" is always the part of a whole, just as a "cause" is always the cause of some effect. Here the link between opposites is stable and invariable, and there are no qualitative or quantitative differences in the link. The link is given, and the opposites do not need to adapt to each other or trouble each other. In this sense, they are indeed linked "indifferently."

But there are two other kinds of link that do not form a stable union. On the contrary, they are dynamically interdependent; and so in these cases the opposites do not coincide indifferently, but constantly adapt to each other, trouble each other, either coming into conflict or striving for reconciliation.

2. The mutual repulsion or struggle of opposites. Examples are superfluous here, since the whole "world that lies in evil" provides a vast number of them. All the conflicts within the internal and external worlds, as well as the conflicts between them, belong to this kind of oppositional relationship. And it is precisely because we come across this stage everywhere in the dialectical development of opposites that Heraclitus could say that "strife is the father of all things." In this kind of relationship, the opposites are indeed linked, even fettered to one another, but the link between them is inconstant and mobile; they are linked to each other not by "indifference" but by "hatred." "The opposites are mutually destructive of each other," as Aristotle says. Hobbes has in mind a similar condition in his remarkable dialectic of society as the "war of each against all." Here the opposites devour each other: "man is a wolf to man."

A tragic contradiction that demands resolution and promises salvation also belongs to this category of opposites. The essence and meaning of this kind of opposition can be expressed dialectically as: mutual exclusion, "either/or," the impossibility of coexistence. Mutual exclusion may be real or ideal, that is, the impossibility of coexistence may involve either statements or things, forces, living creatures. Both belong to the same broad kind of opposition, to the same broad species. There is real mutual repulsion and there is logical mutual repulsion: Kant uses both of these expressions. It is precisely the concept of "mutual repulsion," notwithstanding all the differences in its real and ideal application, that essentially defines this kind of opposition. Therefore it is absolutely incorrect to think that there is only "logical" and no "real" contradiction: living people can contradict each other, and contradictory ideas can wage real war against each other, can end up in a relationship of real mutual repulsion.[5]

Contradiction in itself is a negative value that we desperately try to avoid. Insofar as the opposites cannot bear each other, the contradiction becomes unbearable. In this sense contradiction is the source of suffering and tragedy. It is impossible to come to rest on a contradiction, to get stuck on it: it cannot be acknowledged as "final" — and therefore the establishment of a different link between the opposites is required. And if contradiction means mutual repulsion, that is, strife, then this different

---

5. The most widespread error is the total separation between ideal and real mutual repulsion, the disregard of both basic categories of mutual repulsion. The absolute separation of the logical and the real is in itself already incorrect. Contradiction and resistance participate in the category of "confrontation," which in no case applies to every kind of opposition, because "to be opposed to," "to stand one against the other," in no way signifies "to resist." The first group showed us another category of oppositions, because the south does not "resist" the north, just as the effect cannot "resist" the cause, even though it is its opposite. Yet every judicial trial shows us the extent to which "contradiction" and "struggle" are closely linked to each other, since both sides stand in contradiction to each other: each side says "this is mine, not yours": and this contradiction is real resistance — that is, strife and war. Here mutual exclusion is ideal and real in equal measure. A sharp distinction between logical and real contradiction is always directed against Hegel and is rooted in an error that is precisely the opposite of his, that is, the error of neglecting both these aspects of mutual repulsion — contradiction and resistance. It is only fair to stress, however, that Hegel's error is less severe than that of his opponents, since Hegel recognized the all-embracing unity of mutual repulsion, while his opponents never did. His contribution lies therefore in recognizing the real contradiction, while his error lies in his claim that the logical law of identity (and contradiction) can be restricted and then discarded in this way. Both the one and the other must be preserved, however, as Plato's dialectic requires (especially in the *Sophist*).

resolution of the contradiction can only be peace. Thus we arrive at a new relationship of opposites:

3. The harmony of opposites. Harmony is not identity: it is opposition and at the same time mutual connection, since "opposition is in accord with itself, and from the striving of opposites in different directions the most beautiful harmony is born — and all this comes about through strife" (Heraclitus). This is a new relation of opposites, in which they do not exclude each other, do not annihilate or devour each other, but mutually nourish each other — "opposite nourishes opposite," as Aristotle says. What gives birth to friendship and the harmony of love — similarity or opposition? asks Plato, and he answers: "the most opposite is the most dear to the most opposite" *(Lysis)*. Harmony is born from strife — and the stronger the difference, the deeper and more robust is the union that overcomes it.[6]

The very same elements of being that were formerly capable of making war on each other now enter into a relationship of complementary distribution. A happy new combination has been found, a combination that the alchemists used to call the "sacred marriage" of the elements. This happiness is essentially a miracle, in which it turns out that the "third" *is* given: it is the birth of a new level of being that did not exist before. It is hard to comprehend how this could happen, since at certain moments the transition or mutation is still completely outside the purview of consciousness — even irrational. We can be sure of only one thing: herein lies the mystery of creative uplifting, of sublimation, of the "supersession" of the lower through the higher. The whole hierarchical structure of being as it rises from atom to living cell, from animate life to the living spirit, with all of their ever new conflicts and resolutions — this whole structure becomes possible only if it is all based on the third kind of oppositional relationship: the harmony of polarity. It is here that we must seek out the "philosopher's stone," the stone of wisdom. If it were located in the first kind of relationship — in the indifferent coincidence of the opposites — then there would be nothing to seek: the "philosopher's stone" could be found in every pebble on the street. To look for it in the second kind of opposition — in strife and contradiction — would make no sense either, because the "philosopher's stone" is called on to "supersede" this condition

---

6. One must not forget Spinoza's psychological proof of why former enmity can turn into an especially strong love and friendship (the theme of *Romeo and Juliet* and *Tristan and Isolde*). An enemy is a potential friend and enmity is conquered by love — this is what is meant by the Christian "love for one's enemies."

and to rescue us from it. The meaninglessness of contradiction acquires a meaning by going beyond its limits and finding a resolution to it. The meaning of strife is in the new harmony of peace. To seek for meaning in war itself, in war as such, would be perversion and demonism; for this would be like trying to find a remedy in real contradictions.[7]

The Stream of Becoming and Universal Harmony

All living creatures, all spiritual phenomena, are systems of harmonious polarity, where the three-part structure — the [initial] bifurcation and its reconciliation in the third — constitutes, of course, only the principle and rhythm of the highly complex differentiation and integration of being (the complex process of separation and unification). Jung made his greatest contribution to philosophy and psychology when he discovered the system of harmonious polarity in the soul — first and foremost, the polarity of consciousness and the unconscious. This discovery commits us to further dialectical development, to a dialogue with philosophers and a dialogue of philosophers with the leading representatives of psychology.

Yet the structure of the soul is not a stable equilibrium or a harmony established once and for all. It is only a posited harmony. Harmony always exists and yet at the same time it never does; it is in the process of becoming, of emergence and decay, the continuous overcoming of conflict. The soul is simultaneously harmony and dissonance; it is a system of opposites that "nourish each other" and "devour each other," a system of antinomies that are forever being resolved. Hence the soul's need for salvation and its intrinsically tragic nature. This is because the opposing forces of mutual repulsion and harmony that rule over the soul form a relationship that is not constant but variable, that simultaneously falls apart and unites. Harmonious systems are born from strife and fall apart through strife, their elements either clash with and destroy each other or they are mutually integrated (united). This is precisely the Heraclitean stream of coming into being and passing away, enmity and harmony, death and birth, war and peace. We find this strife-filled rhythm of becoming, this rhythm of resolutions and dissolutions, in every realm: in biology, psychology, sociology. Is there any meaning in this play of opposites? Or, perhaps, does "eternity play with the world, as a child plays with sand"

---

7. The contradiction of war is expressed in the words: "He who takes up the sword will perish by the sword" [Matt. 26:52].

(Heraclitus)? The eternal change of this rhythm compels us to doubt its meaning. This play can be interpreted as eternal recurrence, or as the eternal construction of the new, or as disintegration. It is on these grounds, in their ultimate interpretations and solutions of these matters, that the great religions go their separate ways.

If there is any meaning, then it can be found only in the transitional movement from the second to the third kind of oppositional relationship, that is, in the transition from mutual repulsion to harmony. This movement is a movement toward values. This is where the immanent value system (the axiology) of being[8] is located. Yet the movement toward values heads off into infinity, since any differentiated harmonious system conflicts with any other system, and may require unification (integration) and therefore a more all-embracing system of systems. Such a movement is precisely defined by the idea of an actually infinite integration, the idea of universal harmony. No doubt Leibniz is correct when he defines perfection as the greatest unity of the greatest diversity, or the maximum integration of the maximum differentiation.

Yet universal harmony is the precise philosophical expression for designating the Christian kingdom of God. The last two chapters of the Apocalypse provide the symbolic image of it. In Plato the kingdom of justice is also conceived as a harmony of opposites, as "symphony and symmetry." We need only add to it the idea, absent in ancient Greek thinking, of actual infinity. It is already contained in the concept of the "messianic kingdom" and in the symbol of the "Pantokrator": God will become all in all. The Neoplatonists were also familiar with this idea of concrete total unity: "one thing and all things, total unity." Nicholas of Cusa investigated and grounded the idea of actual infinity using the Hellenic and Byzantine dialectic of opposites, and correlated it with the Christian doctrine of the "kingdom of God." Thus he arrived at the sublime idea of the "coincidence of opposites." God rules over his kingdom, retaining the infinite diversity of opposites by means of their coincidence. Leibniz generalizes these ideas and links the mathematical concept of infinity to the idea of perfection, thus arriving at the concept of universal harmony. The Kantian antithetic and dialectic formulate the basic contradiction, ignored and passed over by Nicholas of Cusa and Leibniz — namely, the contradiction between what is and what ought to be. For Kant total unity (the all-embracing synthesis, "universal legislation") is a value, but it is not

---

8. The kind of axiology that not only experiences and reveals values, but also conceives of and understands them.

given, it is posited. It is present here only "to the extent that it is not" (Fichte); it is not what is (being), but only what ought to be. We must hold on firmly to this idea, with tragic courage and ethical faith, "even if it will never be realized."

But since it is never realized, we may lose courage and faith, and look on the task of realizing it as heading off into infinity, as an unfulfillable task, as "bad infinity," an infinity of perpetual emergence and perpetual decay. Any harmony is bound to undergo the tragic fate of failure — and therefore it makes no sense to turn the wheel of life. This is the other, antithetical perception of life — the Hindu solution.

The Mind-set of Hinduism: The World as Contradiction

Universal harmony, the "kingdom of God," is regarded in India as an illusion, as an intrinsic deception. This is so not only in Buddhism, in which detailed proofs for the nonexistence of God are adduced, but also in both the Upanishads and the philosophical systems of Vedanta and Yoga, which acknowledge the Absolute (Brahman) or God (Ishvara) as truly existing. Ishvara, the Lord God, rules in eternity and in his transcendence: far below him the stream of the world and of humanity clamors in "Samsara," in the eternally recurrent cycle of emergence and disappearance. In this stream roams the wandering soul, lost in the world. And the wandering world keeps rushing onward — it will never arrive at the "kingdom of God," at the mansion of divine greatness and divine glory. It will eternally remain a chain of events without purpose and without end, always aimless, never enlightened. For India, the world and history have neither value nor purpose — revealing a complete antithesis between the Hindu worldview and the Christian one with its positive attitude toward the value of the world.[9] From the Hindu viewpoint, deification through the "restoration of all things," the kingdom of God, makes no sense at all.

In India this mind-set is conditioned by a particular interpretation of polarity and the interaction of opposites. The first kind of relationship, the coincidence of opposites, is almost completely ignored; the third kind of relationship, the harmony of opposites, is not an object of faith among Hindus. They recognize only the second kind of oppositional relationship — mutual repulsion and contradiction. They do not believe in harmony,

9. This accounts for India's failure to develop any science and technology based on opposing categories like cause and effect or the polarity of forces.

because harmony is merely a passing moment. Thus the conviction arises that every system is bound to undergo the suffering and destruction brought on by internal and external conflicts. All of human experience — sickness, old age, death, suffering — serves as proof of this. All these phenomena are merely different aspects of the real contradiction.

The Hindus assume that any opposition inherently results in mutual repulsion, enmity, hatred, and suffering. Only the Absolute — Brahman in his eternal identity — is devoid of suffering, free from contradiction and immortal: "In the beginning there was only one without a second" (Chandogya Upanishad 6.2.2). "What is different from this [i.e., Brahman = Atman] overflows with suffering" (Brhadaranyaka Upanishad 3.4.2). "He plunges from death into new death who thinks that anything diverse is here" (Brhadaranyaka Upanishad 4.4.19). The following aphorism of the Yogi Patanjali is particularly characteristic: "Bifurcation, which causes hatred, appears in consciousness as pain." In short, "opposition is dissension, discord, and pain." "This world undergoes ceaseless suffering through binary oppositions" (Ramayana 11.84.20).

Liberation from Opposites as the Path to Salvation

A solution to the real contradiction is impossible, and yet there is a desire to hold on to the opposites. The only way to resolve contradictions and achieve deliverance from them is to dissolve the opposites into identity, into indifference, or to "supersede" once and for all the very process of contraposing one thing to another. This is the celebrated doctrine of Vedanta — the Kevala-advaita — the doctrine of unqualified nonduality: plurality is an immense cosmic illusion, an illusory delusion. We find this idea everywhere in the Upanishads:

> In reality there is nonduality
> Duality exists only in the schismatic world
> The schism of the Singular, of the Eternal
> For if schism were present in reality
> Then what is eternal would be mortal. (Mandukya-Karika 3.18-19)

> That which is free from good and evil,
> Free from what has happened and what has not happened,
> Free from the past and the future
> That which you see as such — speak it out! (Katha Upanishad 2.14)

This is the freedom from opposites that constitutes the essence of true being, the essence of Brahman:

In the Spirit the following may be observed:
There is no plurality here.
One should regard as Unity
. . . the great I. (Brhadaranyaka Upanishad 4.4.19-20)

In this ultimate unity of the Absolute, every opposition and contradiction disappears and, consequently, so does any kind of suffering:

All complaints are renounced
In him there is no more care . . .
Where there are no more cares
Nothing is taken, nothing is given . . .
Here there are no desires, no lusts . . .
only Unity/Singularity. (Mandukya-Karika 3.37, 38, 39, 45)

The wise person strives for a perfect imitation of the Absolute, even for perfect identity with it (for Atman is basically identical with Brahman), and thus one achieves liberation from opposites, "absence of duality," and thereby the only possible "salvation" (cf. Mandukya-Karika 2.35, 36).

This merging and dissolving of everything in the supreme identity of unqualified nonduality (Kevala-advaita) is achieved through various paths: through the sensory identification of the self with universal suffering, through compassion ("this is you"),[10] and through the theoretical identification of subject and object by means of their nondifferentiation. My "I," Atman itself, is such a focal point of identification from which all opposites are engendered and to which they can all return. This point is beyond the boundary of oppositions: it transcends them all — especially the basic opposition between the cognizing subject and the cognized object. If the "I," Atman, remains in this state of transcendence and does not engender opposites, then: "There is nothing second, other, different that he could see, smell, or touch, no one with whom he could talk that could be heard, nothing that could be thought and nothing that could be felt or cognized," as it says in a celebrated passage of the Upanishads (Brhada-ranyaka Upanishad [4.5.15]).

Objectification is posited here, but so too is subjectification, the

---

10. I.e., *Tat tvam asi* — "That art thou." Trans.

consciousness of the "I" with its functions of intuition and cognition-purgation, with its fear, lust, and suffering. "If there were anything other [i.e., a duality of some kind], then the one would see the other . . . hear, think, feel [the other] — the one would perceive the other. . . . But when everything has become Atman, who is there for one to see and by what means? . . . What is there to greet and by what means? . . . Who is there for one to think of and by what means? Who is there for one to touch and by what means? Who is there for one to perceive and by what means? By what means can one perceive him by means of whom one perceives this whole world? By what means in truth cognize the cognizer?" (Brhadaranyaka Upanishad [4.5.15]).

But if the very process of opposition is "superseded," then all opposites — all things contraposed to other things — disappear, and consequently all objects as well. The world of the object disappears — and yet at the same time the world of the subject disappears along with it:

> No soul is created,
> There is no kind of creation in the world,
> This is the supreme salvific truth,
> That there is never any coming to be. (Mandukya-Karika 3.48)

Any becoming — the whole rhythm of emergence and disappearance, birth and death — disappears along with the opposites. The illusion of diversity, the illusion of an internal or external "world" vanish like a dream.

The Transcendence of Selfhood

Nonetheless, one might ask: So then, what is left? Nothing at all perhaps? Does salvation really mean dissolution into nothingness? Southern Buddhism apparently does not draw this conclusion, but the Upanishads along with the systems of Vedanta and Yoga that are based on them think otherwise: for them, the state of salvation is not nothingness, but something extremely positive — supreme bliss: it is not emptiness but plenitude. "So I say, after death there is no consciousness/awareness" (Brhadaranyaka Upanishad 5.5 [4.5.13]). "Where a man sees, hears, or discerns no other thing — that is 'plenitude' (something greater than being). But where one sees, hears, or discerns some other thing — that is 'scarcity.' Now, 'plenitude' is the immortal, while 'scarcity' constitutes what is mortal" (Chandogya Upanishad 15ff. [7.24.1]).

When all opposites and all worlds have dissolved, what remains is "selfhood" (the "I"), Atman, Purusha ("man in himself"), but in an unusual state that seems strange and terrifying — even to the Yogi himself. Even the wise Maitreyi falls into deep confusion when her husband tells her that in this state consciousness does not exist. It is compared to a dreamless sleep, to lethargy (Chandogya Upanishad, 4.3) but at the same time this state is distinguished from sleep and lethargy as a state that is higher, amazing, difficult to achieve, in no way comparable to states that are lower, commonplace, and accessible to everyone.

The Sarva Upanishad distinguishes four states of Atman: wakefulness, sleep with dreams, deep sleep (without dreams), and the fourth: "Turiya." The last is defined as a "spiritual state, similar to an observer that stands over against existence, while itself signifying indifference, and that has liberated itself from any kind of existence; and this spiritual state is called Turiya."

Strictly speaking, there is no way to describe or define selfhood when it is in a state of ultimate transcendence and salvation. The definition that I offered is quite inadequate. The Brhadaranyaka Upanishad, in the last analysis, gives a negative definition: "neither this nor the other" (just as in apophatic theology) — *neti-neti* [not — , not —] — and this is perhaps the most profound definition that one could come up with. This state must be achieved and experienced through Vedanta or Yoga or some other mystical doctrine. The comparison to a deep sleep indicates one very important thing: in its ultimate state, selfhood is not self-consciousness: it is the unconscious. A deep sleep, however, is something simpler, lower, and might be called the subconscious. In contrast, selfhood (Atman, Purusha) might be called supraconsciousness.

The similarity to deep sleep, to death, lies in the loss of consciousness ("after death there is no consciousness"). However, another supraconscious state of "selfhood" is possible. If selfhood goes beyond the boundaries of all oppositions and rises above them, then it goes beyond the very positing of an opposition between the conscious and the unconscious. Yet Indian philosophy never went as far as this thoroughly modern conclusion. It clearly formulated a different conclusion: the transcendence of selfhood, the "supersession" of opposites, signifies not death but immortality — for death, after all, is the opposite of birth. Death and birth, emergence and decay, constitute a game of opposites, and the game can be terminated by the nondifferentiation of *advaita*. Selfhood makes an exit past the boundary of the rhythm of death and birth, and consequently becomes immortal. But one could also say that selfhood is now "lifeless": because, to the extent that it is liberated from the rhythm of life, it is also liberated from the rhythm of death. All this differs radically from the Christian idea of immortality and salvation.

The Pessimism of the Hindu Worldview

This idea of the dissolution of contradictions, of "nonduality" *(advaita)*, that we encounter in the Upanishads and Vedanta also lies at the basis of the whole Hindu worldview. "Freedom from opposites," "imperviousness to the opposites (nirvana)" — this is the path to salvation that turns up everywhere: in the laws of Manu, in the Bhagavadgita, and in the Mahabharata as a whole. The very system of Yoga defines the highest state of bliss, samadhi, as a "state of imperviousness to opposites." Samadhi can be defined as "curtailment," "withdrawal," limitation. This is opposed to "unfolding," the "development" of contradictions, of opposites, of plurality: "when in the 'psychic world' the conscious relation to any separate object whatsoever is terminated and psychic concentration sets in, then this is the movement of consciousness which is called 'limitation'" (aphorism of the Yogi Patanjali, 3.11).[11] This state of limitation is "free from the opposition between consciousness and the mentally realized object" (3.3; 1.43). The "development" of diversity and, most importantly, the opposition between subject and object is thereby taken away from us. These customary activities in the "psychic world" are overthrown, and the psychic world sinks before the face of the "one who understands the world" (Purusha, 1.41). This "limitation" is achieved through a "concentration into internal unity." This is the Yogi's path to salvation. Here too "nonduality" is taken as principle and method: "a single understanding of two that seem to be absolutely identical" (3.53).

Here, in classical Yoga, we recognize the same Hindu theme: the world will dissolve through the dissolution of opposites. Thus, all at once, "worldly confusion" as the "cause of bondage" will disappear (2.24), the "quenching of thirst" will be achieved (3.50), and the "will to life, cramped by convulsive fear," will cease to exist (2.9). Suffering will be removed through indifference. This kind of salvation through the identity and indifference of opposites is antithetical to the Christian idea of the bliss of "a new heaven and a new earth" and to the Hellenic harmony of opposites as well. Therefore Paul Deussen is wrong when he simply identifies the

---

11. Hauer, *Der Joga als Heilweg*, p. 105.

deep pessimism of the Upanishads with Christianity, and defines the final purpose of both as "salvation from being here and now" (referring to Schopenhauer and quoting the biblical phrase, "the whole world lies in evil"). Christianity is not resignation at all, but tragic optimism — tragic hope, tragic faith, and tragic love.

The Symbol of the Bow and the Lyre
in Ancient Hellenic Philosophy

The Hindu idea of salvation and liberation is the direct antithesis of the Hellenic-Judeo-Christian one. The Judeo-Christian idea is the idea of creation. The world is not an illusion: it is the real creation of God, the "cosmos." All the manifold forces and elements of being are good and valuable in themselves. Having created the world, God saw "that it was good": the only bad part is a particular inclination toward mutual destruction and discord. The idea of creation is first and foremost the idea of the affirmation of the world: an ultimate "yes" embraces all of being, with all of its opposites and levels, in a single and indivisible love. Love is the affect [emotional impulse] of being. At the same time, it acknowledges the intrinsic value of the human being's likeness to God and the creative power of humanity as manifested in art and culture.

What is specifically Hellenic-Christian is the dialectic of opposites and their union through harmony. I have already mentioned that the establishment of harmony is always, in essence, the miraculous solution to a riddle, the dawning of an illumination; it signifies an artful device. This is the miracle of creation, the miracle of art.

In terms of "common sense," the only way to resolve the antinomy, the real contradiction, always seems at first to be the elimination — in whole or at least in part — of thesis and antithesis. Both sides are affirmed and admitted "in part." However, this is a bad solution and an invalid one in terms of dialectical reason. Kant saw early on that when dealing with a real antinomy, thesis and antithesis must be preserved at full strength and with their real proofs. If both must remain true — in a different sense — then this reveals the unity of opposing meanings in the same entity.[12]

Similarly, the antagonistic forces and elements cannot be "mixed together" or quantitatively diminished; this leads not to a happy solution

---

12. For example, man is free and not free; he is an immanent (empirical) and a transcendent being.

but to the minimizing and sidestepping of the conflict. Likewise, the complete partition of the elements, their total separation (as opposed to their "mixture") — as propounded, for example, by Manichaeism with regard to matter and spirit — is not a successful solution either, but merely an admission that a solution is impossible. Only when the opposing forces are completely laid bare, when the resistance is kept taut, can harmony sound forth. This harmony is something new, something that has never existed before, that suddenly breaks through where earlier there had been strife, destruction, and mutual suppression.

Harmony is difficult to cognize and almost impossible to comprehend. A remarkable symbol of Heraclitus allows us to see and understand the third kind of opposition in its mysterious polysemy — and this is the symbol of the bow and the lyre: "We do not understand how the antagonistic [force] agrees with itself: this is the harmony of opposing tensions similar to the bow and the lyre."

The bow is a system of forces at war with each other — and the more powerful the tension of the antagonistic poles, the better the bow. To lessen or destroy the tension between the ends of the bow means to destroy the bow itself. But the bowstring can be converted into the string of a lyre. The lyre is constructed on the same principle as the bow: it is a bow with many strings — one might even call it a transfigured or "sublimated" bow. Here we can vividly hear and contemplate how "the most beautiful harmony arises from strife." Beauty, the good, the whole system of values are all based on this principle. The symbol of the bow and the lyre is polysemic and all-embracing like the Platonic Eros, to which it is essentially linked. Ancient Greek and Hellenistic thought sensed the meaning of this symbol and knew how to elaborate it dialectically. We find it in Plato, Aristotle, Plutarch, Simplicius, even Synesius.

In the Greek worldview, harmony has a cosmic significance. The sage can hear the harmony of the spheres in their motions.[13] The cosmos is "beauty": hence its "symphony and symmetry," so like the lyre's. "Many-sounding and multiform, according to Heraclitus, is the harmony of the cosmos, like the harmony of the bow and the lyre" (Plutarch). "The cosmos is not a simple unity, but something which has been united out of a great number of things, and the separate parts dwell there in concord and in strife" (Synesius). However, not only the cosmos but art, architecture, and technology as well employ the principle of the bow (the "arch") and build according to the principle of counteracting forces (on buttresses).

13. A symbolism we owe to Pythagoras.

It is not so easy to observe this same principle in the inner world, in the microcosm. Plato was the first to observe it, when he portrayed the soul as a chariot harnessed to two horses, one white and one black, and beheld in this symbol the contradiction between the soul's opposing forces and their harmony. As the lyre allows the strings to sound forth, so too is lyric poetry the sounding of the soul. This sounding always proceeds from the tension of opposites, and the concrete abundance of the soul is never mono-valent but always "ambi-valent," more often full of contradictions and, at its best, similar to counterpoint.[14]

The bow and the lyre are identical in their principle, but they are still opposites, like life and death (for life is harmony). Heraclitus expressed this rhythmical play of opposites when he said: "the name of the bow is life and its business is death." (The Greek *bios* means both "bow" and "life.") Heraclitus and Hegel groped after the deepest mysteries of the dialectic, but both of them are guilty of treating it as a game and applying it incorrectly. The "identity of opposites" is an ambiguous, erroneous expression, since coincidence is not identity, and opposites are, in fact, not identical, but opposite.

Plato is still the greatest dialectician, categorically rejecting the frivolous treatment of opposites and the nonobservance of the law of contradiction. At the same time he has a profound understanding of the hidden meaning of Heraclitus's symbolism. He preserves for us the following aphorism of Heraclitus: "That unity that strives for disunion reunites with itself, like the harmony of the bow and the lyre" (*Symposium* 187A). Plato then provides us with a gloss on this passage: Heraclitus expressed himself badly, although he has in mind something that is true. The incompatible and the contradictory cannot be united in harmony, insofar and as long as they are not in accord with each other (187B).

We need a special art like music or medicine to help us, so that the hostilely incompatible may be converted into the lovingly concordant and harmony may be established (187C). Plato thus affirms the inviolability of the law of contradiction; for if contradiction is not perceived as contradiction, then resolution and harmony lose all their meaning and value. The bow and the lyre are not identical, since the lyre is a new invention, a transfiguration and sublimation of the bow. Harmony is something different, a new relation of opposites, the third kind of opposition. Health and beauty, music and medicine, according to Plato, are based on it, and so too

---

14. "Two souls live in my breast, and one wants to separate from the other" (Goethe).

is the mutual complementarity of the relation between man and woman — and this is what we perceive and experience as love and eros.

We should never identify and confuse the "mutual nourishing of opposites" with their mutual devouring, by proclaiming the "unity of opposites" and thereby "superseding" the law of contradiction. If this is done, then all the seriousness of the dialectical process turns into a sophistical game and a hopeless imitation of the Hegelian style and the Hegelian error of his epigones.[15]

We find a dialectical investigation of this "most beautiful harmony, that arises out of opposites and strife" in Aristotle as well. In his ethics we find this famous saying of Heraclitus in the following context. Aristotle is posing the Platonic question: Who partakes of love and friendship — people who are the same or those who are opposites? Euripides is cited first: "the dry earth loves the rain and heaven loves to rush down upon the earth in the form of rain" (*Nicomachean Ethics* LVIII, chap. 1, toward the end). Then Heraclitus[16] is quoted a bit later (LVIII, chap. 8): "but in reality an opposite does not seek out another opposite as such, but only what is linked to itself; it strives toward the middle, for this is the good; for example, the dry strives not to get wet, but seeks out an intermediate condition, and the same thing goes for the hot and all the others."

Consequently, Aristotle understands the harmony of opposites as the mean between them, and it is clear from the context that this "mean" refers to the sought-for synthesis of opposing elements and forces. Aristotle's "golden mean" has been misunderstood and disparaged because

15. We find this first and foremost in Ferdinand Lassalle in his great monograph on Heraclitus. He completely misses the point of the symbolism of the bow and the lyre, despite his enormous erudition and the vast number of his references, since he assumes that Heraclitus's basic principle is the "identity of opposites." Lassalle simply uses the expressions "identity of opposites" and "unity of opposites" indiscriminately. If one does that, everything is lost: the bow and the lyre express the identity of opposites, strife and harmony are one and the same thing (*De philosophie Herakleitos des Denklen von Ephesus* [Berlin, 1858], 1:90). Everything that is true and profound in Hegel is thereby lost. There is a perspicacious remark in Plato that can be applied to both the followers of Heraclitus and the Sophists as well as to the Hegelians, namely, to those who fool around with antinomies and think that they can abolish the law of contradiction: "to argue that identity is opposition and opposition is identity, that the large is the small, the similar is the dissimilar, and the complex is the simple, and to rejoice that opposites continually pop up in discourse — this is not genuine dialectical method, but the pastime of an amateur who barely understands the analysis of being" (*Sophist* [259C-D]).

16. "Opposition is in accordance with itself and from the striving of opposites in different directions is born the most beautiful harmony."

people insisted on equating it with "mediocrity"; but Aristotle's mean actually signifies the center, the middle of the target — and it is not easy but extremely difficult to hit this center: you have to aim very well. Therefore Aristotle himself stresses that his "mean" does not signify "mediocrity" but the pinnacle, the extreme summit, of value. "In no way is it a mean between virtue and vice, between value and negative value — that would be mediocrity indeed; what I am talking about is the mean between two opposing vices."

With this last definition, Aristotle thinks that he has reached the truth. But this is not so. Between two opposing vices and two negative values there can only be zero indifference, not a golden mean. His "middle" becomes true and valuable only when it signifies the center that binds opposing forces and aspirations together and holds sway over them.[17]

An example from Aristotle's theory of virtue will suffice to make this idea clear. Generosity with money [Aristotle's magnanimity] is not the null point between avarice and wastefulness, but a synthesis of two functions that have positive value despite their opposition — namely, the acquisition of money and its expenditure, production and distribution. Without both of these functions, a patron, a Lorenzo de Medici, let's say, would be inconceivable. Covetousness and wastefulness alike are the real contradiction of these functions, since in neither case does the spending of money properly correspond to its acquisition. This example has a deep psychological meaning, since an analogous situation occurs when we deal with the accumulation and squandering of "libido," that is, psychic energy. These functions may be either in contradiction or in harmony with each other.

Thus Heraclitus's symbol already contains the true and profound meaning of the "golden mean," the middle path. The middle path signifies a transition from mutual repulsion to the harmony of opposites — and great art is needed to hit on this path.

The symbol of the bow and the lyre has many other meanings. The arrow is placed at the midpoint of both the bowstring and the arc of the bow, and it must hit the middle of the target. Apollo is portrayed with a bow and a lyre — he is the god of the muses, Apollo Musagetes, but at the same time he is an expert archer who always hits his target (Plato, *Cratylus*). There is another god, Eros, who is depicted with bow and arrow.

---

17. This is the genuine meaning he ascribes to his notion; thus the dialectic can and should be further developed along these lines. In the interpretation of Aristotle in his *Ethics* Nicolai Hartmann discovered this and proved it with brilliant precision (pp. 512-20).

Pausanias describes a famous picture in which Eros shoots an arrow, then puts down his bow and takes up the lyre. The lyre belongs to him too, for he is at heart a "lyric poet."

The Harmony of Opposites and the Christian Idea of Salvation

In conclusion we must now pose the ultimate question: Is this Greek dialectic of opposites, this coincidence of opposites, really in keeping with the spirit of Christianity? Can it really be applied to the Christian idea of salvation? The greatest Greek fathers of the church answered this question with a resounding yes: they were Greek dialecticians who believed in Christ and thought of him as the coincidence of the opposites of divine and human nature. These opposites are linked in the Divine Human "without separation and without confusion," as the celebrated Chalcedonian formula goes. Vedantism proposes another resolution to the problem of the Divine Human: here the opposites merge into one like a drop of water in the ocean.

Christianity is dialectical through and through: it moves in the realm of ultimate concepts, which are antinomic. It discovers and experiences the most sublime antinomies — the world and the soul, immanence and transcendence; and it promises to find a resolution to them: it has a premonition of this solution and a hope of finding it. The apostle Paul is the first philosopher of Christianity as well as its greatest dialectician. Luther said with good reason: "faith is a dialectic of sorts." The ultimate unity of ultimate opposites — the unity of the Absolute and the relative, of heaven and earth, God and humanity — is the ultimate problem of dialectics and the first experience of Christian revelation.

The transition from the second kind of opposition to the third, from mutual repulsion to harmony, from tragic contradiction to resolution and salvation, is the essence of the "good news." How is it possible to wrest harmony, peace, and love out of separation and discord, out of strife, war, and hatred? This is the most elementary and fundamental problem of humanity in all the domains of its internal and external world. Christ himself is the living answer to this question, since he himself is the living harmony of opposites. He himself is peace. This is how Paul understood him: "He is our peace, who hath made both one, and hath broken down the middle wall of partition between us; having abolished in his flesh the enmity . . . to make in himself of twain one new man, so making peace." He "reconciled" both opposites "by the cross, having slain the enmity thereby." Paul sees in this the meaning of Christian doctrine: the abolition of enmity in peace, in universal harmony. "And he came and preached peace to you" (Eph. 2:13-22; cf. John 14:27).

The Gospels acknowledge that the principle of the harmony of opposites applies to both inner peace and external and social peace. "From whence come wars and fightings among you? Come they not hence, even of your lusts that war in your members?" Thus impulses contradict each other within the human being as well as in social interactions; the internal conflicts of the soul are transformed into external conflicts and drag all of humanity down into tragic contradiction: "Ye lust, and have not: ye kill and desire to have, and cannot obtain: ye fight and war, yet ye have not, because ye ask not. Ye ask, and receive not, because ye ask amiss, that ye may consume it upon your lusts" (James 4:1-3). Here we have the dialectic of opposites that devour each other. And to this "anarchy" of the lusts is opposed the harmony that is contained in wisdom and justice, and that signifies peace (James 3:16-18).

But this internal conflict of the soul is perhaps nowhere expressed more powerfully than in the seventh chapter of Romans, for it is the fundamental conflict of self-consciousness with the unconscious. The ancient pagans early on gave expression to this tragic contradiction in the soul: "I see the better and I approve it, but I follow the worse" (Ovid).[18] Consciousness of the law is present, but so too is unconscious resistance to the law. This is Paul's basic thesis. The law is the law of "my mind" and I am aware that the law is good and valuable. I also have a conscious desire to do what is good and what conforms to the law — and even so what happens is the exact reverse! Everything happens in defiance of my consciousness: "for I do not do what I want, but I do the very thing I hate" [Rom. 7:15]. Thus what I do, I do in spite of my consciousness and against my own will. In Paul's view the "I" is nothing other than the center of consciousness and mind. He draws the quite valid conclusion that it is not the "I" which is acting here but something else: "it is no longer I that do it, but sin which dwells within me." Where exactly does sin dwell, if the conscious "I" is overflowing with good intentions and respect for the law? The only place in which it could be dwelling is in the unconscious. Paul lacks this term, however, and so he says that I am "in captivity to the law of sin which is in my members." We can easily discern that what is implied here is the realm of the psyche, since it is a question of our desires and "lusts."

18. Medea in the *Metamorphoses*. Trans.

In this remarkable dialectic of the split in the soul, Paul discovered the law of unconscious antagonism: "another law . . . warring against the law of my mind." This is the law of the "forbidden fruit" (Rom. 7:7-24). All of this together is nothing other than an expression of the antagonism of the unconscious toward consciousness. This struggle, according to the apostle, is resolved through the harmony of opposites and through sublimation by the inspiriting of the body and the soul.

It is now clear that the keen and artful dialectic of the ancients was destined from the very beginning to investigate the tragic conflicts and mystical antinomies of Christianity and to make its solutions "conceivable." The great church fathers Dionysius the Areopagite and Maximus the Confessor were classical dialecticians in the Platonic and Neoplatonic spirit. It will be sufficient just to underline some ideas from this tradition. For Maximus evil and sin are an ontological crack, a discord in the cosmos and in the microcosm, in the world and in humanity, and humanity is summoned to overcome this dissension. Christ shows how this is possible, and he brings this possibility to fulfillment. Christ is the genuine coincidence of opposites. "He is the wisdom and thought of the Father who holds all of being together. . . . He creates the tension between opposites . . . and dissolves the war in being and binds everything together in peace, love and inviolable harmony" (Maximus the Confessor, in Migne, *Patrologia graeca*, 91:1304-14).

Thus we are lifted up from the Heraclitean lyre to the idea of universal harmony — and this lifting (*anagoge*, "sublimation") is the way of dialectics. It leads us from the despair of ancient tragedy, the despair of Hinduism's resignation, to the tragic optimism of Christianity. The postulate of "a new heaven and a new earth" remains intact — even more powerfully than ever before. The idea of universalism is not an abstraction but a genuine reality. There are no isolated, self-sufficient systems of harmony, neither in individual psychology nor in the life of society, the nation, and the state. Everything is connected with everything, "everything breathes in unison," "everyone is responsible for everyone and everyone is to blame for everything" (Dostoevsky). That is why bliss can be yielded up, as the alchemists put it, through "universal medicine," through universal salvation and redemption. For the European alchemist, whether he is nowadays a psychologist, a sociologist, or simply a philosopher, the "philosopher's stone" sought by the ancient alchemists can signify nothing other than the principle of universal harmony. Thus it is easy to understand why Jakob Boehme found the "stone of wisdom" in Christ himself.

CHAPTER 8

The Relationship of Subject and Object and Its Significance for the System of Philosophy

Knowledge[1] begins with the differentiation of the subjective and the objective, which are separated out, born from the depths of the boundless (the incomprehensible), as light and darkness are born from chaos. Consequently, knowledge is the contraposition and juxtaposition of subject and object, a subjective-objective system. But this system is, above all, a system of warring opposites: what truly exists wages relentless war against what seems to be and it must win this war if any kind of knowledge is to be possible. Victory in this conflict must go to the objective side. But this victory does not simply wipe out the opponent: the subject is, so to speak, taken captive by the object; it is turned over to the custody of the victor; it is assimilated into the victor's realm — the subject itself becomes a kind of object. Thus the system of warring opposites is converted into a system in which the opposites have been unified and identified with each other. In the phase of conflict, the subject is construed as the enemy of the object; it is that which only seems to be, the "merely subjective." In the phase of reconciliation, the subject is construed as a kind of object, as "consciousness" (the object of psychology, and therefore of ethics as well). In Schelling's terms, the phase of conflict must be expressed by a contraposition of subject and object, and the phase of reconciliation by a juxtaposition of "in-

---

1. There is a discrepancy between the two editions of Vysheslavtsev's text at this point. The Chekhov Publishing House version has *znanie* ["knowledge"], the one published by the Izdatelstvo "Respublika" in Moscow has *znachenie* ["meaning, significance"]. In context, the former seems to me the more likely reading. Trans.

108

tellect" and "nature." Schelling errs only in his dogmatic rationalism, his assumption that these systems have now been finalized, sealed up once and for all. But they have not been sealed up; the opposites are still warring with each other; the subjective and "what seems to be" are not yet overcome, the unity of "nature" and "intellect" not yet revealed. Between the organic processes of nature and consciousness (the state of consciousness) falls the infinite problem of irrationality. The enigmatic darkness of the boundless breaks through all the boundaries of the system, breaks through the transparent crystals of reason.

If we turn now to the way in which this subject-object identity is realized ontologically, we see that the identity in this case is biased and leans to the side of the object. "Nature" gives birth to the "intellect," to "consciousness" with all of its true and false "representations." Thus nature is the protagonist of the drama, the starting point, the principle; and this is why logic in the strict sense of the word is the logic of the sciences of nature. Whatever the birth of the intellect might portend is yet unclear. If the whole meaning and value of the organism are expressed in its nervous system, and the whole meaning of the nervous system is that it makes consciousness possible, where then is the value of consciousness?

In the process of development, the meaning and foundation of every level are found in the level immediately above it. What level then is higher than conscious organic nature? This remains incomprehensible for the doctrine of being [i.e., ontology]. The meaning of conscious nature is revealed where the logos of being becomes the goal and the beauty of the world, that is, in teleology and cosmology, in those philosophical disciplines that are commonly called ethics and aesthetics. Here consciousness has a completely other and positive meaning: everything that was rejected by logic and cognition as only subjective, as the mere play of sensation and representation, as fantastic images — all of this now acquires an independent meaning. For art and the aesthetic perception of the world, colors and sounds will no longer be just the deceptive appearance of a particular system of motions, just as subjective goals and intentions — the "prototypes" of the creative imagination — will not be so for ethics. Consciousness has no positive meaning in logic because in logic it must completely submit to being; it must humbly and passively assimilate the object into itself. For logic, the ideal subject is one that is absolutely imperceptible, that sinks into the object; a correct representation will be one that is no longer a representation but the actual object of reflection itself. A perfect mirror only reflects; it contributes nothing to the picture; therefore it is totally imperceptible, and becomes perceptible only when it tarnishes. The identity of subject and object leans here to the side of the object.

But another interpretation of this identity is possible. The process of likening object to subject, their unification, may occur on the territory of the subject. What if the world of subjective aspirations, the world of fantastic images, is introduced into the kingdom of being? What if the subject is no longer content with passively reflecting and assimilating the object, but demands that the object submit to it, assimilate it, and reflect its capricious fantasies? We have such an identity, such a likening of object to subject, in any kind of action. In sculpture the marble takes on the form of the artist's subjective visions; in ethical action the objective world takes on the form of the desired goal. A bridge, as an objectively real fact, a fact of experience, is a reflection of the bridge as blueprint, the subjective prototype that lives only in the consciousness of the builder. Here the other kind of subject-object identity is graphically revealed — and it is an ethical, teleological identity.

The opposition of subject to object and the principle of their unity runs through the whole system of philosophy. Ethics encounters the subject and object of aesthetic contemplation in exactly the same way [as ontology encountered the subject and object of ethics], and in exactly the same way their unity is realized in it. The subject-object problem is fully resolved only in the whole system of philosophy: only here is the whole sense of this opposition and the whole meaning of the sought-for unity revealed. Consequently, we have before us three meanings of the subject, three meanings of the object, and three meanings of their identity. If in ontology (in theoretical philosophy) identity leans to the side of the object, and in teleology (in practical philosophy) it leans to the side of the subject, then perhaps only in cosmology (in aesthetics) do we get complete identity or unity while preserving the balance of opposites. In ontology, identity is the universality of the object — the object has turned all that is subjective into a modification of its own, into its own kind of being. In teleology, identity is the universality of the subject — the subject has made the object into a means of its own, an embodiment of its own goals. But now in cosmology, identity is the balancing of both sides, universal equilibrium. In cosmology [aesthetics], the subject is no longer obliged to vanish humbly when confronted by the object, as in logic: it is not obliged to renounce the play of its own fantasy, its own subjective colorings and sounds, because all of that lives on in the object of beauty. On the other hand, neither is the object obliged to become merely the means to subjective goals: the object of beauty is independent of the subject; it is a goal in itself. Beauty is what I like; it is my beauty; in this beauty my spirit recognizes itself, its own cherished searchings and strivings. But at the same time, beauty is pure objectivity: it is not just "my" beauty, but the beauty of the world, the beauty of the statue. "Mine" and "not mine" lose their meaning most of all when confronted by the beautiful. Aesthetic delight itself cannot be owned, but neither am I obliged to renounce it completely. What am I listening to in music? My harmony, the harmony of sounds woven by me — or the mysterious harmony of being? Neither the one nor the other, because both the one and the other. I recognize in the harmony of being my own harmony, and in my own harmony I experience the harmony of being. Here and perhaps only here, the "I" and the "not I," "mine" and "not mine," merge completely. When I contemplate the beauty of the starry heavens, when I hear the harmony of the heavenly spheres, the dichotomy of spirit and nature vanishes: "Everything is in me and I in everything" (Tyutchev).

Thus three different meanings of subject and object correspond to three different meanings of identity. In logic the subject is the source of error and the object is "what truly exists" (inorganic, organic, and conscious nature). In ethics the subject is the dramatis persona, the bearer of "prototypes" and the ideal, while the object is the realm of means, the arena of activity. In aesthetics both of these meanings are wondrously united in the subject and object. The subject of aesthetic contemplation is similar to the subject of cognition, because it comprehends beauty, sinks into it, renouncing its own selfhood; and at the same time it is similar to the ethical subject: it acts, it is a creator — and it is not only the artist who creates, but any spectator or listener as well. In just the same way, the object of beauty is similar to the object of knowledge in that it truly exists, it is self-sufficient and independent of any subject (as the truth also is), and at the same time it is similar to the practical object, for it is a creation, a making, a work of art, the embodiment of an idea.

The solution to the celebrated problem of subject and object resides in the principle of the unity of opposites. But this unity can be established only at the point when the whole meaning of the opposition between what objectively exists and what subjectively seems, being and appearance, has been exhausted and so arrives at the system of being, the system of the objectively existing, which encompasses the objects of "external and internal experience," physical and psychological being, spirit and matter. Ethics has as its basic postulate the opposition between the acting subject and the acted-upon object, between person and thing. Finally, aesthetics postulates an opposition between the spirit that creates and contemplates and created and objectively contemplated beauty. We must go through all the levels of these oppositions in order to bring to realization the identity of subject and object. All these levels are present in the system of philosophy; moreover, the higher level always presupposes and contains the lower one. We need to contrapose being and appearance in order to set aside everything that seems and appears and to reveal the system of being that encompasses the spiritual and the material. We need to behold both the opposition and the indissoluble bond between consciousness and the material world, between the soul as the bearer of aspirations and creative designs and the body as the instrument of the soul, as the active power, in order to proceed towards the ethical contraposition of person and thing. Finally, we need to go through all these levels and have all this material in front of us, in order to enter the kingdom of aesthetics. After all, how can we have comedy and tragedy without a cast of characters, without ethical individuals composed of body and soul? And are tragedy, comedy, and beauty really just an illusion, an apparition? Are tragedy and beauty really not present in being itself? Thus ontology (logic) is the condition of possibility for teleology (ethics), and both the one and the other are the condition of possibility for cosmology (aesthetics). After all, what goals and ideals of being could there be if there were no being of any kind? What beauty could there be if there were no nature, no humankind, no reality, no ideal?

The problem of the identity of subject and object is being resolved at every one of these levels. As we saw earlier, this problem is an infinite task, or idea: more precisely — three infinite tasks, three ideas — truth, the good, and beauty. Each of them in its own way expresses the unity of subject and object. The infinite task of identity must be posed in such a way that it is not impossible, irresolvable, or meaningless. Above all, it would lose any meaning if the identity of subject and object referred to their simple analytical identity (A = A), their indistinguishability. Then there would be no problem whatsoever: everything would turn into a dead unity, in which nothing could be born, for nothing would separate out; in which there would be no system, no juxtaposition of opposites, no life — only a dead, indifferent calm. On the other hand, the task will also be unresolvable if we replace this dead identity with a dead contraposition [of opposites], with the severance of one side from the other. If we dogmatically rip subject away from object and isolate them both into independent, separate things, then we end up with a theoretical and practical skepticism. If subject and object are ripped apart, then there can no longer be a transition from one to the other. But this independence of theirs, this isolation and segregation, is a falsehood of finite reason. In fact, subject and object are indissolubly linked in their opposition, and the transition from one to the other is constantly taking place. Further, it is not only reason that serves as our guarantee for the indissolubility of the dialectical link of opposites: their ultimate unity, their fusion, lies hidden in the irrational. The infinite task consists in converting this indeterminate unity (unity in the boundless) into a unity that is determinate, separated out, into a system. The critique of bad infinity must eliminate the false interpretation of the idea of an "infinite" task. At the basis of any potential infinity lies actual infinity. When applied to our present task, this guiding thought means that a universal system of objective being, encompassing both spirit and matter, is not an unattainable ideal, forever ripped away from us, toward which the process of cognition strives in vain. On the contrary, this actual infinity of the object is always with us and we are within it; it is all of being, the being that encompasses both the process of cognition and that which is cognized. This idea is not at all an illegitimate hypostatization (the imparting of an isolated existence to any kind of abstract representation), but on the contrary, the necessary hypostasis of the Absolute. The same is true with regard to the infinity of ethical progress and the infinity of the idea of the good.

CHAPTER 9

Self-Knowledge

The Task of Self-Knowledge

"Know thyself" — this is the place where philosophy, religion, and psychology converge. For Socrates self-knowledge means both work on oneself and the forging of oneself. It lies at the foundation of all culture, all practical and creative activity; for, in the final analysis, every act is work on oneself; and culture, art, and technology are nothing other than the self-perfection of the spirit, its eternal experiment on itself, just as science means eternal experiment. Analytical psychology is also an experimentation with the soul, that is, work on the soul, the care of the soul, and so it converges with religion and asceticism.

The first thing we need to do here is to weigh up the vital meaning, the personal ethical meaning, of self-realization. "Realize thyself" — it is an imperative, a command; and it requires an inner transformation, a new birth as it were. It is a liberation from unconsciousness, and a coming round to oneself — the basis and principle for a creative life of self-definition and self-formation; for selfhood, as Jung says, is the goal of life.

Coming to self-awareness is the effort to gather up and correlate all the powers and functions of the soul: that is, it is "yoga," a sort of "burden" or "yoke." But at the same time it also means liberation, for it is imposed on me by my genuine "I" ("My yoke is easy and my burden light," Matt. 11:30). With such a bridle, the warrior holds together the two horses, white and black — consciousness and the unconscious — that are harnessed to his chariot, and drives them into the battle of life.

A stern call: "realize yourself." It never loses sight of the state of delusion and blindness. The message of the Delphic oracle addresses those na-

114

tions and peoples who lack a sense of measure and moderation, and who are plunged into the chaos of the unconscious because of their self-conceit and overweening pride. Such were the Hindus and Greeks, such are the Russians as well. This is why the call to self-awareness sounds so forcefully in Dostoevsky. This man, who best portrayed the demonic forces of the soul, knew well that possession is overcome only by way of self-awareness, the knowledge of oneself. This is his main ethical idea, expressed in his Pushkin speech: "The truth is not outside you, but in yourself; find yourself in yourself, subdue yourself, master yourself — and you will behold the truth. This truth is not in material things, it is not outside you, it is not somewhere beyond the sea, but first and foremost in your own labor over yourself." We find the same thing in the notebooks for *Demons:* "Golubov's ideas are humility, self-control, and that God and the heavenly kingdom are within us in our self-control, and freedom is there too."

This call to master oneself rings out most powerfully when a person or a nation is threatened by danger, when culture is threatened by decay. This was so in the time of Socrates and Plato; and it was so in the twilight of Roman civilization, when the Stoics proclaimed wisdom's task to be self-knowledge, and Christianity began to preach the infinite value of the soul and the kingdom of God "which is within you." We find the same mind-set in India as well, where the inherent tragedy of earthly existence became apparent precisely when the incursion from the north of the warlike tribe of Indra played itself out. At the height of the war, when destruction threatened whole kingdoms, there arose the most profound meditation about Atman, the self-knowledge of the Bhagavadgita. The same historical rhythm, the same dialectic, may be observed in our epoch as well. Under conditions of general crisis, the problem of self-knowledge is raised anew in all realms of the human spirit.

What does this coincidence of crisis and self-knowledge mean? Paul, the first and greatest Christian philosopher, expressed it symbolically: the last judgment can burn to ashes and extirpate the whole edifice of human culture, whether it be built of straw or wood, silver or gold; nonetheless, "he himself [the one who builds] will be saved, but only as through fire" (1 Cor. 3:15). He himself will be saved, as Noah was saved from the flood.

Selfhood cannot perish from tragic conflicts. On the contrary, the sublimity of tragedy consists in this, that tragedy always gives us an intimation and premonition of upward flight, an ascent *(anagoge)* to something higher and unknowable. This is the spirit's only consolation, the consolation of the Paraclete: tragic contradiction is in principle always resolvable, even if at any given moment the solution is not yet visible. And the solution of tragic contradiction means salvation. Selfhood must not perish with the disintegration of the elements, the demise of culture, in death and decay. It can be saved and redeemed, it can rise again from the dead, it can experience the "restoration of all things," and achieve a new harmony in a new heaven and a new earth. This is the mind-set of Christianity.

Philosophically and psychologically, this can be expressed in the following way. Out of the collective unconscious, out of the "subterranean" depths, new opposites and conflicts sprout up that threaten to destroy the whole edifice of conscious culture along with all of its previous solutions and syntheses. In response, selfhood must rise above the plane of consciousness to find a supraconscious solution, that is, the only solution to be hoped for. Selfhood must reach the heights of self-knowledge, lest it suffocate in contradictions or perish from doubt and despair. In so doing, selfhood discovers its own transcendence.

The Transcendence and Immanence of Selfhood

Selfhood crosses beyond (transcends) all the stages of being, all the categories, including the psychic ones. Selfhood is not body and not soul, not consciousness, not the unconscious, not the person, and not even the spirit. What then is it? It is not a "something," not a material thing or an object, not an idea — it is the infinite going beyond the confines of oneself *(transcensus)* and it is freedom; it is absolute beyondness, the "completely other," in the image and likeness of the absolute[1] and therefore in the image and likeness of God, for one may attain it only through "detachment," "liberation." "It alone is wise, and liberated from all things" — this is how we should understand that dark fragment of Heraclitus.

At the same time, it is precisely in the very absoluteness of selfhood, in its "detachment" from all things, in its transcendence (otherworldliness), that its immanence (this-worldliness) is revealed, since the "I" is really in the world, in the body, in the soul, in the spirit, even when my selfhood crosses beyond all these stages of being. After all, it really is my body, my soul, my consciousness, my unconscious, my fate and character, my spirit, my personality; and precisely for this reason all of this is oppo-

---

1. What I have in mind here is the fact that the word "absolute" derives from the Latin *absolvere*, which has a double meaning: (1) to unbind, to release, to liberate; (2) to conclude, to make perfect, complete.

site to me, not identical to me, even if it is accessible to me and I am everywhere to be found in it. In this word "my" the miraculous transcendence and immanence of selfhood manifests itself in full force. Selfhood is like absolute selfhood, for the Absolute is immanent to the whole world, and at the same time transcendent to it. Every speck of being, every fleeting psychic experience, is a "well-grounded phenomenon" [Leibniz], in which a "good foundation" mysteriously lives and acts. This is why Fichte could say: "God is living behind all these images. . . . We see him as a stone, a plant, an animal; we see him — when we rise above ourselves — as natural law and moral norm, — and yet all this — is not he himself." To express it mystically, God is "everywhere and nowhere," just as I myself am everywhere and nowhere. Here is the core of mysticism, here is the fundamental religious antinomy of immanence and transcendence, as it is revealed in both selfhood and the Absolute.

The Discovery of Selfhood

The greatest contribution of Indian philosophy — which could edify gods and demons as well as human beings — was precisely the discovery of this selfhood, this Atman, along with an indication of the only path that can lead to it. This is the path of infinite judgment, negation, and transcendence. The very idea of in-finity and im-mortality is nothing other than an example of the force of negation (not-A), the power of transcendence. Thus we should not be surprised that selfhood, the only thing that possesses a full measure of this force, is experienced and felt, first and foremost, as a selfhood that is infinite and immortal. Selfhood possesses the force and the freedom to go beyond the confines of the entire world, beyond the confines of everything that exists in the world, beyond the confines of my very "I."

This is the most ancient result and discovery of Hindu philosophy, the revelation of Hindu mysticism. This ascent to Atman in the Brhadaranyaka Upanishad reaches its height with the concluding words: *neti-neti*, "not this and not that." This selfhood in the image and likeness of God, this Atman-Brahman, Purusha, Divine-Human is revealed only through "negative theology,"[2] through "learned ignorance." This is also the revelation of Christian mysticism (cf. Rudolf Otto, *Mysticism East and West*), and

---

2. Apophatic, i.e., denying the possibility of defining divinity by means of any kind of positive principle.

perhaps of any mysticism whatsoever, regardless of cultural and religious differences. Pascal also knows that genuine selfhood means "not this and not that"; but he discovers it not through immersion in the self, but through love: "He who loves someone for his beauty — does he truly love him? No: for smallpox, which destroys beauty, compels him to fall out of love with that person. And if I am loved for my judgment, for my memory, am I truly loved? No: for I can cease to have these qualities without ceasing to be myself. So where then is this I, since it is neither in the body nor in the soul?"

Two Approaches: East and West

One may distort the basic religious antinomy, the principle of the coincidence of opposites, by placing undue emphasis on either the moment of transcendence or the moment of immanence. In the Eastern, Hindu experience of alien estrangement from the world, only transcendence counts as truth and value, while immanence is declared to be a nonvalue, an illusion. In this view, physical being and earthly existence are misfortunes and delusions. This age-old Hindu motif of pessimism can also be heard far beyond the borders of India — in Orphism, in Platonism, even in Christianity.

In contrast, the Western worldview and culture face the opposite danger, the danger of taking immanence as the supreme value and rejecting transcendence as illusion and bad metaphysics: physical being and earthly existence are the sole happiness, and the rest is delusion. This involves not only the immanence of the "I," but the immanence of the Absolute as well. In this view, selfhood must be sought in the body and the soul; the Absolute must be sought in matter, nature, the world of ideas/ representations. This is the core of Western immanentism with all of its variants — materialism, naturalism, positivism, subjective idealism (the philosophy of immanence), and so on.

Only the philosophy that grew out of Christian mysticism is free from these errors, for it holds firmly to the basic religious antinomy, to the experience of both immanence and transcendence. These opposites cannot be wrenched away from each other. The transcendence (otherworldliness) of the Absolute is just as true as its immanence (this-worldliness). Physical being and earthly existence are not an illusion, but neither are they the sole being or all of being. The advantage falls to the side of infinite transcendence. The incarnation of selfhood is certainly no illusion; selfhood really is present in its incarnations — it is present in the body, in the soul, in consciousness, and in the unconscious. But at the same time selfhood infinitely transcends all the stages of its "descent," its immanence. The idea of physical becoming preserves and retains the unity of immanence and transcendence. Thus the creative activity of culture is made possible, for culture is the incarnation — the immanent activity here and now, in the body, in nature — of the transcendent selfhood that stands above and surpasses everything.

The Miracle of Selfhood

Thus transcendence, in its value and plenitude, has the advantage over immanence, just as "not-A" has the advantage over A — since not-A includes all the other letters of the alphabet — and just as the infinite surpasses the finite. Therefore the error of immanent philosophy is an infinite one; the truth of immanence a finite and limited truth. But any transcendental philosophy, the Hindu or Platonic for example, points to infinite truth and errs only in disdaining immanence, that is, finite value. This advantage of transcendence, which is revealed in absolute selfhood, may best be formulated in the words of Plato: "beyond essence, surpassing everything in power and worth." This truth is foundational for any mysticism; and the differences among the various mystical teachings become apparent only when they descend into the realm of the immanent.

Any contempt for selfhood — which is sovereign "in power and worth," which consists in its otherworldliness, its capacity for *transcensus,* its freedom from everything — is a "fall," a guilt at the loss of selfhood, that threatens selfhood with great dangers but does not mean its complete destruction. Selfhood can never be totally lost; it is always saved "as though through fire" [1 Cor. 3:15]. The "loss" of selfhood refers only to self-forgetting, to immersion in the lower planes of being, to the forgetting of the self's "royal origin," its sovereign freedom. It is as it were "sold into slavery" and "brought up by shepherds" like a lost princess.

Analytical psychology displays a profound understanding of these experiences and knows that the miraculous *transcensus* of selfhood is frequently portrayed in a wise and beautiful mystico-philosophical symbolism. In Orphism the soul forgets about its otherworldliness, its heavenly origin in the Lethe of earthly existence, and then recollects it, discovering the unconcealable, unforgettable, always hoped-for truth about itself, the true nature of its existence. One need only delve into oneself through recollection to find in the depths of one's soul one's own genuine selfhood, which has never really disappeared. Thus the "unborn Atman that never grows old" is revealed. Strictly speaking, the "soul" is never a being of the here and now; it is never a spatiotemporal object; it can never be considered as exclusively "creaturely." It is not considered to be such even in the biblical recounting of the creation of the world. The human soul is not created by God: God "blows" it into the body and the human being inhales it into himself. Atman is the breath of the Deity. The light in the soul is like this — the light of the "Logos" as the divine light, the "spark" of Meister Eckhardt. All those notions of the preexistence and immortality of the soul express nothing other than humanity's inherent transcendence of spatiotemporal being. It would hardly be possible to express this transcendence more forcefully and meaningfully than in the words: "My kingdom is not of this world."

"Where Do We Come from and Where Are We Going?"

My selfhood that is situated in this world is not of this world — this is the greatest discovery made by self-consciousness, which puts into question the whole meaning of life and the world. At rare moments in people's lives they suddenly discover their own genuine selfhood, along with all the mysteriousness of their transcendence and the freedom that soars above everything. In these moments a deep amazement first seizes us: as if we had "fallen straight out of heaven" (a characteristically Orphic expression), we feel as if we are "thrown into the world" (Heidegger), and the question rises up before us: Where do we come from and where are we going? Philosophy begins in wonder. We stand here before the miracle of miracles, which arouses the eros of philosophy and promises the most magnificent revelations. This is the secret meaning of the dictum: "Know thyself." This dictum is transformed from something that is self-evident into a mystical and oracular message, a recovery of sight; for selfhood is not something self-evident, but rather something that is evidently incomprehensible.

In mythology, in mysticism, in philosophy, and, finally, in the poetry of all nations, we constantly hear this eternal question: Where did we come from and where are we going? (Tertullian). "But if I am so wondrous a creature, and where I come from is a mystery. . . ." These are Derzhavin's words; but one could just as well bring in a multitude of citations on this same theme from world poetry, beginning perhaps with Omar Khayyam.

Of course, we find this question, first and foremost, throughout the Upanishads; for it is not just one out of many possible philosophical questions. It may very well be that any kind of philosophy begins with it, and does so because philosophy is concerned first of all with the question of origin, of our own origin. This problem is experienced in a new way in modern philosophy, which now confronts the tragic state of the world, in "fear and trembling" before the setting sun of the West [cf. Spengler]. Hence the modern rediscovery of Kierkegaard, who came to a profound self-awareness through the most profound personal tragedy. This is essentially the same age-old question once again: "Whence and whither?" "Where am I? Who lured me into all this and dumped me here? Who am I? How did I get into the world? Why wasn't I asked first, why didn't they initiate me into the manners and mores of this life? Why did they just shove me into the ranks, as if a trafficker in souls had bought me? . . . Is this a free thing? And if they forced me into it, where then is the Manager? Or is there no Manager? To whom shall I complain?"[3] We need to evaluate and weigh up this unique experience in all of its psychological, philosophical, and religious ramifications. What does this wonder mean, this "whence and whither"?

"I" and Nothing

In these very questions it is already possible to demonstrate and philosophically ground my transcendence, for the very question of origin already signifies the act of transcending, the passage from A to not-A, to the "absolutely other." If in the course of this passage I simply run up against "nothing," this is not an argument against but rather in favor of transcending: I transcend in the direction of "nothing," but in order to discover "nothing" I myself must exist. The metaphysical fear of "nothing" is only possible if "meta-" — that is, a going beyond the limits — is possible. But what then happens is something other than Heidegger's "being toward the end."[4] Transcending (going beyond the limits of) "nothingness" means something other than opposing what exists to what does not exist; for transcendence is always an opposite, a passage to the other, according to the principle of not-A. But if I myself *am* the power of transcendence

---

3. Kierkegaard, *Repetition*.

4. I refer here to Heidegger's doctrine of "being toward death," "being toward nothingness." Cf. his "freedom toward death."

and opposition, then all of my power and worth lie precisely in that I do not identify myself with what I produce. Genuine selfhood inherently transcends any opposite, for all opposites coincide in it and develop from it. When it is in this sovereign position — "beyond the barrier of the coincidence of opposites" — and only insofar as it is able to stay in this position, selfhood is in the image and likeness of God, and surpasses the whole world, for the world is made up of opposites and contradictions. Hence the invulnerability of Atman, which Arjuna discovers in battle: no "destruction" can threaten selfhood, for it rises above all opposites, even the opposition of "being and nothing."

Despite all my fears and doubts, what always stays with me is this "ergo, I exist" — and nothing can threaten it. "Being toward the end [*konec*]" reveals to me my infinity [*beskonechnost'*].

Absolute nothingness is an illusion. Parmenides was right about that. There is no way to make nothingness into an absolute, for the statement "absolutely nothing exists" is patently untrue: my existence refutes it. However, relative nothingness — and here I am referring to the "not-A" — can signify transcendental being. "Sacred ignorance," says Nicholas of Cusa, "teaches us that what our reason takes to be nothingness is precisely the ungraspably Greatest." If transcendence really meant nothingness, then it would simply be destroyed.[5] Heidegger's dialectic is insufficient because he never posits the question of the Absolute.

Analytical Psychology: "I" and Selfhood

The antiquated traditional psychology of consciousness took as its only province the age-old middle plane of the conscious. Hence the mediocrity and banality of this boring and useless science of ideas and mental representations, which in its solipsistic immanence (i.e., taking the person of the cognizing human being as the sole reality) remains totally detached from the living sources of transcending being.

Analytical psychology is the only one that is capable of revealing and shedding light on transcending selfhood. All other psychological doctrines were immanent psychologies, merely psychologies of consciousness, which

---

5. This was correctly understood by Epicurus: he simply wants to destroy metaphysical fear, the fear of death, by destroying the otherworldly, the transcendent: I and nothingness never meet up with each other, for either there is nothing there and therefore I do not exist, or else there is an "I," and therefore not nothing but something.

knew only about the conscious "I." The unconscious is transcendent in relation to my consciousness. This transcendence, however, signifies the "subconscious" that lies at the basis of consciousness as its foundation, as the precondition of its possibility. But there is another transcendence, in another direction so to speak, which leads not to the subconscious but to the supraconscious. What is revealed here is something greater than consciousness and therefore it stands above consciousness: the "value that is located above the conscious I," the "unknown subject that stands above it" (Jung). Both consciousness and the unconscious lie at the base of this subject, who overcomes this opposition by constantly resolving it and realizing the unity of the whole. It is precisely this which is the mysterious, unapproachable, all-transcending selfhood. The greatest contribution that analytical psychology has made to philosophy is this differentiation between the conscious "I" and selfhood. A psychology of this kind takes into consideration and evaluates the mystical experience of supraconsciousness, the philosophical intuition of the irrational, the dialectic of the transcendent. And only this kind of psychology knows about psychology's ultimate realms: the depth of the soul and the height of the spirit.

Selfhood as Both Evident and Unknowable

The transition from the immanent to the transcendent marks all of modern philosophy. Modern philosophy opposes the immanent school, subjective idealism, rationalism. The irrational "thing-in-itself" is no longer banished; it is accepted now with all due respect. The genius of Kant continues to live for us not in his subjective idealism, but in his recognition of the transcendence of "being in itself" in the notion of "noumenal man."

Modern "existential philosophy" also appeals to the fact that there is "that which exists for itself (being-in-itself)"; it also recognizes the power and meaning of transcendence, and we see this in the objective ontologism of Nicolai Hartmann as well. But the appeal to transcendence is made by existentialism more in the realm of the subject, and by ontologism more in the realm of the object. I will not elaborate here on this difference, or on the possible controversies linked to it. It is sufficient to establish that both philosophical tendencies share a recognition of the unknowability and transcendence of selfhood.

"Being as the being of the I," says Karl Jaspers, "is as immediately self-evident as it is ungraspable." "The indubitability of the I," says Nicolai Hartmann, "can coexist with the most total ignorance of what the I is."

123

Selfhood for us is "indubitable," but "unknowable." According to Jaspers, "Reflection on one's self in the guise of an objectifying understanding does not grasp selfhood itself, which evades this understanding, and in its untouchable sovereignty opposes itself to everything that can be known or explained." For Hartmann, "Knowledge of oneself is only a sensation of self-awareness, it is a certain givenness outside the realm of objects." Selfhood is radically isolated from all other kinds of being; it is something impenetrable, for the most part irrational, alogical, and at the same time beyond the limits of the intelligible.

It is amazing that good old Kant can still tell us something of value about this problem. His "paralogisms" and the general formulation of his main ideas in the *Prolegomena* (§§46-49) can be interpreted correctly for the first time. In Kant's view the absolute subject, the "I", the thinking subject (and Kant uses all these terms to designate selfhood) is not given in experience as an object, and therefore not as a substance, as rational psychology assumes. The subject is in fact the unknowable thing-in-itself. This thing-in-itself lies at the basis of the phenomena of our internal experience, the experience of my soul in time, as the unknown "essence-in-itself," in the same way as the thing-in-itself lies at the basis of external experience: "as a physical body designates not only our external contemplation of it (in space), but also the thing-in-itself" (Kant).

At this point we must impart something truly marvelous about this "essence in itself" that lies at the basis of internal experience: it differs in principle from the "thing in itself" that lies at the root of external experience, that is, the cognition of material nature. This "essence in itself" is in fact what we ourselves are. In contrast, the "thing in itself," which lies at the basis of external experience, is for us something alien, something that is opposed to us. Both the former and the latter are unknowable, but we cannot say that both of them are alien or unknown to us. I myself am neither alien to myself nor unknown to myself. I am set up to have a particular kind of cognitive disposition toward myself (Sezeman); I am unknowable to myself, but at the same time I am "indubitable" and self-evident.

The Sense of "Man in Himself"

How does this mind-set work? How is it possible for the incomprehensible to be "self-evident"? Kant responds: not through a concept, not by means of categories, not in acts of objectification, and therefore not by way of rational knowledge — but only by means of a special feeling. "Such cognition," says Kant, "is nothing more nor less than a sense of the presence of being, without the aid of any concept whatsoever." Consequently, there is a sense of myself that expresses the irrational self-evidence of my selfhood. Here "I" myself "sense," as if I sniff it out in the depths of my soul, the mysterious and ungrounded "being-in-itself" of selfhood, since I *am* precisely this selfhood "in itself" and "for itself." This is the unique doorway into "being in itself" opened up by self-realization. It is the access to Brahman through Atman: the way out [*vykhod*] toward noumenal being through the noumenal man,[6] the path to the Absolute through my selfhood. But in no case should this mysterious esoteric path of self-realization eliminate the familiar and generally accepted method of objectification. It must not look down on the observation of the "starry heavens above me." This latter path can also lead to the Absolute. And only both paths together are capable of posing comprehensively the problem of "being in itself and for itself," the problem of the Absolute.

A philosophy that takes an introverted (i.e., turned in upon itself) path toward "being for itself" comes to approximately the same conclusions. There have been centuries (e.g., the 17th and 18th up to Kant) when this problem was totally disregarded. Afterward, it crops up again: the old experiences and reflections — resurrected and experienced anew — come back to mind once more. Present-day philosophy has seen the rise of the problem of anthropology, and here a collaboration between philosophy and analytical psychology is mandatory. Any philosophy that disregards the magnificent discoveries and experiments of the analytical school runs the risk of remaining naive and childish, a fate that has overtaken ordinary psychology. The antipsychologistic attitude toward ordinary psychology was absolutely correct. But no one can regard analytical psychology as naive, either from the philosophical or the religious and mystical angle: it journeys over all the mysterious paths of psychic experience and in so doing it has even discovered the idea — so rarely formulated with precision — of the transcendence of selfhood.

Selfhood as Postulate

For Jung, selfhood is "something irrational, an indefinable existent, which rises above the 'I.'" Thus it is supraconscious, as the sun is "supra-

---

6. Through Purusha, through "man in himself," in Hauer's beautiful translation.

terrestrial." Or it might be better to say: it is more central than the conscious "I," "which is dependent on it and revolves around it, rather like the earth revolves around the sun."

Both the transcendence and immanence of selfhood are expressed in this image, since the sun is transcendent to the earth, and at the same time immanent to it through its light, warmth, and gravitational pull. "The idea of selfhood in itself and for itself," says Jung, "is a transcendent postulate, which can be justified psychologically, but not scientifically proven." Selfhood is transcendent to science: it "takes a step from within science — to get outside it," going beyond psychology; at the same time it conditions its possibility, "since without this postulate I could not even talk about the psychic processes." Selfhood is thus the metaphysical premise without which psychology is impossible. Every science is founded on a similar transcendent value, a "hypothesis" in Plato's sense, a premise. For biology this value is life; for physics, the structure of the atom. To put it mildly, however, not every science is as fully aware of this as analytical psychology has become. The positive sciences often get stuck in a naive immanentism: they take no account of either the transcendental or the transcendent. Therefore we must make a special point of stressing the metaphysical power and significance of transcendent selfhood. If the idea of selfhood is understood here in the sense of a synthesis, in the sense of wholeness or a whole whose parts are consciousness and the unconscious, then there is no way to interpret it in the sense of immanence — as a value that is appended to the sum total by a simple additive process. Every synthesis of opposites is transcendent in relation to those opposites; that is, it forms something new, something totally different and higher in comparison to them. Every wholeness is transcendent and metaphysical (as Kant demonstrated, taking as his example the idea of the universe as a wholeness), for we encounter no such wholeness either in experience or in the empirical sciences. Already in the sphere of organic life, the whole provides grounds for and gives birth to the parts, but not vice versa; and we see this even more clearly in the realm of psychic being. Everything we can say about selfhood — synthesis, wholeness, the center — none of this is adequate, it is all merely images, merely objectifications. Selfhood, though, is impossible to imagine, impossible to objectify. The individualized "I," the so-called personality, is not objectifiable, but it is the "object of a subject that is unknown and stands above it" (Jung). When we say "selfhood," this is not yet objectification. What exactly "I myself" am is impossible to convey in words; rather, I can understand it in silence ("Atman is known in silence"). In science or psychology there is no way of just bumping into selfhood, no way of "proving it scientifically." Whatever you take it to mean, selfhood remains "meta-." Nor is it possible to think of it as the object of rational metaphysics: a possibility that we should reject, as Kant does. But we could say that selfhood is the unknowable "thing in itself" of psychology, that it provides this science with this advantage: that I myself am this being "in itself." This is why analytical psychology is fascinated ("enchanted") by the most ancient symbols of selfhood: it may all be only images, but — as Jung beautifully puts it — images in which we ourselves are present.

Selfhood in the Image and Likeness of God

In the ultimate and most profound self-realization — which is not reflection or self-awareness, for I myself am "unknowable" to myself even if I am both "indubitable" and self-evident — I can discover yet one more hidden meaning: my own freedom and transcendence and, in this sense, my "likeness to God." But this freedom is not absolute: I sense that it is bound up with a mystical feeling of dependence. I am not self-sufficient, not complete, not finalized, not locked inside myself, but, so to speak, opened up to something "utterly other," like a window that looks out on the infinity of the heavens. I am in the image and likeness of God, but I am not God.

At this point, relativism and positivism might challenge us by retorting that the idea of God is just an illusion, as is our feeling of dependence and our religion. Our response should be emphatic: if the Absolute is an illusion, then everything is an illusion, for the Absolute lies at the basis of everything, embraces everything. And if everything is an illusion, then the very word "illusion" loses any meaning, since illusion can be conceived and proclaimed only in opposition to what truly exists. The exact same thing goes for the "phenomenon," which is conceivable only in opposition to what exists in itself. Illusion, phenomenon — all this is a relative matter, and in order to relativize we need to presuppose the Absolute, that is, what exists "nonrelatively."

Thus, if Freud has discovered yet again that God in heaven is merely an illusion (or so he would like to think), then in terms of dialectical self-realization this means that our traditional representation of God is totally inadequate to that which exists in itself. In contrast, the Absolute, the genuine Divine Being, is something "totally other." Every denial of false Absolutization is an affirmation of the genuine — even if unapproachable — Absolute. As Bonaventura paradoxically formulates it: if there is no God, then God exists.[7]

When we relativize (compare) something, we absolutize it at the same time; when we absolutize it, then we simultaneously and necessarily relativize it. These two functions are essential for the spirit in all realms of knowledge and in the bargainings of our conscience. This is why Scheler is right to say that the human spirit encompasses the sphere of the Absolute and stands in a necessary relationship to the Absolute. If this relationship is lost, then the false absolute immediately pops into view, and the absolutization of false idols ensues. Thus the Absolute can in no way be ripped away from me, it is indissolubly connected to me; it is transcendent and at the same time immanent to me, that is, it speaks in the depths of my "I." But its "Word" is not easy to understand, since it speaks in the language of symbols and parables — a language whose meaning has been lost in the darkness of infinity — and points to something unknowable.

Two Interpretations of Selfhood as the Image and Likeness of God

Here is the ultimate and most intimate thing, the fork in the path where religions come to a parting of the ways, where mystical experiences and revelations start to diverge from each other, where philosophical ambiguities come to light. There is no way to deny our dependence on the Absolute, but we can offer two different and opposing interpretations of it. We could put the question this way: Is this dependence, in the final reckoning, a dependence on my own absolute selfhood, or is it a dependence on an absolute selfhood that is utterly different from mine? Vedanta and Sankhya proceed along the first path, while the Judaic and Christian religions and Ramanuja in India take the second.

Both solutions are absolutely foundational for the disposition of the psyche and the spirit, and thus for psychology and philosophy and, consequently, for culture as a whole. A disposition is always an ultimate solution, a relation to the Absolute. Any disposition or worldview is always the expression of a transcendent feeling of dependence, whereby the problem of the Absolute reveals itself to man, and on the basis of which man

---

7. This is the true meaning of the ontological argument: it is impossible to comprehend the Absolute, it is impossible to reduce it to an illusion. The Absolute, just like the thinking "I," holds out against a phenomenological reduction.

achieves self-realization. How he lives, what his sense of himself is like — all this depends on how he experiences and interprets his own feeling of dependence.

The Absolute — from whose viewpoint we are all subject to relativization and on which we depend in all religions — is selfhood. Expressed exoterically,[8] this is the person, the personal God. From the esoteric point of view, on the other hand, this is the transcendent "I," which goes beyond the person, just as my own selfhood is transcendent to my person. Remarkably, even in philosophy or metaphysics, the Absolute cannot be signified otherwise than through the concept of "selfhood." Yet the Absolute is unconditioned and therefore independent. It is being itself or that which exists by itself and which we are constantly seeking even if "basically" we constantly have it. For all his denial of the anthropomorphic notion of the Deity, Spinoza cannot define his absolute substance otherwise than as "what exists in itself and is known through itself." Kant with his "thing in itself" proceeds in the same manner. The Absolute is precisely "what exists in itself and by itself." But I also exist "in myself" and "by myself." Is this supposed to mean that I am the Absolute, or that I only resemble the Absolute? Am I god, or only a creature in the image and likeness of God? But this likeness must consist in the fact that both God and I are selfhoods. Is the divine selfhood something different, even totally different from my own selfhood, or is it a selfhood identical to my own? This is the most profound esoteric question, the ultimate enigma of mysticism.

If we take the second possibility as our postulate, then Atman turns out to be identical to Brahman, Purusha is transformed into the ultimate uncreated absolute being, man becomes the only god, the "pith and measure." In his inner selfhood and only in this selfhood of his are heaven and earth united (Wilhelm). Given such a solution, the feeling of dependence no doubt designates only a dependence on our own hidden selfhood. We could also go along with Freud, and define this feeling as a dependence on our superego, which we hypostatize into the "Heavenly Father." Here, despite all their differences, Indian and Chinese mysticism merge with the Western European deification of man. Such a confluence holds a special power of attraction for modern man, who is incapable of an act of naive faith and therefore seeks out a new mysticism in order to save himself from atheism. In India and China, in the guise of a new revelation, he fi-

---

8. Vysheslavtsev's text reads *ezotericheski* both here and in the next sentence. O. Meerson suggested the emendation of the first instance and I concur. Trans.

nally discovers that there are religions without God, and that his own self-hood is the supreme, and perhaps the only, selfhood, and the ultimate miracle and mystery on earth.

Dependence on the Absolute

The mysticism of immersion in oneself is a true mysticism, but taken in isolation it cannot be acknowledged as the exhaustive truth. My self-hood is not lonely and cannot remain lonely. Any immersion into the self is not content with forming a relation to itself or even with a relation to its neighbors, despite all the self's love for them. It necessarily strives to perform an act of ultimate *transcensus*, a flight [*vykhod*] toward the Absolute. If the self is made into an absolute, selfhood gains nothing, but loses everything. Metaphysical megalomania led to the fall of the archangel. In the extreme absolutization of my finite knowledge, I become ridiculous, a suitable butt for Socratic irony. Through self-absolutization, I lose my own selfhood, for I forfeit my capacity for self-realization, for self-knowledge. Self-realization begins by saying: you are not absolute. We should not deny or falsely interpret the experience of transcendent dependence as the ultimate and most profound mystical experience. We feel this dependence everywhere in the supreme moments of our spiritual life: thus art is experienced as inspiration, science as discovery, moral action as vocation, religion as revelation. Similar experiences are everywhere and always felt by us as a compelling suggestion from above. I am not locked inside my own selfhood; I go beyond its confines and discover the sublime mystery of the Absolute, my basic cause and the causelessness in which my being is rooted. I am, and I am myself, but not "through myself" and not according to my own will. This is clearly revealed in the ultimate questions — "whence and whither," the question of my beginning and my end. I am not forbidden to pose these questions, nor is transcendence sealed off from me.

The final result of my self-understanding is that I truly find myself in my extreme apposition to the Absolute, whom I — conscious of my power and dignity — can address as "Thou." For if the Absolute is a monad, then I am a monad; if the Absolute is God, then I am a "humanized God" (Nicholas of Cusa); if God is selfhood, then I also am selfhood. Finally, if God is the mystery and depth that has no beginning, then I also am a mystery and have no beginning. The human being and God form a unity of opposites, but not an identity. They stand facing each other in intensive strife and intensive love. This is the difference between the Christian-European solution to the God-man problem and the Indian-Chinese solution: in the latter all opposites mingle together like a drop of water in the ocean; in the former they are united "without separation but also without confusion." The God-man problem is the central problem for humankind, and thus it becomes the central question for any psychology or philosophy, precisely because the human "soul is Christian by its very nature," because no soul is perfect without Eros striving toward the Absolute.

CHAPTER 10

The Meaning of the Heart in Philosophy and Religion

The Heart as Man's Hidden Depth

The concept of the "heart" occupies a central place in mysticism, religion, and the poetry of all nations. Odysseus pondered and made decisions in "his dear heart." In the *Iliad* a stupid person is called a man with a "foolish heart." In Latin *cordatus homo* means not a "cordial man" but a reasonable man. The Hindu mystics located the human spirit, one's genuine "I," in the heart, not in the head. And we come across the heart on every page of the Bible. It apparently signifies the organ of feelings in general and religious feeling in particular. The difficulty, however, is that not only feeling but the most varied kinds of conscious activity are ascribed to the heart. Thus, to begin with, the heart reasons. In biblical language "to say in one's heart" means "to think." But furthermore, the heart is the organ of the will; it makes decisions. Love emanates from it: people love God and their neighbors by means of the heart or from the heart. It is said that we "have someone in our heart" (Phil. 1:7; 2 Cor. 7:3) or "we are of one heart with someone" (Acts 4:32). Finally, the heart is the location of that intimate and hidden function of consciousness — the conscience: in the words of the apostle, conscience is the law delineated in our hearts. The most varied feelings that surge through our soul are likewise ascribed to the heart: it is "abashed," it is "frightened," it "grieves," it "rejoices," it "makes merry," it is "distressed," it is "tormented," it "laments," it "feels delight," it "weakens," it "shudders." It is as if the heart were consciousness in general, everything that is now investigated by psychology. Indeed, the Bible treats

132

the concepts of "heart" and "soul" as at times interchangeable, and the same thing goes for the concepts of "heart" and "spirit."

But our difficulties increase when we are persuaded that the heart embraces the phenomena not only of psychic but also of physical life. All of life's phenomena emanate from it and revert to it, they have a physical effect on the heart. Whenever we are fortified by food and drink our heart is fortified; every burden burdens the heart (Luke 21:34); every assault on our life is an assault on the heart (Exod. 9:16). This is why it is said: "Keep your heart with all diligence; for from it flow the sources of life" (Prov. 4:23). Given this endless variety of meanings, the symbol of the heart threatens to sprawl all over the place, to become totally indistinct, to turn into a mere poetic metaphor. But this is not what happens: in religious language the heart is something very precise, one might even say mathematically precise, like the center of a circle from which an infinite number of radii can stream forth, or the center of a light from which an infinite variety of rays can emanate.

The Bible ascribes to the heart all the functions of consciousness: reflection, the resolutions of the will, sensations, the manifestations of love or conscience: above all, the heart is the core of life in general — physical, spiritual, and psychic. It is the center first and foremost, the center in every possible sense.[1] Thus there is talk about the "heart" [*serdtse*] of the earth, the "heart/pith [*serdtsevina*] of the tree" (Matt. 12:40). A question naturally arises: if this is so, then isn't this expression — the "heart" — the same one that is so familiar to psychology as the principle of the unity of consciousness, as the center of consciousness?

This is not quite the whole story: there is something here that is deeper, more religious, that remains inaccessible to a scientific and empirical psychology. There are deep reasons why the religious symbol of the "heart" has been adopted here, and not the concept of the soul or consciousness or mind, or even the spirit. Indeed, the heart signifies a certain hidden core, a hidden depth, inaccessible to view. It is in this sense that the Bible speaks of the "heart of the sea," the "heart of the earth," as that which is hidden in their mysterious depths; to an even greater extent, one

---

1. The question of the biblical meaning of "heart" has been posed by Father Pavel Florensky in *The Pillar and Ground of the Truth* (Moscow, 1914), in connection with an article by P. D. Yurkevich, "The heart and its meaning in the spiritual life of man according to the teaching of God's word" (Publications of the Kiev Theological Academy, 1860, book 1), to which he often refers. However, the only thing one finds in these authors is a posing of the question and a collection of citations.

may speak of the heart of God himself. Leon Bloy calls the heart of the Deity an "abyss," and many mystics talk about this "abyss" as the ultimate irrational depth of the divine center. But the same thing can be said of the human heart, as the hidden center of personhood. It is, first and foremost, inaccessible to someone else's view; we cannot penetrate into people's hearts from the outside. The hearts of our neighbors are not transparent to us.

But we must not assume that man's ultimate depth is sealed off only from other people; to a significant extent it is ungraspable even by man himself; we do not know how to — and sometimes we do not want to — understand ourselves; we are afraid to peer into the abyss of our own heart. A deep wisdom is contained in the oracular saying that Socrates loved to quote: "Know thyself" — a wisdom both Hellenic and ancient Indian. But people do *not* know themselves, and not only in the sense of their temperament, their passions, their defects — no, in a much deeper sense: they do not know their genuine selfhood, their genuine "I," what the Hindus call "Atman," what Christianity calls the immortal soul, the heart, the heart of the soul. Socrates and the Indian sages knew that man is separated from his selfhood by the daily vanities of life, by his concern for his body, by his concern for his pleasures, for material things, material gain. Christ says: What use is it to a man if he gains the whole world but loses his own soul? He is talking here precisely about that ultimate mysterious center of the personality, where all its value and all its eternity reside. To find one's eternity is to find one's genuine "I," to gaze into the depths of one's heart. Not many people succeed in doing this. It is experienced, first, as a feeling of the most profound astonishment, perhaps like a new spiritual birth, or a sudden recovery from congenital blindness. The man who truly wishes to gaze into his own depths must necessarily become a religious person, he must experience a religious feeling, a feeling of reverence, of mystical trembling in relation to himself and to the unfathomable depth of his heart, he must see in himself "an entire world full of infinity" (Leibniz). For, after all, religion is simultaneously a recognition of the divinity of God and the divinity of man himself.

Religion is finding God in oneself and oneself in God; and atheism is not only a lack of faith in God but is bound to be also a lack of faith in man, a lack of faith in oneself, a lack of faith in one's absolute value and one's absolute eternity. Atheism assumes that "I" am only my body, my passions, my desires, my movements and actions in the world, and naturally all of this is transitory and destructible and rushes past like smoke. There is nothing in this of my genuine selfhood. When atheism contemplates the world, it constantly moves around the periphery, on the surface; it constantly places its faith in outward shows, in visible appearances; atheism is the denial of the mysterious center of personhood and, consequently, a denial of the mysterious center of the universe. For atheism there is no such thing as the "heart of the earth," the "heart of the sea," the "heart of the heavens," nor does it believe in the existence of the human heart, for atheism is constantly skimming over the surface and never descends into the depths; and, to be sure, nothing is easier than skimming over the surface. The superficial thing is the easiest thing, the most generally accessible. Atheism is the most banal of worldviews, the worldview of the third-rate hack. Aristotle says that philosophy begins in wonder, and we might say that religion begins in a feeling of mystery, a trembling before the mysterious, veneration before the mysterious. In this sense, atheism and positivism are worldviews that are just as devoid of religious feeling as they are of philosophical interest; they wonder at nothing and venerate nothing.

The Heart as the Organ of Religious Experience

We must necessarily acknowledge the heart as the basic organ of religious feelings. In the simplicity and accessibility of this word, this symbol of the "heart," which crops up everywhere in simple conversational speech, lies its supreme religious value. A person "without a heart" is a person without love and without religion; to be without religion is, in the final reckoning, to be heartless. It is false to say, as some people do, that there is some kind of nonreligious heartfelt emotion in the form of humanitarianism, solidarity, class consciousness, and so forth. The greatest crimes have been committed for the sake of such humanitarianism, and they have been vindicated by declamations of love for humanity, by rhetoric in the spirit of Rousseau and Robespierre. The first thing that can be said about the people who make these claims is that they have no heart and thus they have lost the mystical bond to their neighbors and to God; they have, naturally, lost their genuine "I" as well, they have forgotten all about it, they do not even suspect its existence.

But it is only there, in the depths of this "I," in the depths of the heart, that a genuinely real contact with the Deity (God, who is felt by the heart — Pascal), a genuine religious experience is possible; and without this contact and this experience there is no religion and no genuine ethics. The Gospels continually declare that the heart is the receptacle for the divine Word and the gift of the Holy Spirit, the organ into which divine love

135

pours. And this contact with the Deity is possible because there is the same mysterious depth in the human heart as there is in the heart of the Deity. Here the whole meaning of the expression "the image and likeness of God" is revealed, here man has a sense of his own divinity, here one depth reflects the other; and until man meets up with this depth in his own essence, he does not understand what the depth of the Deity means. One needs to be deep oneself in order to sense this mysterious depth.

This is why religion has taken up the symbol of the heart. The innermost center of personhood is expressed in it. The heart is more incomprehensible, impenetrable, mysterious, hidden, than the soul, than consciousness, than the spirit. It is impenetrable to another's gaze, and, even more startling, to one's own gaze. It is just as mysterious as God himself, fully accessible only to God himself. The prophet Jeremiah says:

The heart is deep[2] above all things . . . who can know it? I, the Lord, search the heart, I try the reins [kidneys] (Jer. 17:9-10)

for the righteous God trieth the heart and reins (Ps. 7:9)

I am he which searcheth the heart and reins (Rev. 2:23)

the Lord searcheth all hearts, and understandeth all the imaginations of the thoughts (1 Chron. 28:9)

[God] knoweth the secrets of the heart (Ps. 44:21)

An exceptional significance attaches to the human heart: its secrets are fully known only to God. We are then bound to feel a reverent trembling before this mysterious depth in our own heart and in the hearts of our neighbors. Here is the true beauty, the true and eternal value of the human being. The apostle Peter — this nearly prosaic apostle — has astonishing words, full of inspired poetry, devoted to this "hidden man of the heart." He starts out by talking about human beauty, about the beauty of

2. The Slavonic text, which Vysheslavtsev uses here, reads *gluboko*, which would mean "deep, unfathomable." The Septuagint, from which the Slavonic Bible is translated, reads *batheia he kardia* = "deep [is] the heart." The Hebrew word is *'aqob*, which means "crafty, tough," "bumpy, uneven ground"; the root also produces a verb that means "to grasp by the heel, to cheat." The Russian Synodal translation renders it as *lukavo*, "crafty." KJV has "deceitful"; NRSV, JPS, Jerusalem Bible, "devious." Trans.

women and their unconscious efforts to adorn themselves. Here are his words: "Ye wives . . . whose adorning let it not be that outward adorning of plaiting the hair, and of wearing of gold, or of putting on of apparel; But let it be the hidden man of the heart, in that which is not corruptible, even the ornament of a meek and quiet spirit, which is in the sight of God of great price" (1 Peter 3:1, 3-4).

Everything of value that can be said about the heart is gathered together here: the heart is the secret center of the human being; it "keeps quiet," and apophatically proclaims its depth; hidden within it is an incorruptible beauty of the spirit, an authentic beauty; and this incorruptible spiritual center is absolute value, it is "of great price in the sight of God." The prosaic apostle has succeeded in finding the most poetic words for this mysterious depth.

The Heart in Indian Mysticism

It is striking to compare Christian and Indian mysticism on this point. At first, we will be struck by the concurrence of the paths and even of the mystical symbols. This is inevitable if the one and only true God is the goal of all mystical aspirations; it is a concurrence in the truth. But we should not conceal from ourselves the most important divergences of these religious paths. If Christianity is the plenitude of the truth, then it would be improbable if other peoples in their religions had never come near this truth in any way; it is hard not to notice such approximations in the mysteries of Egypt and Greece, in Platonism and Neoplatonism, and, finally, in Indian mysticism.

On the other hand, if Christianity is the actual plenitude *(pleroma)* of the concrete living person of the Divine Human, then it is singular and unique and individual. We cannot replace it with all sorts of eclectic generalizations in the spirit of theosophy, which in its tasteless mishmash of styles loses any feeling for individuality, nationality, personality.

The "hidden man of the heart" is the center of attention in Indian religiosity. The Hindus are great masters at investigating the ultimate, hidden center of our "I," our selfhood. The whole of Indian wisdom aspires toward it.

What is selfhood? It is the luminous "I" [*purusha*, "man"] that is cognition, which is amid the breath of life, within the heart. (Brhadaranyaka Upanishad 4.3)

137

This Atman [the basic term for hidden selfhood] of mine within my heart is smaller than a grain of rice, smaller than a mustard seed, smaller than the kernel inside that grain. This Atman of mine within my heart is larger than the earth, larger than the spaces of the air, larger than the heavens, larger than all the worlds. (Chandogya Upanishad 3.14)

Man [*purusha* — another term for innermost selfhood] is barely as large as one's little finger, his innermost selfhood eternally abides in the heart of everything that is born. (Katha Upanishad 6.17)

Through the mind that governs the heart (cf. "the mind that stands in the heart") is granted the revelation about it [i.e., Atman]. (Svetasvatara Upanishad 3.13)

Smaller than the small and larger than the large is the selfhood that reposes on the heart of this creature. (Svetasvatara Upanishad 3.20)

This quality of being infinitely small and infinitely large demonstrates the ultimate centrality of our "I": it is a center, a point, it has no dimensions ("the kernel of the grain"); and yet innumerable radii stream out from it toward the world, toward the heavens; rays of cognition and rays of strenuous aspiration.

Christian Love and Buddhist Compassion

In Christianity mystical contact with God and one's neighbors comes about through the agency of the heart. The heart is the organ that establishes this special intimate bond with God and with one's neighbors that is called Christian love. It differs from any other non-Christian love by virtue of its mystical depth; it differs in that it is a bond of depth with depth, a bridge thrown across the abyss from one heart to another. But up until the time of Christ or outside Christ, love of any kind has only been comradeship, the frenzy of passion, or, at best, pity, compassion. All these are superficial contacts between one person and another: contacts of body or soul, but without touching the hidden, spiritual center of the heart. This is the love of atheists.

The Buddhist love-as-compassion is not like this at all. It is, naturally, opposed to any kind of self-interested passion, to any kind of friendship or comradeship. Yet this Buddhist love differs in the most profound way from Christian love, with which it is often conflated in the tasteless popularizations of theosophy. The expert on Buddhism, Barthélemy-Saint-Hilaire, calls this feeling "compassion without love." Love reposes on a faith in the absolute value of a real person. There is no such faith in Buddhism. In Christianity love is the mystical bond between one individual depth and another, the bridge between two abysses; in Buddhism it is the declaration of the identity of two suffering selfhoods, equivalent in their suffering and therefore com-passionate. That they are individuals who are opposites and face to face with each other is denied. Buddhism[3] says: you are I and therefore I love you and feel sorry for you; Christianity says: you are not I, and therefore I love and feel sorry for you. This is an enormous distinction. In Christianity my "neighbor" is an individual, a person who is opposite to me, irreplaceable and unique; in Buddhism the multiplicity of differing individuals is an illusion, *maya:* in fact they are all one, identical in their essence, undifferentiated in their heart. There is not nor can there be any kind of individual immortality, and consequently no love of any kind for the immortal, singular, and irreplaceable individual. Here the unity of opposites that constitutes the essence of love does not exist; there is no "coincidence of opposites"; here persons are identical to each other in an indifferent, equivalent suffering, whose terminal point is the total "withering away" of any individual difference in nirvana.

These particular features of Buddhism are rooted in other deeper and older religio-philosophical systems, which in turn have their ultimate grounding in the Indian Bible — the Upanishads.

Here the mystical contact with God is of a different kind from that in Christianity, and consequently there is a different kind of contact with our neighbor as well. What fascinates us in Indian mysticism is the inspired surging into the depths of the heart and the finding in it of the immortal luminous point, our true "selfhood" (Atman), reminiscent of the "spark" of Meister Eckhardt, and even, as it were, the "true light that enlightens any person coming into the world." The solid achievement of Indian mysticism will forever be its unmediated contemplation of the indestructibility and immortality of the "I," which can be perceived here and now without having to wait for the moment of death. Further, the assertion that contact with the Deity is realized only at this ultimate point, only in this "depth of the heart," also relates Indian to Christian mysticism.

---

3. The original text reads "Hinduism." Trans.

Two Types of Indian Mysticism

The European may not immediately notice the striking difference between East and West. The impassive purity of India's detached spirit and the brilliant wisdom of its unspoiled imagistic speech summon up a veneration into which Christian experiences are involuntarily poured; just as in a beautiful but alien temple of an alien style and spirit, our own native and primordial prayers come back to our minds. Even the greatest philosophers and experts — Schopenhauer, Hartmann, Deussen — assume that it is all essentially the same thing. But in fact it is totally different.

Indian mysticism proclaims the immanent identity of the ultimate center of my selfhood with the ultimate center of divine selfhood. It is not that I find God in myself by coming into contact with God in the depth of my own heart, but rather that I myself turn into a god! I myself — not, of course, in the sense of my body or soul, and not in the sense of my empirical personality or character (not even in the sense of "divine humanity"), but in the sense of the ultimate irrational center of my "I." This center of mine is identical to, coincident with, the divine center. At this high level of speculation, the human "I" coincides with the divine "I" to the point where they cannot be distinguished from one another.

For the unaccustomed and the uninitiated, this can seem strange and wild, but this is how it is. It is useless to dispute it. "Atman is Brahman." I myself am the one and only deity. This is the central idea that runs throughout the Upanishads. It is a system not of the unity and coincidence of opposites, but of the identity and indifference of opposites and, in the final analysis, of the illusoriness of opposites: the diversity of opposites turns out to be an illusion.

Now this identity — "Atman is Brahman" — can be interpreted in two ways. The ontological center of gravity may lie in the first or the second term. "Atman is Brahman": this can be understood to mean that my supreme "I," detached from its outer shell, perceives its identity with God, and dissolves into him without remainder, like a drop of water in the ocean, like a grain of salt in salty water. Then only Brahman, only God exists, and not man: here we have the system of Vedanta.

But if we switch around the terms of the identity, then the ontological center of gravity will lie in Atman. "Brahman is Atman": my supreme "I," detached from everything, will be the genuine, supreme, ultimate reality. Then only man will exist, and there will be no God; we have the atheistic system of Sankhya. Atman (the favorite term of Vedanta, where it is always identical with Brahman) here changes its name to Purusha, whose original meaning in Sanskrit is "human being," but which, as a philosophical term, designates the innermost "I." Purusha is that same "innermost man of the heart" which was designated in Vedanta by the term "Atman."

Thus we have two types of Indian mysticism: theosophical pantheism and "anthroposophical" atheism. Remarkably enough, the atheistic Sankhya is regarded as a canonical system, that is, as grounded in the sacred books, the Upanishads. This is as if to say: yes, the identity of Brahman-Atman can be interpreted in this way, in the direction of a human "immanentism" and atheism. This is the same line of thought that we encounter in the first period of Fichte and that provoked a fully justified charge of atheism against him.

The Reformation-like popularization of Buddhism wavers between these two classic and profound resolutions. The Buddhist nirvana can be interpreted either as an atheistic "extinction" of consciousness or as a pantheistic dissolution in the absolute. Buddha very wisely forbade his disciples to investigate this question.

We could appropriately search here for the source of the religious vagueness of theosophy and anthroposophy, concerning which it is not easy to decide whether they are pantheistic or atheistic. The whole business is made more difficult by the extreme philosophical dilettantism of these schools, which self-indulgently dredge up out of cultural time and space anything that suits their fancy.

We see now that the mystical contact with God in Indian mysticism is absolutely peculiar to it. It is not at all the Christian love that unites the depth of the heart with the depth of the Deity. Here there is neither God nor man, no God-Man or God-Son relationship, no love, no harmony of opposites ("coincidence of opposites"), for there are no persons — Father and Son — who are opposite to each other. What we get is undifferentiated identity.

This identity is not regarded as love, it is not inclination, attraction, aspiration — it is a blissful calm in detached indifference. This is why the "heart" in Indian mysticism also has another meaning: it refers only to the inner world, the hidden centrality, the heartlike form of Atman in relation to all things. But there is none of the emotional, erotic, or aesthetic coloration that is inevitable in the Christian heart and that is ultimately transformed not into the identity of unison but into the harmony of tautened strings opposing and according with each other.

CHAPTER 11

What Am I Myself?

The Problem of Divine Humanity

The biblical idea of "image and likeness" expresses first and foremost the essential similarity between man and God. Man is a "lesser god," a *micro-theos,* for it is said, "ye are gods; and all of you are children of the Most High" [Ps. 82:6]. The idea of likeness to God is, of course, essential to Christian, and indeed to any religious, anthropology; but it is just as essential to a nonreligious anthropology. This might seem quite strange and unexpected, and yet it is so.

"Image and likeness," as the essential similarity between man and God, is an axiom that is never questioned by either the religious or the religionless (atheistic) consciousness. Nicolai Hartmann is absolutely correct to point out that the human being, as a spiritual person, ascribes to himself all the attributes of the Deity: mind,[1] freedom, consciousness of values, foresight, and prophetic insight. Both the theologian and the athe-

---

1. It is important, especially for this chapter, to clarify the concept of "mind," which is how I translate the Russian *um,* which itself is often the equivalent of the Greek *nous.* A helpful definition is given in the glossary to the *Philokalia,* volume 1, translated by G. E. H. Palmer, Philip Sherrard, and Kallistos Ware [New York: Faber and Faber, 1979], p. 362: *nous* is "the highest faculty in man, through which . . . he knows God or the inner essences or principles of created things by means of direct apprehension or spiritual perception." It "does not function by formulating abstract concepts and then arguing on this basis to a conclusion reached through deductive reasoning, but it understands divine truth by means of immediate experience, intuition or 'simple cognition.'" It is "the organ of contemplation, the 'eye of the heart.'" The adjective *umnyi* I have generally translated as "noetic." Trans.

142

istic philosopher — Feuerbach and Marx — agree equally on this. The only question is whether God created man in his own image and likeness, or man created God in *his* image and likeness.

In any case, human beings possess an ineradicable tendency to place themselves in some relation to the Absolute, to the ideal, to the ultimate truth, to the essence of being. To understand the human being means to understand his relation to God. Even atheists do not doubt this. The problem of humanity is the problem of Divine Humanity. Feuerbach labored over a resolution to the problem of Divine Humanity; and so have labored and labor still the modern psychologists, Freud and Jung. God is the "superego," our ego's ideal, the archetype (prototype) of the father, they tell us. Well now, this is not all that far from the truth, the religious philosopher will respond. In any case, the problem of Divine Humanity is at hand whenever the question arises of the comprehension of the soul in all its dimensions.

The Absurdity of Psychologism

True enough, the whole question revolves around whether God is only "existence in our psyche [*dusha*]," only a subjective illusion, only an immanent phenomenon in our soul. But this "only" should be cast aside as the crudest sort of psychologism, as an explanation by the method of "nothing other than," against which Jung himself has directed his irony. The Absolute is precisely that which infinitely surpasses any "only"; it is revealed in our psyche by a certain sign and symbol, but a symbol that transcends, that points toward something transcendent. The human being always transcends himself and his psyche, and this is indicated by concepts like the "superman" or the "superego." The quests of science have aspired toward the transcendent, the otherworldly, just as the aspirations of ethics and religion have aimed at the ideal of perfection.

Any immanent idea, image, or symbol can be doubted, cast under suspicion as subjective, with no objective meaning. But one thing is beyond all doubt: these immanent ideas "have the intention" of transcending, of expressing something objective. *Transcensus* remains beyond any doubt: it is indicated by a gesture — by hands raised to heaven, by a word, by a symbolic act of religion, or of art, by a cognitive mathematical symbol. It makes no sense to reduce the absolute to the immanent ideas about it, because all symbols and ideas of the absolute presuppose (postulate) a way out [*vykhod*] beyond the confines of the subjective (a *transcensus*).

To explain the idea of God psychoanalytically as the transfer of the "Father" complex to our higher "I," or to reduce the idea of God to the archetype (prototype) of the Father, does not at all entail, as Freud thought, the reduction of religion and God to a subjective illusion, to a mere "existence in our psyche," to purely immanent images and experiences. The existence in my psyche, in my consciousness and subconscious, of the father and mother complexes, of prototypes of father and mother, does not at all mean that real mothers and fathers who are transcendent to my psyche do not exist; it does not mean that their existence is reducible to my complexes and is merely "existence in my psyche." From the fact that the archetype of the soul is projected onto woman, it does not at all follow that a woman is only a subjective illusion. From the fact that the archetype of the "healer" is projected onto the psychoanalyst, it does not at all follow that this doctor is not a doctor, but only a "complex." On the contrary, the archetype in this case is projected, as it were, right where it belongs. Archetypes in general can have transcendent cognitive meaning as symbols, and they do constantly have it. All our cognition and activity begins with archetypes.

This is where all the absurdity of psychologism — not psychology but psychologism! — becomes apparent. The psychological reduction of everything to the subjective and the immanent has no right to assume a pose of Mephistophelean irony, for it becomes comic itself when it claims to discredit and eliminate the objectively true and the transcendent. The genuine reality of father and mother is not eliminated because I project onto them my own complexes and the archetypes of the collective unconscious; the genuine reality of the world is not at all eliminated because the Greeks projected onto it the archetype (prototype) of the psyche and regarded it as an animate creature; lastly, the genuine reality of the Absolute is not in the least eliminated because the archetype of personhood, the archetype of the Father, is projected onto it. We maintain that this transference is fully grounded, for the archetype of the Father is an adequate symbol of the Absolute. There are quite profound reasons for symbolizing the Absolute by the archetype of personhood. There is something in personhood itself that resembles the Absolute. Indeed, the person exists in itself, through itself, for the sake of itself, and one may say the same thing about the Absolute. The person is the first cause and the final goal of its own activity, and there is no other way for us to symbolize the Absolute than as the first cause and the final goal of being. Personhood is the creative freedom we have had from the beginning and an end in itself. The same thing may be said of the Absolute: everything that exists proceeds out of it and for the sake of it. In a word, personhood is self-construction, selfhood —

and the Absolute is self-construction, selfhood. Existence in itself and for itself — this is what they have in common. There is no other model (paradigm) for the Absolute.

The Mystery of Creation

Thus the idea of the image and likeness of God is unveiled: God and man are similar to each other. No one doubts this: neither the credulous Greek poets (as the apostle Paul pointed out), nor the skeptic Xenophanes, nor Feuerbach, nor Freud and Jung. But which of them actually created the other: did God create man or man God? Who comes first, who is the prototype (the archetype), who is the originally existing and who the reflection? It is sufficient to pose the question in this way to eliminate the perplexity about Divine Humanity. In his metaphysical question of "whence and whither?" man strives to project the originally existing and ultimate meaning of existence. In this very question, in his basic sense of himself, he recognizes his dependence, his conditionality, his nonprimariness. "But if I am so wondrous a creature, and where I come from is a mystery, and I have no power on my own to exist" [Derzhavin]. That man has not created himself is abundantly clear to him. To claim that he has created the Absolute would entail the claim that he has created the whole world and himself to boot. Such a claim is foolish ("The fool says in his heart — there is no God," Ps. 13:1; 52:2). Man has not created himself out of nothing, but discovers that he has been created and asks in amazement: "Who with hostile power called me forth out of nothingness?" [Pushkin].

I have sprung up out of the unknown depths of being, but not by my own power; and I am summoned to an unknown goal ("life, why were you given to me?" [Pushkin]). This is indeed the mystery of creation, the miracle of creation, our sense of being created and the wonder of it, which gives birth to the process of contemplation — in essence, all science, all philosophy, all theology. Here is the foundation adamantine for the "ontological argument," which constitutes the great tradition of Russian philosophy. The ontological argument is a pointer toward this ontological foundation, this "sufficient reason"; for "any phenomenon is a well-founded phenomenon" (Leibniz). Man springs up out of the unknown Absolute; any doubt about it is impossible: on the contrary, here lies the unshakable foundation for all our doubts, for what we doubt is not the foundation of existence, but how to think about and conceptualize this foundation. What kind of "ideas," what symbols and hieroglyphs, can best express the

145

Absolute? That is the question, that is where doubt is possible. Did a "hostile power" call me forth from nothingness, or the love of a Father for his son?

The Commensurability between Man and the Absolute

All our faith in "revelation" affirms only that the Absolute is revealed or, more accurately, glimpsed, in some symbols (in the Credo [= *simvol very,* "symbol of faith"]), in some "word," in some "dogmas," but in others the Absolute is concealed and obscured. Is this a vain faith or a true one? If there do exist such "words" about the Absolute, which reveal something about it, then it means that there is a commensurability between man and the Absolute, regardless of all the incommensurability between them; if God can say something to man and man can say something to God, then they have something in common, and what they have in common is the logos, mind. Likeness to God is the essential premise of any religion, any revelation, especially of the true one. But here is the remarkable thing: likeness to God is also the prerequisite of any knowledge, any science; for if the mathematics of the divine Architect of the world were to have nothing in common with our mathematics, then knowledge of the world, astronomical knowledge, would simply be impossible. But this would mean that every single experiment would fail, no technology would be possible, no human creativity could exist, since the earthly architect by the power of his reason alone could build nothing that could remain standing for even a moment in the face of the heavenly Architect. Human creativity presupposes foresight and prophetic insight — but these are divine attributes. God is the creator, the poet of being; but man is also a creator, the poet of culture — insofar as he cultivates and does not destroy the Eden that has been created for him. If he possesses an imperfect (albeit truly godlike) poetry, if he possesses not an absolute — and even an infinitely small amount of — foresight and prophetic insight, then this only goes to prove that he is not absolute, but absolutely in the image and likeness of God: not God, but rather an icon (image) of the Deity.

The Viewpoint of Christian Anthropology

Likeness to God is the basic premise for understanding man's essence. Outside of the problem of Divine Humanity, man is inconceivable, for "here he stands" in an essential bond with the Absolute; he is rooted in it and affirmed in it.

If we reject the first solution to the problem of Divine Humanity, the "Man-God" solution, which explains our likeness to God by the fact that man creates God in his own image and likeness, then we are left with the second, the God-Man solution, which asserts that God creates man in his own image and likeness. The first solution is an immanent one: man is locked inside his consciousness and identifies God with his own "concepts" and "notions" and fantasies about God. A thoroughly consistent immanentism is solipsism, that is: only my consciousness exists; the world is only "my idea" and God is only "my idea." The second solution is a *transcensus* (a going beyond the confines of the subjective). In any quest, in any creative act, in any aspiration, man transcends himself (goes beyond the confines of himself). The Eros of the Absolute, the aspiration toward depth and height, is *transcensus*. Man is not the "original" and he is not self-sufficient; there is a being that is deeper and higher than he is. Yet he finds in himself the reflection and the seal of this ultimate depth and height. This is the viewpoint of Christian anthropology.

From the viewpoint of patristic anthropology, man is an "icon of the Deity," and this is the solution to the riddle of his mysterious essence. But we can understand its meaning only if we unfold the whole hierarchical structure of the levels of being into which man is interwoven and which he bears and reproduces in himself. It is in this sense that the church fathers call man a microcosm, a lesser world containing the elements and structure of the greater world, but who also bears in himself something else that goes beyond all natural and cosmic limits.

The human being is plural, that is, it is impossible to reduce him to a single element, a single substance. Materialism is just as false as spiritualism. Nor is it possible to understand the human being as a combination of two juxtaposed substances — a thinking one and an extended one — as Descartes does. Man is made up of three hierarchically ascending levels: the body, the soul, and the spirit. The soul is higher in dignity than the body and "animates" the body; the spirit is higher than both body and soul and it "inspirits" the body and the soul. This is Paul's notion, and it is the point of departure for patristic anthropology. Emil Brunner regards it as the viewpoint of natural common sense, which is closer to the truth than the various sorts of scientific monism. This is correct, but only in the sense that this three-part division provides the whole complex hierarchical structure of the human essence in concentrated form. In order to unfold this structure in its full scale, we must inevitably enlist the whole modern science of man: biology, psychology, philosophy. The church fathers always relied on the most advanced science of their day; they bequeathed this method to us, and we too should rely on the most advanced science of our own time.

The Hierarchical Structure of the Human Being

The "body" embraces not one but two levels of being: it contains the physicochemical processes as well as the processes of organic life. In the light of modern psychological discoveries, the "psyche" also loses its simple unity: it is not exhausted by consciousness, just as the "spirit" is not identical with consciousness. There is in fact a psychic unconscious, but even this has two levels: the collective unconscious and the individual unconscious. The conscious psyche also has two levels: the animal and the spiritual psyche (the conscious spirit). But the conscious spirit is not the summit of the human essence either. Still higher is the supraconscious, the "deep" supracognitive "I," "I myself," or selfhood.

Thus we find in the human essence seven ontological levels (levels of being):

1. Man is physicochemical energy.
2. He is "animate" energy, *bios,* the living cell.
3. He is the psychic energy that forms in its hidden depths the collective unconscious, as the common soil on which the individual soul grows and develops.
4. He is the personal unconscious, which rests on the foundation of the collective unconscious.
5. He is consciousness, the conscious soul; and, first of all, the nonspiritual animal soul, which is defined as the egocentric mind-set. This is the soul that is ruled by "interests" like the calculation of pleasure and discontent, that interprets and evaluates everything only in accordance with the vital center of consciousness.
6. The human being is spiritual consciousness, the spirit, the spiritual person, and as such the builder and bearer of culture. The feature that distinguishes this level from nonspiritual, animal consciousness is that here the egocentric mind-set has been abandoned. Perception and evaluation are no longer subjective but objective. For the spirit, there exists not only what is "useful" and pleasant for the vital consciousness, but also what is in itself, that is, "objectively,"

valuable and true. (Utilitarianism and the ethics of "interests" are the viewpoints of animal consciousness.) Among the Greek and — following in their footsteps — the Latin church fathers, this level of spiritual consciousness is strictly differentiated from the nonspiritual animal soul, as the logological [pertaining to the logos] (verbal) from the nonlogological (nonverbal); it is the capacity to perceive and express the rational word and its objective meaning. When Paul says: "he that is spiritual judgeth all things" [1 Cor. 2:15], he is referring first and foremost to this capacity for all-round objective judgment, which is inherent in the spirit.

7. But spiritual consciousness, the "conscious I," the "thinking I," the spiritual personality, as the creator of culture, is not yet the ultimate, highest, and deepest level in the human essence. It is hard to say anything about this ultimate depth, except that it is — I myself, the human being "in himself," selfhood. Selfhood is the seventh level, the ultimate and highest mystical level in the human essence. Science and rational thinking cannot reach it or give proof of it, and therefore psychology cannot grasp it, as Jung has by now clearly proclaimed. Selfhood is meta-physical and meta-psychic, something that is "meta-" in every possible sense, the ultimate *transcensus.* Only revelation and mystical intuition can point toward this ultimate depth.

In practical life, in our cognition of the world, even in cultural creativity, this level can pass totally unnoticed. This is why consciousness, the "conscious I," the spirit, the mind, spiritual personhood [i.e., level 6], has almost constantly been regarded as the highest level in the structure of the human being and the ultimate manifestation of his essence. But reason and consciousness are not man's highest level: irrational and supraconscious selfhood is the highest. The great mystics of all times and among all peoples search for it, make conjectures about it, and express it in their strange paradoxical language. The favored symbol of the "heart" points to this mysterious depth, accessible only to God ("God alone knows the secrets of the heart," says the Bible [cf. Ps. 44:21]). Selfhood is the "hidden man of the heart." Thus not only is God ungraspable, but the human being as well; and in this godlike ungraspable depth of his the human being also encounters God, in the depth of his "heart." This is why the mysticism of the heart plays such an enormous role in the collective experience of Eastern Christianity. This is why the Eastern fathers and the Russian hermits after them adjure us to "stand with our mind in our heart," or to "immerse our mind in the depths of our heart." This indicates that "mind" is not the ultimate depth nor the ultimate fulcrum.

The hierarchical structure of the human being shows us that he bears in himself all the levels of cosmic being: he is "dead matter," living matter, an animate organism, animal consciousness. The cosmic elements and earthly animal-vegetable life are contained in him, they pervade him and interact with him. The human being presupposes and contains all the "days of creation" and the whole of that cosmic hierarchy of being which has been unfolded in them. In this sense he is a microcosm, a lesser world linked to the greater world. But he is something greater still: a micro-*theos,* a "lesser god," linked to the Almighty God. When the creation of man and nature is completed, then creativity begins — the creativity that issues from man himself, by virtue of his spiritual personhood and freedom. It is this that makes him "godlike." The sixth and seventh levels of the human essence lift him above nature and place him at the summit of the hierarchy. But the true summit of the hierarchy has not yet been reached. Man has a sense of something higher than himself, thanks to which he "sublimates," in the name of which he acts and makes sacrifices and sacrifices even himself. Man himself is the "altar to the unknown God" [Acts 17:23], and he finds this altar in the depth of his own selfhood, as the ultimate word of "self-knowledge," as the ultimate wisdom of eternal Athens. The unknown God leads him out of the abyss and lifts him up to himself. This is what is revealed to him in the ultimate question: "Whence and whither?" And man experiences this leading out and lifting up *(anagoge)* as a twofold dependence: as his own createdness and as a summons to create (for man creates, in the true sense of the word, not according to caprice or arbitrariness, but because he is a creator "by vocation").

Thus man is not the beginning and not the end of being — this is abundantly clear to him. He is not the alpha and not the omega, not the first cause and not the prototype — he is only an iconic reflection. This is why he does not crown the hierarchy, nor does he ground it: he is not the "sacred principle itself," although he stands closest to it in the cosmic hierarchy. This fact alone, this inseparable link and closeness, poses the problem of our "likeness to God." We cannot help but examine this problem within the framework of the hierarchical structure of the human being, of the cosmic hierarchy.

The Light of Consciousness and the Might of Freedom

The hierarchical structure of the human being is the nexus binding together all the problems of his existence and purpose in life. We will leave aside all the complexity of these problems and touch here only on the problem of "image and likeness." After all, what is it in man that makes him God's image? Not his body, of course, but his psyche; and not his animal psyche, but his reasoning psyche: his mind, logos, spirit — this is what is godlike in man. This has been the general conviction of the church from the very beginning; this is the doctrinal starting point for the Eastern and Western church fathers. The mind is something beautiful; it is what we have that is in the image of the Creator (Basil the Great). God is mind and man is mind: this is the only reason why God could even be united to man [in the Incarnation], since man is most closely akin to him. "In both [God and man] the nature of mind holds sway. God is the light of the mind, the lamp of the mind, and the human mind is illumined by the prototype of the light" (Gregory the Theologian [Nazianzus]). The image of God consists of the mind, the spirit, in that which differs from nature and rises above nature (Gregory of Nyssa). This deification of the logos, the mind, is what the Eastern fathers inherited from Athens, preserved in Byzantium, and transmitted to Western theology and, more than that, to all of Western scholarship and culture.

On the other hand, man's likeness to God consists in his freedom. This is what Macarius of Egypt forcefully proclaimed with inexorable consistency. No natural entities are free — neither the sun nor the moon nor the earth nor the animals; but God is free and man is free: "you are created in the image and likeness of God, because God is autocratic and he does what he wants. If he wants, by virtue of his power he could send the just into Gehenna and the sinners into his kingdom. But this he does not approve of and he does not choose to do, for the Lord is just. You also are autocratic, but fickle by nature, and therefore if you wish you can perish, you can blaspheme, poison and murder, and no one can prevent you from doing so. And yet if anyone wants, he can submit to God and enter upon the path of righteousness and rule over his lusts."[2] The godlike essence of freedom in man is proclaimed by Gregory of Nyssa. It consists in his inde-

---

2. Saint Macarius, Homily 15, in Migne, *Patrologia graeca*, 34:592. A theme for future investigations is outlined here: freedom is an ontological likeness to God, and it is preserved even in sin and transgression. Righteousness is an ethical likeness to God, and it can be forfeited, for our nature is "fickle" and we can abuse the gift of freedom.

151

pendence from material force, his capacity to decide and choose out of his own resources, out of his own essence. If there is no freedom then there is no mind either, for then the gift of making decisions and judgments would be an illusion.

Joining both these elements of spirituality together, John of Damascus defines the divine image in man as mind and freedom. Consequently, the divine image does not simply dwell "in the psyche" (cf. the crude definition of Tertullian); it dwells in the spirit. It dwells in the two highest levels of human essence (the sixth and seventh levels on our scale). The human being is a spiritual person, self-consciousness, "I"; and in this he is like God. The person in whom the spirit dwells is the light of consciousness and the might of freedom. This "light" and this "freedom" are not things and not substances and not the properties of objects — it is my light and my freedom; more than that, it is I myself. When the human being says: "I exist," he is exactly like God, who says "I am that I am" [Exod. 3:14]. To understand what I myself am, is to understand my likeness to God.

Creative Freedom

Here we should touch on yet another new element in the likeness to God. The personhood of man is not a detached spirit, a detached mind, a detached freedom. This would be the Indian understanding of man, not the Christian one. In Christianity the spiritual person is an incarnate spirit, an incarnate mind, a creative freedom — the freedom to incarnate his own ideas. This is witnessed by the hierarchical position of the personal spirit in relation to body and psyche, in other words, in relation to the first levels of the human essence. Spirit rules over the lower levels in man's essence. If the human being, as Gregory of Nyssa pointed out long ago, is a microcosm and contains all the elements of the universe, if he is the ultimate creation in the hierarchy of being and therefore "embraces life of every kind in himself," then this is precisely what constitutes his hierarchical advantage, his authority over the world, his capacity for creativity. A detached, abstract spirit is incapable of either ruling or creating. That man possesses a body through which he is linked to the cosmos, to nature, is not only his weakness but his strength. That he is mineral, vegetable, and animal enables him to make contact with all levels of being, to understand them, to inspirit and transform them. The beauty of mind, says Gregory of Nyssa, is reflected in man's whole constitution and "enhances what is immediately below it by means of the higher level" — thus effecting the hierarchical "sublimation" of the levels of being, their elevation *(anagoge)* to what is highest in man, and to the Most High through man.

The human being, as Vladimir Solovyov wittily remarked, is not some kind of angelic cherub just cobbled together out of winglets and a pretty head, and this is a great advantage to him. Saint Gregory Palamas developed the same thought in all seriousness: man is created in the image of God to a greater extent than the bodiless angels. Why is this so? Because he is created to rule (whereas the angels, the "messengers," are created in order to serve). "In our psyche there is a governing and ruling part, and another part which is subservient and obedient, namely: will, appetite, sense perception, and everything else that, being lower than the mind, God has made subject to the mind; and when we are incited by the disposition to sin, we rebel not only against God-*Pantokrator* (the 'Almighty God'), but also against the autocrat ('self-control') that is inherent in our very nature. By virtue of this principle of authority in us, God gave us dominion over all the earth. But angels do not have a body joined to their spirit and subject to their spirit, therefore they do not rule but only carry out God's will." It is precisely this capacity in man's nature, that he contains the lower levels of being in himself, that makes his freedom a creative freedom. This is how Gregory Palamas expresses it:

> We alone of all creatures have a faculty of sense perception in addition to our noetic and rational faculties. This faculty of sense perception, joined to the Logos, creates the multifarious sciences and arts and forms of comprehension; it further creates our capacity to till (cultivate) the fields, to build houses, and in general to create out of what does not exist (albeit not out of absolutely nothing — for only God can do that). And all this has been given only to humankind. And although nothing that has been created by God can perish or arise all by itself, still one thing combined with another takes on a different form through us. And the invisible word of the mind not only subdues the motion of the air and becomes the sense of hearing, but it can even be written down and can be seen in the body and through the body; all this God gave only to humankind, for the sake of faith bringing about the bodily advent and manifestation of the sublime Logos. The angels have never had anything like this.[3]

3. Gregory Palamas, "Physics, Theology, Morals," chap. 63, in Migne, *Patrologia graeca,* 150:1165.

I have cited this remarkable passage because it gives an entire Orthodox philosophy of culture, a philosophy of creativity. It is based on the
idea of our likeness to God: if God is the Creator, then the human being is
also a creator, a "poet" of culture. But the human being creates not absolutely, not originally, not out of nothing — he only "forms" things out of
the lower elements, lifting up to a higher level and incarnating what is
"given" to him "from on high." If God is incarnated, then the human being is also incarnated, for every spoken word (logos) is an incarnation of
meaning; and all of culture, with its technical enterprises, its arts and sciences, is the incarnate spirit, the incarnate wisdom of the human being,
who is "in the image and likeness" of the divine Logos.

The Human Likeness to God Is All-embracing

Thus we ask ourselves once more: What precisely is it in man that is worthy of being called the image and likeness of God, the "icon" of the Deity?
Wherein does his human dignity and worth reside? My answer is this: spiritual personhood possesses this dignity and worth — it is this that is "of
great price in the face of God," as his image and likeness. All the great
church fathers come to this conclusion, but not all of them unveil the
axiological treasure (values) laid up in personhood, in selfhood, with
equal profundity.

To say that man's godlike personhood is simply the psyche, as
Tertullian does, tells us almost nothing; to say that this personhood is a
"rational animal," as Thomas Aquinas, following Aristotle, does, is to
speak in platitudes (which, nonetheless, allude briefly to man's hierarchical structure). To say that this godlike personhood is mind, freedom, creativity, dominion over the lower forces of nature, is to grasp something essential about personhood, but in no way to exhaust its treasure or to
comprehend its mystery. Gregory of Nyssa, perhaps, rises above all the
others in providing us with an ultimate grasp of this concept. The image
of God in the person receives from him the broadest, truly all-embracing
meaning. Thus, first of all, the person is capable of loving and herein resides his likeness to God, for God is love and man is love. Where there is
no love, the features of God's image are distorted. Further, the person
strives for immortality and herein is a likeness to God, for human immortality is bound up with the eternity of God. But there is even more: "we
should acknowledge as the image of God in man everything that reflects
the divine perfections, that is, the sum total of the gifts and blessings em-

bedded in human nature." Man resembles God because he is "adorned with life and logos and wisdom and all beautiful and divine values." This whole treasure of personhood, says Gregory of Nyssa, is expressed in the book of Genesis by a single phrase with many meanings: created in the image of God. This is why man's likeness to God is all-embracing and not confined to any one feature.[4]

We should not be surprised that God's image in man, as we take a closer look at it, expands to the point of boundlessness, and thus loses, as it were, its determinate quality. After all, its prototype is God's very divinity, the Absolute itself, in all its boundlessness, in all the inexhaustibility of its potentialities. The person is like God in precisely this way: it is a unity (a monad) embracing the "entire world full of infinity" (Leibniz). The person cannot be defined by a system of concepts. Concepts cannot express the ultimate mystery of the person. The question, What is the person? can be answered in only one way: the person is "I myself." But to comprehend what "I myself" am means to comprehend my incomprehensibility. It is not so easy to get a sense of what the ultimate mystery of the person is; and it is especially hard to find it "in one's self." Such terms as "self-knowledge" or "self-consciousness" throw us off the track, for it may seem that knowledge and consciousness are the subject that turns me myself into my own object. But this is just what cannot be done. My knowledge and my consciousness belong to me, but I myself do not belong to them; they are my "properties," my instruments, my functions, and I myself am far from being exhaustively defined by them. This identification of me myself with my "self-consciousness" and "self-knowledge" is precisely what modern psychology has done away with. I have a subconscious in addition to my consciousness, my knowledge coexists with my unknowability. "I myself" rise above all these opposites, I transcend them and therefore I am supraconsciousness. If "I myself" eternally evade any positive identification and realization, if "I myself" never come into conscious awareness, then this is an advantage to me and not a defect: there is something in me that exceeds any cognition, and this mysterious surplus is what makes me magnificently unapproachable. "God dwells in unapproachable light" [1 Tim. 6:16], but man also discovers in his own depths an "unapproachable light." This is the ultimate, sublime mystical element in his likeness to God. God is transcendent — and I myself am transcendent; God is mysterious and I myself am mysterious; there is a hidden God

4. Cf. G. V. Florovsky, *The Eastern Fathers of the Fourth Century* (Paris, 1931), pp. 157-59.

and a hidden man. We have a negative theology that points to the ultimate mystery of the Deity; there should also be a negative anthropology pointing to the mystery of man himself.[5]

This sublime mystical element in our likeness to God has been formulated in all its clarity by that church father who elevated the human being in his "likeness to God" above everything else, namely, Gregory of Nyssa. His reasoning goes like this: The image ought to have all the essential features of the prototype. But for God the ungraspability of his essence is essential, and so this must be reflected in the ungraspability of man himself, as the image of the Deity. "Who hath known the mind of the Lord?" [Rom. 11:34] says Paul. "And I will add to this," says Gregory of Nyssa, "who has grasped his own mind?" The mysteriousness and ungraspability of "noetic" personhood consists in its complex multifacetedness, and at the same time in the simplicity and "noncompositeness" of its ultimate unity. Here we have the likeness in ungraspability: "our spiritual nature, being in the Creator's image, evades our grasp, and thereby fully resembles that which is higher than we are; our very ungraspability reveals the imprint of what is unapproachable [i.e., divine] in our nature."[6]

5. The classic model of such an anthropology is in the Brhadaranyaka Upanishad with its final "not, not" *(neti-neti)*.

6. Gregory of Nyssa, "On Responsibilities," chap. 9, in Migne, *Patrologia graeca,* vol. 44.

CHAPTER 12

Pascal

The Infinitely Large and the Infinitely Small:
The Limits of Reason

It is not by chance that I have chosen Pascal as the theme of this chapter. The profound philosophical and mystical experiences of this man of genius touch on the problems of modern existential philosophy — in other words, they are quite relevant today. If we ask why, our answer should be: because they deal with the fundamental idea of modern philosophy — the idea of transcendence. But with this concept we enter into the domain of modern existentialist philosophy. The problem of transcendence has been raised by Nicolai Hartmann, Heidegger, Jaspers, Sartre. We do not need to be frightened by this terrible word "transcendence." "There is nothing beyond this world!" a lady of a skeptical and materialistic turn of mind once said to me. Regarding this claim, we could learn a lot from Pascal.

Pascal was clearly quite a child prodigy. When he was twelve years old he worked through Euclid's geometry up to the thirty-second theorem by himself, without the help of a teacher and to the great astonishment of his father. He was not yet seventeen when he published his work on geometry, which sent Descartes into raptures. A year later he invented the first calculating machine. Further epochal discoveries in the physics of air pressure, barometric measurements, and so on followed. Thus, right up until his death he continued to be one of the greatest mathematicians of his epoch. His mathematical investigations included an early notion of the differential and integral calculus. Creative scientific work constituted one of his basic missions throughout his life. In the two years before his death, just for amusement, he derived the most taxing mathematical equations in the field of cycloids.

What is it that constitutes the basic problem of all these scientific investigations? The wonder and mystery of mathematical and astronomical infinity — infinity, as the eternal symbol of the Deity. "The eternal silence of these infinite spaces," he says, "makes me tremble." In connection with the mysterious infinity of the world, Pascal poses the problem of the "infinitely small." What does science teach us? Pascal asks. It reveals to us, he answers, an astronomical infinity in which the center is everywhere and the circumference nowhere. What, in the face of this fact, is the earth? What are cities and states? What is man? But the same kind of infinity is in the infinitely small — the infinity of the microscopic structure of matter. Thus we exist between two infinities, two limits, two abysses. "What is man? He is the midpoint between nothing and everything." Man is infinitely removed from any understanding of these extremes. He has no hope of understanding the beginning and end of things, the principle and ultimate goal of existence. Only the Creator of these wonders can understand and encompass them. Only an infinite reason can encompass the infinity of all things. Therefore, all the sciences are confronted with infinite tasks. We are limited, finite creatures, in both our body and our spirit. All the extremes do not, as it were, exist for us. Our knowledge is part knowledge, part ignorance. In any cognitive act, every advance turns into a new problem and any firm result evades us.

We find in Pascal a real criticism in the spirit of Plato and Kant — here too is the idea of an infinite task and the limitations on cognition. How can the part know the whole? Yet the parts are connected with each other in such a way that only the whole ("total unity") can give us genuine knowledge. Only the infinite Mind/*Nous* can encompass both infinities, the understanding of which evades human reason. Man stands before the absolute mystery of genuine being, and science — precisely the most exact of the sciences, mathematics, astronomy — leads him to the limits of his cognitive functioning.

Has science made any progress since Pascal's time? Has science succeeded in understanding what he regarded as a mystery? Modern physics is moving along the same path that Pascal took. "The human world lies between the infinitely large and the infinitely small," says the English natural philosopher Sir James Jeans. "It lies between the world of the electron and the world of astronomical nebulae." One might add that, after the revolution undergone by modern physics, these two worlds have become even more of a mystery to us. "We are like children," says Jeans, "who are playing with pebbles on the seashore while before us rages the ocean of unknown and ungraspable truths."

The Logic of the Heart: The Theory of Values

Pascal's thought oscillates, as we can see, between science and religion. Science leads him to the idea of transcendence, and transcendence leads him to the scientific problem of the limits of human reason. Yet Pascal's life is not wholly defined by this interest in science and religion. Pascal was a true man of his own time; the worldly interests of the social circles around him were not foreign to him. The fashionable world of the French baroque spread out before him, with its salons, the scintillating pleasantries of its drawing rooms, the lavish costumes of its fashionable beauties, the refined wit of salon philosophers and French freethinkers, with the hypocrisy of churchly officiousness — in short, with all of its esprit and emptiness, all of its positive and negative values. The task set before him was to distinguish in this world the beautiful from the repulsive, the lofty from the base, and, finally, good from evil. All this required judgments — not theoretical judgments as in science, but judgments of value. The posing of the philosophical problem of values was his invaluable contribution to the history of human thought.

Those concepts by which Pascal designates judgments of value prove that he anticipated what has been accomplished by modern philosophy. He was the first to express the thought that value judgments are judgments of our intuition, and not judgments of mathematical ratiocination. Values are not perceived by theoretical reason: they are intuited. This requires us to possess, however, a very finely tuned capacity for intuition. Such intuitive activity is not a woolly sentimentality, it is not subjective fantasy, but a certain specific capacity for judgment. Kant called it "practical reason."

Pascal was, first and foremost, interested in moral values, then aesthetic values, and lastly political and legal values, and so on. Every thing can prompt us to ask: Does it have any meaning, any kind of value? The differentiation between the positive and negative value of good and evil is a judgment of a specific kind — not a judgment of reason, but a judgment of the heart. Judgments like these have a self-evidence of their own, they can be proved in their own unique way. "These proofs," says Pascal, "are of a different kind from those we use in geometry." "The heart has its reasons (logic) that reason knows nothing of." The heart has its own ordering of ideas, different from the rational ordering.

It is perhaps astonishing that French philosophy, which has investigated and interpreted every squiggle in every line of Pascal's works, has not noticed this striking discovery of his: the logic of the heart and the value judgments based on it. In their handsome edition of Pascal's complete works, Brunschvicg and Boutroux noted that he came close to discovering the theory of the infinitely small, that is, the differential and integral calculus, but they say not a single word about his theory of values. Paul Valéry completely overlooked this side of Pascal's way of thinking. He claimed that Pascal's very attempt to make a distinction between the spirit of geometry and that refined spirit of the conscience which characterizes the establishment of value judgments results in a distinction that is essentially muddy and unclear. If we pick up the revised edition of the French philosophical dictionary (edited by André Lalande — a work awarded a prize by the French Academy) and look up the word "value," we find that this concept was supposedly invented in Germany by the theologians Albrecht Ritschl and Wilhelm Herrmann. From them it was passed on to Harnack and Höffding. There is not a word in this dictionary about the idea of value in Pascal. Nor is anything said about Max Scheler or Nicolai Hartmann. But Scheler was actually the first philosopher to discover Pascal's idea about the "logic of the heart." He constructed his own theory of values on the basis of this idea, a theory that was further developed by Hartmann and reflected in the psychology of Jung. Scheler showed that values are arranged in a specific hierarchical order. This idea about the order of values was also anticipated by Pascal. In Pascal's view moral values are higher than others. Moral judgment is more important for human beings than the theoretical judgment of science, since it determines their whole life and fate. We can see here an anticipation of Kant's doctrine of the "primacy of practical reason," something commonly overlooked in the history of philosophy.

Even above moral values Pascal places religious values, and the chiefest of these is "holiness." Only the absolute person of God possesses holiness in the full sense of this word. This is the loftiest discovery that can be intuited by the heart. "It is the heart," says Pascal, "that discovers God, not reason at all." The heart loves the Supreme Being, "as luminous natural light." Through morals Pascal discovers the Transcendent Holy One summoning us to perfection — namely, God the Father. For Pascal, as for Dostoevsky, without God there is no good or evil — without God everything is permitted!

The Three Levels of Personal Values

The kingdom of values opens up to us a new realm that lies beyond the borders of mathematics, physics, biology — in short, everything that has to do with the "Existent." The sciences of nature have nothing to do with judgments of value, they do not talk about what is just or unjust, what is good and what is evil, what is beautiful and what is repulsive. They have nothing to do with what ought to be, they only determine what is. What is virtue, sin, transgression, recompense, happiness, misfortune — there is no talk about these questions in mathematics, in physics, in astronomy — and the same is true of biology. Whether the snake is good or evil, beautiful or repulsive — zoology is not concerned about such questions. In terms of judgment, scientific truth has nothing to do with value. The laws of nature established by natural science are indifferent to good and evil. The natural sciences are "beyond" good and evil.

There are various systems of values among various peoples and cultures. Their ultimate foundation is the great religions in which values are revealed, for example, in the Ten Commandments of Moses. The hierarchy of values is always crowned by the affirmation of a supreme value, which is felt to be the highest holiness, the highest perfection. "Be ye perfect, even as your Father which is in heaven is perfect" [Matt. 5:48] — this is the best expression of the thought that we can formulate. Pascal was convinced that the hierarchy of values was established by God and given in Christian revelation. From the viewpoint of the Christian religion, personal values are higher than impersonal ones. The person ranks higher than any material body in this world — higher than a star, than the earth, than the firmament. Higher, because the person knows all these things and, in addition, knows himself, while bodies know nothing. We can set up three levels of personal values: (1) the greatness of earthly sovereigns, the rich and powerful of this world, the lords of humanity — this greatness is in the end physical, not spiritual. (2) The greatness of human genius: Archimedes, Plato. This is the greatness of the human spirit. (3) Finally, the greatness of holiness, surpassing the others in its radiance. Such is Jesus Christ and the assembly of the saints, surpassing everything else in value.

The Experience of the Otherworldly: "Pascal's Wager"

This was something that Pascal recognized — and we come now to that religious experience of his which could be called sublime. We are talking about the experience of transcendence, expressed in the words: "my kingdom is not of this world." The "transcendent," the "otherworldly," is revealed to us through self-knowledge, through astonishment at our own existence, expressed in the familiar questions: "Where do I come from and where am I going?" To pose such questions, we must perform an act of *transcensus* with regard to ourselves, we must relate ourselves to the world, to infinity, to God. Pascal knew these experiences and expressed them with great power: "I see the incredible spaces of the universe in which I am contained, and I sense that I am attached to a single point in those spaces, without knowing why I am fastened to this place and not another, without knowing why, out of that infinite stream of time that preceded me and that will go on flowing after me, it has been decreed that I live in this small segment of it and not another." "I only know that, having made my exit from this world" — and this is the spot where the transcendence that we were talking about is revealed — "I will fall forever either into the abyss of nothingness, or else into the hands of a wrathful God."

The very same question was posed by Kierkegaard and Dostoevsky (see above). Modern existentialism also poses it, in Heidegger and Sartre. We are confronted with a sort of mysterious "either/or": either God and immortality, or nothingness. Transcendence can mean either the first or the second — moreover, science and reason are powerless to give us a solution to this dilemma; this solution is given by the heart, by religion.

We find an original solution to this dilemma in the argument that commonly goes by the name of "Pascal's wager." The argument may seem like a paradox, even a joke. It is aimed at that salon atheism that was widespread among the upper echelons of French society in Pascal's day. But at the same time a profound and serious problem lies hidden beneath the surface of this argument. All of human life is like a game in which we place our stake on the various possibilities before us. What should we count on in life, where should we place our life's stake — on God and religion, or on godlessness? In answering this question Pascal employs his favorite science, mathematics. He proposes to resolve the question by applying the theory of probability to it. He assumes that the existence and the nonexistence of God are equally probable — mathematically expressed, the chances are fifty-fifty. Now we place our stake on the first probability and take a look at what we can lose on this wager and what we can win. We can lose nothing (we lose zero), and we win everything: the infinity of a future life, bliss, immortality. Then we place our wager on the second supposition, on atheism. With such a wager we cannot lose anything, since we turn into dust, into nothing; but at the same time we win nothing either, since "nothing," "zero," is not a gain. Clearly, if this is how matters stand, we ought to place our stake on the existence of God, and not on atheism. What do you lose, says Pascal, if you set out on the Christian path and acknowledge God and immortality? What horrible thing can possibly befall you if you choose this path? "You will be faithful, honorable, humble, grateful, well-disposed toward other people, you will be true, sincere friends. True, you will not be afflicted by a passion for sensual pleasures, but do you really have no other kind? I assure you that you will only win in this life." It is stupid to take chances on finite benefits if you can gain infinite ones. This joke of an argument takes a serious turn, since every thinking person, in the final reckoning, has to choose what kind of disposition toward life he ought to adopt — the whole form of his life, his whole fate and character depend on it. If I stand face to face with "nothingness," then I ought to say, "Eat and drink, my friends, forever and ever, smashing all the vessels." "I built my trade on 'Nothingness,'" says the absolute atheist Stirner. "The otherworldly is an empty phantom." But if this is so, then everything is permitted — any desire, any crime. There are no commandments, no positive imperatives, nothing that is held sacred. If I stand facing God and his kingdom, then there is a positive imperative, there is a higher calling for humankind, there is love, there is faith and hope.

Personally, for Pascal himself, there was no such wager. For him the question had already been resolved through a religio-mystical experience, through the "logic of the heart." But one cannot talk about that sort of thing in salons.

The Greatness and Insignificance of Man

What is the nature of the deep religious experience of Pascal that underlies, in the final analysis, all of his apologetics and the path of his own life? It is the experience of the tragic. Contradiction is tragic — the human being lives in contradiction, and the contradiction is not a logical but a real one, intuited in the soul of every human being, in the whole of his life, in his fate. We are talking about the struggle of opposing forces and strivings that are unfolded in the innermost human essence, in his heart. "The Devil," says Dostoevsky, "is doing battle with God, and the field of battle is the human heart." The heart intuits the positive and negative values that are unfolded before the human being; it intuits the human being himself and all humanity. The deepest human experience is the greatness and insignificance of man.

Man searches for life and happiness, and finds suffering, illness, and death; in his breast he nourishes the ideals of the good, of beauty and holiness, and in reality he meets with the radical evil of his own nature. Hardly anyone has had a more powerful sense of this tragedy than Pascal himself — and not only in himself but in the whole of humanity. "What a chimera is man," he exclaims, "what a bundle of contradictions, what a monster! The judge of all things — and at the same time an earthbound worm; the witness of the truth — and at the same time the cesspool of ignorance and error; the pride of the universe — and at the same time its worst refuse." The more man intuits his own impotence, the more keenly he senses that mystical force that is "not of this world."

The tragic condition of man is ennobled because the breath of the Holy Spirit, the Paraclete, the Comforter, is intuited in him. Any dissonance is the birth of harmony. For Pascal, tragic experience means the birth of Christ in the heart. The divine call is not a rational decision but the grace of God. Without reason having any part in it, God directly influences our heart, inspires it. Those to whom God has granted this experience in their heart are blessed indeed and endowed with a sense of the incontrovertible genuineness of what they have experienced.

This bliss was granted to Pascal in the deepest mystical experience of his life. Eight years after Pascal's death, his servant found a "Memorial" sewn [into his clothing], a short record that described this deepest experience of his soul, a reminder to himself, a sort of epitaph on his own monument. It begins strikingly: "In the summer of 1654, Monday, November 23, from about half past ten to half past midnight. Fire. The God of Abraham, Isaac, and Jacob — not the God of the philosophers and scholars. Certainty, certainty. Feeling. Joy. Peace. The Lord God Jesus Christ. The universe and everything else totally forgotten, everything except for God. . . . The greatness of the human soul. . . . Joy, joy, joy, tears of joy."

I will not cite the rest; everyone can read it through for himself. The important thing is that we are dealing here with a genuine mystical experience. The whole of Pascal's subsequent life vouches for its authenticity. For the rest of his life, every step, every thought of Pascal was a development and illustration of what he learned on that night. His withdrawal into the seclusion of the Port-Royal monastery, his active participation in the struggle of the Jansenists, his polemics against the Jesuits, the defense of Christianity in his *Pensées*, and, finally, the ecstasy of faith and love in the last months of his life — all of these were the outcome of what he went through on the night of November 23.

What is particularly important about this mystical experience is

Pascal's renewed sense of the greatness of the human soul. Not one more word about human wretchedness and insignificance. The deposed sovereign feels that he is sovereign once more. This greatness is sensed by Paul as an ascent to the seventh heaven.

To those who view mysticism with scorn and contempt, and yet cling to the idea of grace, we must say that the supreme and ultimate grace of God is expressed precisely in mystical experience. Pascal knew this — he who talks about his own mystical revelation as a "year of grace," "hours of grace." A dry theological scholasticism is often linked to the idea of grace, but what is even worse is that many devout mystics are infected by a mistrust of human nature, a lack of faith in man. The Christian religion is faith in God and faith in man. How else can the "Son of God" be called the "Son of Man"? How is it possible to love man without believing in him? What is there to love in man, if it is genuine love that we mean? Not "dust and ashes," after all. What is loved is his true selfhood. It is not easy to say what exactly it is, this selfhood, since it is invisible and rationally unknowable. There is an otherworldly man as well as an otherworldly God — "the hidden man of the heart in the incorruptible beauty of his meek and quiet spirit." This mystical essence of the human being is inaccessible to physics or psychology; it is revealed only to the heart. Pascal discovered this mystical essence through love, as Descartes discovered the "thinking I" through the instrument of reason. Pascal himself was a "hidden man of the heart," and so he is beloved and dear to us. Alongside his scientific genius, his rich knowledge of humanity, his beautiful style, we sense a hidden, divine selfhood, the fiery core of his love and his abundant soul, a core that radiates light into the world across the centuries.

CHAPTER 13

*Descartes and
Modern Philosophy*

Descartes's Basic Intuition

The main task I have set for myself is not at all to refute Descartes but, on the contrary, to uncover what is valuable in his work for Russian and world philosophy. Essentially, he has only furnished us with one fundamental intuition, but it has, in truth, an eternal value.

For me the genuine philosophical method is intuition and dialectics. Intuition produces discoveries that keep leading us all ever higher toward the Absolute. No such discoveries can be produced with syllogisms and system building. Thought suffocates in closed systems; it strives to break out of the frame by way of new discoveries, which inevitably appear as new intuitions.

Descartes's basic intuition lies buried (and deeply buried) in the words that we all read in our school textbooks: "I doubt everything; I think, therefore I am." Here, it seems to me, is the knot binding together the dialectical chains — the most modern and the most ancient — which lead us into the unknown.

Descartes's doubt is a particular, a unique doubt, totally unfamiliar to either science or everyday life. Common sense does not allow it, for it goes contrary to our natural inclinations. But this unique operation is quite familiar to philosophy; it is as old as philosophy and mysticism themselves. Through this doubt we are initiated into philosophy; and the first initiation was due to Plato. But the philosopher who in our day has marvelously refined this operation of universal doubt is Husserl. He

166

called it the "phenomenological reduction," whereby the entire world is reduced to "phenomena" [i.e., appearances].[1]

For Kant too the world of the senses is the object of science — it is "nothing but pure appearance, nothing but an idea." And Schopenhauer says: "the world is that idea which I create for myself about it; it is my representation of things." Finally, the ancient wisdom of India also claims that the world of the senses, nature, is nothing but an illusion, a dream, maya. At two points this Hindu reduction comes close to Descartes: first, there is the comparison to a dream (a thought that struck Calderón: "life is a dream"), and then there is the ultimate goal of doubt, the goal of this whole unique operation: we doubt in order to find the genuine "I," the "thinking I," "Atman."

We know how Descartes finds it: his universal doubt embraced all human judgments, all the exact sciences (since they presuppose an objective reality); in the end, it even embraces the whole world as it presents itself to us, the world in time and space. What if the whole world is not reality, but a dream, an illusion? Let us suppose so. But there still remains at least one reality: the "I" that sleeps, that dreams, that has illusions. "There is some powerful deceiver whom I do not know . . . who is constantly deceiving me. Consequently, since he deceives me there is no doubt that I exist; and let him deceive me as much as he wants, he will never be able to make me nothing as long as I think that I am something" (*Meditations* II). This is the genuine thought underlying this celebrated dictum: "I doubt everything; I think, therefore I am."

The Hindu says: the world of the senses is nothing. Yet out of this "nothing" something still persists, and this is the illusion that presents itself to me; after all, a hallucination is also a reality of sorts, a "well-founded phenomenon" (in Leibniz's phrase). Here we have the result of the "phenomenological reduction," and it is I, I myself, with my ideas, with my phenomena/appearances.

Husserl defines the result of this Cartesian doubt or "reduction" in one phrase — "I think" — since "I think" in Descartes refers in fact to all of consciousness, encompassing not only my thoughts but also my will, my actions, my feelings (*Meditations* III): in the final analysis, everything that is now customarily called the life of the psyche. Here is the remarkable and curious thing about it: this whole world of things, indeterminate and doubtful insofar as it is based on the transient flux of appearances — this

1. We owe the word "appearance" to Plato; he was the first to say that "the world of the senses is reduced for us to appearances — to that which appears and is born."

world gives us something that is absolutely determinate and real, since the real presence of appearances is indisputable even when their objective meaning is indeterminate. If I sleep, if I dream, if I have hallucinations or false and unreal ideas, then all the same I have one absolute reality, one absolute truth. This is simply the truth of the presence of these suspect and unreliable appearances (Solovyov).

Here is how Descartes himself set forth this amazing discovery: "Let us suppose that the things which I imagine are not true, nevertheless this ability to imagine really exists in me and forms part of my thought: I see the light, I hear the sound, I feel the warmth. But I will be told that these notions are false, and that I am sleeping. Let it be so; still, at the very least, there is no doubt that it seems to me that I see the light, hear the sound, feel the warmth; and this is what cannot be false" (*Meditations* II).

The Earth of Objects and the Sun of the Subject

Instead of the totally unreliable world that surrounds me when I meditate, I find a different reality, reality in another dimension. I discover this new reality by turning toward myself: in my very self I discover the "stream of pure experiences with all that is present in it — and this stream is 'self-evident'" (Pascal). The immediate intuition of experiences never deceives. The immediate *données* of consciousness, as Bergson calls them, are always genuine and real.

My thinking, that is, my consciousness, along with everything immediately given in it, appears to me as a new dimension, or, more accurately, as a different point of view. Finding this new dimension was extremely difficult. Kant says that this discovery is like the Copernican one, but it was Descartes and not Kant himself who made it. The first dimension, or the first point of view, is naive realism (Kant's term) or naturalism, which takes as its starting point the world of things, the earth of objects. This viewpoint is perfectly natural for common sense — but philosophy is not common sense and common sense has no need of philosophy, as the death of Socrates proved. The second viewpoint, Copernicus's or rather Descartes's viewpoint, is phenomenalism (what Kant calls empirical realism — "appearances/phenomena alone exist"), which takes as its starting point not the earth of objects but the sun of the subject, the sun of spirit and reason.

Along with this "phenomenological reduction" my thinking shows me yet another new and strange thing: and this is my "I." There is endless

168

talk about it, but it never shows itself clearly. On the contrary, it is in hiding — and nonetheless it is regarded as "self-evident."

For this "I," it is necessary to oppose the reduction to appearances, it is necessary that this "I" be opposed to doubt. The "I" can reduce everything to appearances, except itself. The "I" will never show up in the "field of appearances"; it always remains invisible and, perhaps, incomprehensible. One might say that it is a being of another dimension from that of all appearances — the third dimension.

Plato's famous myth provides a convenient illustration of what I have just said. I am seated in a cave and I see shadows on the wall — and this is the world of appearances; but among these shadows I will never see my genuine "I," just as the audience in the theater will never see itself on the stage.

It is self-evident that my body, my movements, my habits, even my character and my "soul" will appear in the "field of appearances": all of these are "visible" and empirical — but none of them is my genuine "I." My whole body is not "I"; it merely belongs to me, just as my clothes are not "I." My ideas, my sensations, my thoughts — none of these is "I" either: they belong to me, but I can exist without them.[2]

Yet Descartes made a discovery that exceeded the power of his understanding, and that still exceeds the power of modern philosophy. Right up to the present day we do not know what exactly this genuine "I" is. We find the most profound analysis of this problem in Indian philosophy and in Christian mysticism, for example, in Meister Eckhardt. Let me quote a remarkable passage from Pascal. He asks: What is it that we love when we love somebody? "He who loves someone for his beauty — does he truly love him? No: for smallpox, which destroys beauty, compels him to fall out of love with that person. And if I am loved for my judgment, for my memory, am I truly loved? No: for I can cease to have these qualities without ceasing to be myself. So where then is this I, since it is neither in the body nor in the soul?"

Take a good look at these words: "neither in the body nor in the soul." That I can say *my* soul [i.e., that my soul belongs to me as my clothes do] — means that my genuine "I" is unapproachable. It is in a dif-

---

2. By the way, the whole of the philosophy of the Upanishads is nothing other than the genuine path that leads to the discovery of this mysterious "I." It is found by sweeping aside everything related to the realm of appearances, for this "I" goes beyond the confines of all appearances (Husserl); otherwise it would be possible to plant this "I" among appearances and expose it to doubt along with everything else.

ferent dimension, the third dimension — above the stream of experiences and, in the final analysis (and here is Bergson's error), above space and time.

Solipsism and the Overcoming of It

This new dimension is quite marvelous. The choice of a new viewpoint was a very propitious one. Consciousness clearly embraces the whole world — physical bodies, animals, people, stars, the heavens: consciousness is the "mirror of the Universe" (Leibniz), it is the "whole world full of infinity." In a certain sense, one could say that I am omnipresent, omnipotent. Everything that exists belongs to me (the Upanishads). I am microcosmos and micro-*theos*.

Yet there is something unbearable in this situation, in this position of sovereignty: I am thus seated on a throne of absolute solitude; I have entered into the vicious circle of solipsism. Only "I" truly exist, and all the rest of the world is my ideas, my notions, the *"données* of my consciousness" ("a monad has neither windows nor doors," says Leibniz).

The internal dialectic of thought forced Descartes into the vicious circle of solipsism (and this is his great contribution, for all subsequent philosophy has been forced to follow in his footsteps). Descartes knows all about the thesis, "I am alone in the world" (*Meditations* III; *Discourse on Method* IV), and he finds a very original method for overcoming it. God alone can help us to break out of the vicious circle of egoism and solipsism. The world, nature, other people are incapable of doing so, for they are all "I": they are my ideas, my appearances. But God is not I, since I am not God.

We are told: All that may very well be true if God in fact exists, but go and prove it to us! Didn't Kant refute all those theological proofs of God's existence (including Descartes's)? Here again we can see the greatness and originality of Descartes. For him God, the Absolute, requires no proofs. On the contrary, it is the world, it is nature, that must be proven. We can doubt that things exist, but we cannot doubt the existence of Absolute Being. The Absolute cannot be reduced to anything; just as I am not subject to a reduction to appearances, neither is the Absolute, and to an even greater extent. For Descartes the reality of the Absolute is an immediate intuition: its self-evidence is revealed whenever the self-evidence of my "I" is.

The Axiom of Dependence

Let us examine once again the first of these intuitions. How does this "I" appear to me? As a creature who doubts, who seeks the truth, who has desires, "who strives unceasingly for something better and thirsts for what is much higher than he himself." In other words, the "I" is a thing that is "imperfect, incomplete, and dependent on something else." Doubt is imperfection ("knowing is much more perfect than doubting," *Meditations* IV); when we desire and strive for something, it means that we are experiencing deprivation and dependence. But imperfection is inconceivable without perfection, just as the finite is inconceivable without the infinite, and just as the relative exists only in contrast to the Absolute. Nothing but the self-evidence, the intuition, of each of these opposites can immediately reveal that they belong together, since opposites are inseparable. The fundamental intuition that reveals the relativity (the nonabsoluteness) of my existence is simultaneously an intuition of Absolute Being, the intuition of my dependence: for the relative is dependent on the Absolute, as the finite is on the infinite.

We have now arrived at what I call the "axiom of dependence," or, if you prefer, the "axiom of religion," for religion is precisely a "bond," "dependence" (Schleiermacher). A few citations from Descartes will show the dialectic leading to the axiom of dependence.

> How could I know that I doubt and desire, that is, that something is lacking in me and that I am not entirely perfect, if I had no idea of the existence of a being more perfect than I am, in comparison with which I could recognize the deficiencies of my nature? (*Meditations* IV)

> When I meditate about myself, I not only know that I am something which is imperfect, incomplete, and dependent on another . . . but I simultaneously know that the one on whom I depend possesses all those higher properties to which I aspire . . . possesses them not just in potentiality but . . . actually . . . and to an infinite degree, and that, consequently, He is God.

> When I observe my doubt, that is, when I observe that I am something which is incomplete and dependent, the idea arises distinctly in my mind of a being who is complete and independent, that is, God. (*Meditations* IV, French edition)

Finally, here is the axiom of dependence in its most definitive and concise form:

It is perfectly evident to me that I depend on a being who is different from myself. (*Meditations* III)

This dependence proves to me that I am not "alone in the world," that I am not the "only being in existence"; it liberates me from the vicious circle of solipsism. With all its enormous range of time and space, the world of the senses is incapable of doing so, since all of it is merely my ideas, merely my appearances: it is all within me, immanent to me and not transcendent.

I become independent of nature and the world of the senses through the following method of reduction: I am "superior" to everything else, it is they who depend on me. They are contained within the compass of my consciousness. (*Discourse* IV, *Meditations* III)

As a result of the "phenomenological reduction," after everything has been exposed to doubt, only two beings remain indubitable: "I," who am not the Absolute, and the Absolute, who is not "I"; the "I" being dependent, and the Absolute independent. One might say, along with the blessed Augustine: "I know God and the soul: and what else? — absolutely nothing!"

The Irrationality of the Bond with the Absolute

This dependence on the Absolute is something unique in the world; it is totally different from any other natural dependence, for example, a dependence on things, people, nature. We must liberate ourselves from any other dependence in order to become aware of this dependence on the Absolute, to contemplate it. The mystics' "path of purification" is a method of achieving "independence from objects," independence from the world. The "path of purification," philosophy's "dark night," is doubt. It liberates us from all temporal, material, natural things, reducing them to appearances; it gives us the opportunity of elevating ourselves to the third dimension, where the soul feels that it is dwelling in a spiritual atmosphere of thought and freedom — high, high above the world of appearances. This is the striking dialectic of Descartes, the dialectic of all the great mystics, Hindu and Christian alike. Having reached the heights of independence, they reveal their own absolute dependence, for they have met up with the Absolute.

It is precisely here that one can pinpoint the difference between this Russian interpretation of Descartes's philosophy and the interpretation offered by the celebrated German philosopher Husserl. Our Russian interpretation is more ontological, more absolutist, more mystical, and much more faithful to Descartes himself. Husserl claims that a phenomenological reduction of the Absolute is possible. We assert, however, along with Descartes, that it is impossible. You cannot abolish the Absolute. As soon as you assert something relative, you are presupposing the Absolute; as soon as you assert the finite, you are presupposing the infinite. The Absolute cannot be abolished: when it is denied in its true form, it will appear in another, false form. If you say that there is no God, there is nothing but matter, then matter becomes your Absolute. If you assert that there is no God, there is nothing higher than myself, nothing higher than humanity — then "I" or humanity becomes the Absolute (the "Great Being" of Auguste Comte). Finally, you say: if there is essentially nothing, then we fall into the abyss along with the world. If you get the idea that in saying this you are talking about some sort of radical atheism, you are making a grievous error, for you have come upon a very mysterious Absolute: the Great Emptiness, absolute nothingness, and this is the Absolute of one of the great religions, Buddhism.

What is especially remarkable is that genuine atheism is impossible. Atheism is in fact idolatry and fetishism.

The axiom of dependence mentioned above is self-evident, but it is not rational. The mystical intuition of the Absolute is irrational. It is an encounter with the "hidden God." Face to face with this God, we experience a strange sense of deep wonder, or terror at the abyss. This is called the *mysterium tremendum* (Rudolf Otto), or the feeling of absolute dependence (Schleiermacher). Sometimes the irrationality of the Absolute appears to us as a great question, strange, disturbing, terrible: "I see these terrifying spaces of the Universe, in which I am enclosed . . . all the eternity which preceded me and all the eternity which will follow after me . . . and I ask myself: 'where did I come from?' and 'where am I going?'" (Pascal, *Pensées* [194]).

My whole life, my fate, what direction my path will take, all depend on how I answer these questions. This is the intuition of dependence, whose voice is heard by every human being at some point in life. In theological language, this feeling of dependence is the immediate intuition of a created being who senses that he is bound to a being who is not created, to the Creator; and this bond is what we call religion.

This bond with the Absolute is unique, mysterious, irrational, inexpressible in terms of categories like causality, substance, and purpose. Thus Kant is right as opposed to Aristotle and the Thomists. Only religious symbols and myths are capable of expressing this bond.

The Two Parts of Descartes's Philosophy

Descartes's philosophy consists of two parts, which are unequal in value. The first part is his doubt, his "I think," his "phenomenological reduction," his doctrine of dependence and freedom. Within this realm Descartes is one of the greatest philosophical geniuses. In his greatest works we can easily trace the deepest current of philosophical and mystical thought, a current that we encounter in the Upanishads, Plato, Plotinus, the blessed Augustine, Anselm, Bonaventura, and Duns Scotus. This is the splendid perspective in which Descartes appears to us. His "I think" is a whole critique: it is all of Kant in embryo; it is Fichte and all the problems of German idealism; finally, it is the neo-Kantian movement and the immanent school of philosophy.

But there is still another marvelous thing: Descartes towers above all this. The most powerful school of modern philosophy, phenomenology, may be nothing but a broad new interpretation of his "I think." This latter philosophy is deep, but it does not reach the ultimate depths. The "I think" is not yet exhausted, it has not yet been sufficiently plumbed; the greatest service it performs is to pose the problem of the subject — of the "I." After Augustine, this problem was forgotten for many centuries. They wrote up a philosophy of the object, a philosophy of things, of substances. All of this is philosophy in the first dimension. Descartes found the second dimension — the dimension of the subject, of the spirit. Thus he put forward the problem of freedom and did so with a force surpassing that of Duns Scotus. There is no freedom in the realm of objects, things, substances: it is lacking in the first dimension. One must raise oneself up higher in order to see it: "I doubt, therefore I am free, I am independent of things." Freedom is the essence of the "I." It would be unwise to subject freedom to proof, since freedom is actually the prerequisite for making the judgments by which things are proved or doubted. Descartes elevated the human spirit to a high level, to the level of the angels, higher even perhaps than the Thomist system allows. Yet he raised it in a direction that is absolutely Christian.

Thomas Aquinas reproached the blessed Augustine for constructing a psychology and gnoseology fit for angels but not for human beings.

Jacques Maritain made the same reproach against Descartes; yet Descartes is protected from all of Maritain's arrows by the blessed Augustine's shield.

The "I," the spirit, is not only something angelic: it is also divine, it is God's image, just as freedom is also God's image. This is the first part of Descartes's philosophy and it testifies to his greatness. But even in this part it is possible to make a few reproaches against him from the viewpoint of Russian philosophy: the simultaneous intuition of the "I" and the Absolute is an intuition that is mystical, irrational.

Descartes errs chiefly in regarding the "I" and the Absolute as two rational ideas, as two things, two substances. This is also the error of dogmatic rationalism, which is incapable of grasping the irrational. If something is self-evidently clear and distinct, this does not mean that it is therefore rational. The sky is self-evident and yet absolutely irrational; infinity is self-evident (Schiller) but irrational; Descartes himself admits as much. Finally, light — the symbol of clarity — is the most irrational thing in the world, even in physics. Yet, proceeding on the basis of his well-founded dialectic, Descartes could not claim that the "I" is a "thinking thing," and that God is a substance. The level on which "things" and "substances" exist is transcended by doubt, overcome by the phenomenological reduction.

Then, despite this problem, there is the second part of Descartes's philosophy, and it is his sin, his poverty. This is his doctrine of two substances, his geometrical and mechanistic approach to the phenomena of organic life, an approach that leads him to regard plants and animals as lifeless automata devoid of souls. We can see how arbitrary and dangerous it is, as a rule, to construct philosophical systems. As soon as Descartes starts to build a system, he forgets all about his discoveries: he says that the "I" is a thinking thing, a substance. Whereas in his *Meditations,* the dialectic that unfolds in the words "I think," the phenomenological reduction is not an object, not[3] a substance. As always happens, the disciples inherit and appropriate the master's mistakes and blunders. Cartesianism grabbed hold of and developed only this second part of Descartes's philosophy, which is now worthless. If this is what Thomism is quarreling with, then we are in full agreement with the Thomists. In order to understand the true value of Descartes, we must throw Cartesianism overboard, just

---

3. The Russian text reads *no est' substantsiya* ["but it is a substance"]. This may be a misprint for *ne est' substantsiya* ["it is not a substance"], and I have translated it accordingly. Trans.

as we have to distill the real Tolstoy out of Tolstoyanism in order to appreciate him properly.

The striking thing about Descartes, and what arouses our admiration, is the sincerity and straightforwardness of his thought. To be a real philosopher means to devote one's whole life, to sacrifice one's salvation in order to strive for a self-evident certainty and reach the truth. Descartes made a vow to the Most Holy Mother of God that he would make a pilgrimage if his prayer were fulfilled — the prayer of a philosopher who asked for only one thing, that he might find the self-evident truth. And he did make his pilgrimage: he wandered up and down the valley of doubts, through the dark night of negations — a perilous wandering, which started off from doubt in the very existence of the Most Holy Virgin herself.

This is what I call straightforwardness of thought, the virtue of a philosopher. To show what I mean, I invoke, in contrast to this straightforwardness, the arguments of Job's friends. The friends of Job are liars and flatterers before God: in order to get the benefit of his mercy, they build systems that seal off God's justice and providence behind a barricade of syllogisms. They are scared to say and think what they really see; they are afraid of doubt. Job himself, on the other hand, is bold enough to say that what he sees is neither justice nor providence nor even God: what he sees before him is the image of a "deceitful God."

But this is the miracle that turns the table: God shoves the flatterers aside and graciously allows Job to behold the irrational Absolute. This same grace was also granted to Descartes. The Most Holy Virgin answered his prayer — the prayer of an authentic knight of the truth, a knight without fear and without reproach.

Descartes is the true glory of France and he lives on in contemporary philosophy. He is young and beautiful once again, as Plato said of Socrates; while Cartesianism is now moldering in the dust.

CHAPTER 14

Immortality, Reincarnation, and Resurrection

The Bible on Man's Fate after Death

"What awaits people after death is something they did not expect and about which they had no clue." What did the mysterious Heraclitus mean by these words? Here's what: when we affirm "immortality," it means no doubt something grand and mysterious, but we do not know exactly what it means. We do not know what exactly we are affirming when we talk about immortality, what exactly it is that we wish for and toward which we aspire. The oldest myths and symbols make some guesses about it and perhaps they have guessed something. What is the nature of the philosophical and scientific meaning of these symbols and conjectures, this faith that "hypostatizes our hopes" and wants to give us "evidence of things not seen"?

The distinctive feature and advantage of biblical symbols consists in that they encompass all the problems of the spirit and envisage all the potential ways of solving them. Thus we find in the Bible four viewpoints on the question of man's fate after death, which exhaust all possible solutions:

1. The affirmation of the utter mortality of the soul, in the Psalms[1] (cf. Ecclesiastes) — a doctrine that is fully endorsed by the Sadducees.

2. The possible "transmigration of souls," a faith in the "reincarna-

---

1. For example: "As for man, his days are as grass: as a flower of the field, so he flourisheth. For the wind passeth over it, and it is gone; and the place thereof shall know it no more" (Ps. 103:15-16).

tion" of the former prophets, as the prophetic forerunners of the coming fulfillment of the messianic promises. This includes all the talk about the expected advent of Elijah (Luke 9:7-8, 19; Matt. 11:14; 17:3, 10-12; John 1:21). It would be improbable if such a theory as the one about the reincarnation of souls, so widespread in Egypt, Greece, and India, had remained unknown to the Hebrews, and it obviously found supporters, just as the theory of utter mortality did.[2]

3. The immortality of the detached soul, liberated from its body, immortality in Sheol, in the kingdom of shades, or else in "Abraham's bosom," in a blissful existence. Such a notion of immortality runs through all the Gospels, the Old Testament, and the Epistles. It plays an enormous role in the Christian consciousness of the Middle Ages; and for the majority of Christians it is the fulcrum of their belief in immortality. This theory of "disincarnated" immortality, however, is closest to Orphism and Platonism, and therefore it is not characteristically Judaic and Christian.

4. Finally, faith in the resurrection of the dead, faith in the resurrection of both souls and bodies. It is this viewpoint that is essentially biblical and absolutely distinctive for Christianity. It runs completely counter to both the Platonic and Hindu theory of immortality, for both Greeks and Hindus regarded the resurrection of souls and bodies as absurd: not only impossible, but nothing one should even wish for. In Athens the apostle Paul could preach splendidly about the "immortality of souls" in the sense of the immortality of the disembodied soul: this was an Orphic idea familiar to the local Greeks. But when he started talking about the "resurrection of the dead," about the resurrection of souls and bodies, no one wanted to listen ("we would like to hear you talk about this another time" — as reported in Acts [17:32]). This proved to be the real "foolishness unto the Greeks" [1 Cor. 1:23].

Death Is a Friend and an Enemy: The Apostle Paul's Solution

The remarkable thing is that the third and fourth notions of immortality coexist peacefully within Christianity, whereas they are quite divergent in

2. It does not at all follow, however, that we should understand the words of Christ (Matt. 17:11-13) as the acceptance of the theory of reincarnation by Christ himself. We should interpret them to mean: a man will appear who will truly be "in the spirit and power of Elijah" (Luke 1:17). Such a "reincarnation" can be accepted by everyone.

spirit and even antinomic. This antinomy is hardly even noticed in ordinary Christian consciousness, because for the most part no one takes the "resurrection of the dead" seriously. At best it is a timid hope: Tchaikovsky's "I look for the resurrection of the dead" (in his "Credo") strikes our ear as a strange dissonance, a tormenting question. The immortality of the abstracted soul is much more comprehensible and influential.

But the antinomy is perfectly clear, especially in the concise formulations of the apostle Paul. On the one hand, death is a friend, a value, a "gain," a prize: "to be gone and be with Christ is incomparably better"; "it is better to long to be exiled from the body and to be at home with the Lord" (Phil. 1:21-23; 2 Cor. 5:8). On the other hand, death is the ultimate enemy, who must be "destroyed," who must be trampled down by Christ's death: death must be swallowed up in victory, for death itself would be the victory of hell (1 Cor. 15:54).

Theology has not yet fully resolved this antinomy nor has it been realized by the pedestrian church consciousness. But in 1 Corinthians 15 Paul sets down its solution: "it will not live unless it die" and "what is sown is corruptible, but what is raised is incorruptible," "what is sown is a natural body, and what is raised is a spiritual body." This solution, just like chapter 15 as a whole, tips the balance decisively toward resurrection in a new transfigured flesh — it is even the central notion of Christianity, for "if Christ did not rise and if the dead do not rise, then our preaching is in vain and our faith is in vain" [1 Cor. 15:13-14]. But death is a necessary dialectical moment, subordinate to resurrection and finding its true meaning in it: the metamorphosis of the grain is terrifying and tragic, but it saves and enriches our existence. After all, what "rises up" is more perfect because of the decay of the less perfect.

"Enlightened" Prejudice

We will now take a look at these theological problems, these religious symbols, from the viewpoint of modern philosophy and modern psychology. First, modern science and philosophy ought to shed completely the "enlightened" prejudice that posing the question of immortality is (as they allege) unscientific, since we know for certain that there is no life "beyond the grave," no life "eternal." Not only do we *not* know this: we even know for certain that "immortality" exists at all levels of existence and, so to speak, in all the sciences. Where death has not yet been, eternity exists in the physicochemical realm, in the form of the law of the conservation of energy (for energy is eternally conserved); but even in the realm where death already exists, there is still immortality in the form of genealogical preservation, in the form of the immortality of the living cell; and, finally, death is no more in the realm of the spirit and spiritual entities (the sphere of science, art, history, philosophy, religion).

Even if eternal existence is absolutely beyond doubt in all these realms, it will still seem insufficient to many people. Is the soul "immortal," is the personality "immortal," is there "individual immortality"? These are the questions they ask us. Here modern philosophy and modern psychology have a lot to say.

What Exactly Is the "Soul"?

The problem of the "immortality of the soul" retains its profound meaning in modern analytical psychology. The question that it raised was certainly not meaningless, for there are indeed realms and properties in the "soul," in the sphere of the psychic, which are not subject, as it were, to time and death. The discoveries of psychoanalysis and analytical psychology have succeeded in demonstrating this in quite a new way and from a new angle. The point is that the "soul," the psyche, is much broader, richer, more mysterious, than we had assumed.

People always used to think that "soul" meant consciousness and, therefore, that the death or loss of consciousness was equivalent to the death or disappearance of the soul. But "soul" and personality and selfhood are no longer identified with consciousness at all: consciousness by itself can disappear, can be lost, without any loss of personality or selfhood. This happens to us every night when we fall asleep: if the loss of consciousness is death, then we die and are resurrected on a daily basis. The rhythm of sleep and waking closely resembles the rhythm of death and birth; souls as it were fall asleep in death and are reawakened in birth. Yet this rhythm does not prevent the life of the soul from going on. It is precisely this eternity of the "psychic" and the "spiritual" amid the alternation between death and birth that is expressed symbolically by the idea of the transmigration of souls.

Modern psychology considers that psychic existence is not exhaustively accounted for by consciousness. The psychic embraces both the subconscious and the supraconscious. Therefore, even if death means the loss of consciousness, this still does not at all mean the annihilation of the soul, but may only mean a transition from the conscious to the unconscious. This is exactly what Leibniz thought: after death the soul curls up and goes to sleep, only to uncurl and rise again. What he propounded was not metempsychosis, but the metamorphosis of the person, the monad; for the person always remains himself and keeps on developing in his own way during these metamorphoses.

The Subconscious Does Not Believe in Death

Freud established a curious fact: the subconscious does not believe in death — unconsciously, instinctively, we live as if death did not exist. Consciousness and thought are well aware of the existence of death, but the subconscious "neglects" it, as it were. It is remarkable that when we dream we never see the dead as supernatural phantoms and shades — we see them alive and as they were; sometimes we feel that they have merely been gone for a long time and have just now come back to us. The subconscious, as it were, "represses" their death. Precisely for this reason, as Freud pointed out, people in conversation ban and regard as unseemly any talk about the death of those present.

Therefore, Freud is not being entirely consistent when he talks about the death instinct: how can there be a subconscious drive toward death when the subconscious blocks the very idea of it? Wouldn't it be better to say that the subconscious has a special gravitational pull, that it longs to drag people down into its abyss? Then we could say that there is a striving not only to be conscious and to preserve consciousness, but also an inverse striving for the loss of consciousness, for submersion in the unconscious: a striving for sleep, for nirvana, for the extinction of consciousness as a going beyond, into a trance. This trance can also be experienced in the ecstasy of love (by Tristan and Isolde, for example), and then it is a submersion into the unconscious — not into nonexistence but, if you will, into the most intense existence. These are the mysteries of Dionysus. The kingdom of Dionysus, the trance into the unconscious, takes over when the torch of consciousness is extinguished; and it may be more worthwhile, more beautiful than daytime consciousness with its worries and torments of conscience. Perhaps true reality is here, and the "daytime shadows" — are they only shades and phantoms? This question of Wagner and Schopenhauer takes on a contemporary relevance once more.

The Theory of the Collective Unconscious

Jung's analytical psychology can answer this question of why the subconscious blocks out death, does not believe in it. The answer is contained in the theory of the collective unconscious. The collective unconscious does not die and is not born, nor does it fall asleep, although it does grow and is transformed; it lies at a deeper level than the alternation of birth and death, day and night. Simultaneously we are in it and it is in us; but what exactly is the collective unconscious?

Delving into the depths of our own subconscious, we find there a subterranean stratification of all the layers of our life — this is the emotional-subconscious memory that preserves and remembers everything. But the intellectual-conscious memory knows how to extract only some portions of this material. If we go down even deeper, we would see that in these stratifications of our life — or more precisely underneath them — we can uncover the even more ancient strata of the emotional-unconscious life of peoples and all of humanity. The documents of the collective unconscious are myths, symbols, "archetypes."

We are submerged in this collective unconscious — it is in us and we are in it. In it we can read through the whole spiritual history of humanity, with its "fall into sin," its "enmity toward the snake," its "lost paradise," its Cain and Abel, its demons and gods, its incest, murders, heroic exploits, sufferings, and repentances.

As a geologist reads the whole history of the earth from a stratified cross-section of it — and the whole of this history is present and available in it — so the subconscious provides a present-day sample of the entire history of the soul, past and present. Here the soul is truly pan-temporal, and therefore not subject to time; it bears eternity in itself; one need only know how to see it, how to read its language. Rudolf Steiner's idea of the "Akashic chronicle" is quite true, but Steiner himself has absolutely no method for reading it, since he does not know where to read, in what depths of the soul, and he does not know the script in which the chronicle is recorded. Steiner's psychology knows nothing about the "subconscious" or the "collective unconscious," nothing about how to interpret dreams and symbols, nothing about psychoanalysis, and for this reason he himself is a splendid object for psychoanalysis, but to be the analyzing subject is totally beyond his powers. Steiner is completely under the spell of the chaotic subconscious; his conscious thought is archaic and infantile; he is eternally barred from initiation into scientific-philosophical and mystical esotericism. Steiner has reveries and dreams, and this is a precious source of knowledge, but there are dreams and dreams — some are "prophetic dreams" and some, like Steiner's, only muddleheaded ravings. Steiner's Christology, mentioned by Father Sergey Bulgakov in his article, could serve as an example of the latter. Emanuel Swedenborg was also immersed in reveries, in dreams and delirium, but his ravings are much more talented and symbolic.

Thus all of time lives in the subconscious in an eternal present: thousands of emotions that at one time or another bound children and parents together are alive in every affect toward mother and father; just as the emotions of Cain and Abel are alive in the competition and enmity between brothers. But the main thing is that a presentiment and anticipation of the future, an intuition of the possibilities contained in the present, are living in the subconscious. Here is the key to the secret of predictions.

The main thing that scientific occultism and parapsychology show us is the mysterious and uncharted might of the subconscious. About these real and genuine discoveries the "occultism" of Blavatsky and Steiner is absolutely clueless.

Consciousness and Chronos

Thus immortality appears to us at all levels of existence: at the physico-chemical level (as the eternity of energy), at the biological level (as the immortality of the cell and its transformations), at the psychic level (as the pan-temporality of the subconscious, which lives simultaneously in the past, present, and future without making any rigid distinctions between them). Here is the reason why any "trance" into the subconscious — which we observe in dreams, in reveries, in mediumship, in eros — is first and foremost a loss of the sense of time: "clock time is not observed" there.

A rigid opposition between present, past, and future, on the other hand, is the essential mark of consciousness. It is conscious of the rhythm of day and night, birth and death; it counts out the seconds and "observes clock time"; it keeps track of chronology and is conscious of the irreversibility of the numerical sequence of time. The irreversibility of time exists only for consciousness. Hence the sadness and tragedy of consciousness. On the whole, consciousness is the sphere of tragedy, for it is born from conflict, from the clash of opposites (a re-flection is an activity, a casting back). The first opposition that consciousness makes is the one between past and future, which make contact only in the fragile and ephemeral moment of the present. The original tragedy of consciousness is the tragedy of Chronos devouring his children. This is why Ecclesiastes, that book of unrelenting sorrow, is first and foremost an awareness of the tragedy of temporality: "One generation passeth away, and another generation cometh. . . . For the living know that they shall die: but the dead know not anything . . . for the memory of them is forgotten. Also their love, and their hatred, and their envy is now perished: neither have they any more a portion for ever in anything that is done under the sun. . . . What profit hath a man of all his labor?" [Eccles. 1:4; 9:5-6; 1:3].

This realization of the irreversibility of temporal sequence is the wisdom of consciousness, but in this wisdom there is much grief, and "he who increases his knowledge, increases his sorrow." The collective unconscious is happier and more fortunate. If "death and time rule on earth" [Solovyov], then they rule first and foremost in consciousness and for consciousness, since "time is a form of consciousness."

Memory and History

Thus we arrive at the conclusion that if there is something mortal and temporal, then it is first and foremost our consciousness: it begins at birth and ends with death; it is a small and finite segment of time. Yet consciousness also makes contact with eternity and possesses a pan-temporality of its own, but only when it rises to the level of the spirit. It can assume the "viewpoint of eternity," and this is precisely the viewpoint of the spirit, of spiritual "total unity."

Consciousness knows and sees that an infinity has flowed past before its birth and that after its disappearance an infinite period of time will flow past as well. Its spiritual gaze sees much more than the brief segment of its personal temporal life; it sees, in essence, the infinity of the past and the infinity of the future, the infinity of history that is granted by memory and foresight, by the sense of the past and the striving toward the future. History is in fact the imperfect, moving "image of eternity."

Memory and history are the first overcoming of death and time. This overcoming may be imperfect, but it can infinitely approximate the fullness of "eternal" or absolute memory. Since this is so, we need to remember that history goes in both directions, back toward the beginning and forward toward the end, that it is always both "archaic" and teleological, that the significance of historical study consists not in the contemplation of the past but in the prevision of the future, that is, in the making of history:

hence the eschatological element in "sacred history." The brief moment of our life, of our conscious existence, is inserted and interwoven into the whole space-time continuum, into the history of the world and into the vast expanse of the universe. In this moment we have the node, the focal point, of countless vectors, actions, and reactions emerging from all worlds and times and heading toward all worlds and times. Or, if we take up Leibniz's comparison, this focal point, this center that captures and emits the emanations of energy, is consciousness as a "monad," as the "mirror of the universe," in which the "entire world full of infinity" is reflected.

Going far beyond the limits of his *Monadology*, Leibniz brilliantly intuited the monad's link to the entire universe, the possibility of reading the history of the whole cosmos in every "atom" of being. This idea is scientifically and philosophically irrefutable. It is equally true for astronomy and geology, for biology and psychology. Jung found confirmation for it in the psychology of the unconscious, but it is true even for the psychology of consciousness.

The human being is a microcosm, a vantage point from which a picture of the whole world is unfolded in perspective. We need only know how to read, to decipher, what is in our consciousness and subconscious, in that murky and mysterious mirror where the fullness of being is reflected, albeit without its full clarity. Here is another side of Leibniz's genius: he anticipated the theory of the unconscious. The monad is the focal point for the whole history of development and all the influences coming from every direction, but not everything can be perceived, since these perceptions may be infinitely small; they are contained in the monad unconsciously, and self-consciousness only gradually becomes aware of them.[3]

"Reincarnation" and the Mutual Permeability of Souls

The distinctive universality of the subconscious and consciousness, their concentrated total unity, shows us how the soul overcomes mortality and finitude through the potentially infinite memory and the all-encompassing "focal point" of the spirit. The spirit possesses a focal point of contact with eternity. In light of these discoveries, the notion of utter mortality becomes totally obsolete. But what about the other myths of "life after death," and,

---

3. It must be said that both ideas, (1) the nature of the soul as microcosm, its concentrated total unity, its "potential infinity," and even (2) the unconscious contents of the soul, are already present in the genius of Plotinus. See the *Enneads*.

first and foremost, the myth of reincarnation? At first glance it might seem that the existence of the soul's supraindividual and cosmic memory (the Akashic chronicle) confirms the idea of the "transmigration of souls." But this is precisely what is *not* true: supraindividual and cosmic memory is a memory of other people's incarnations, not my own.

In my memory and fantasy, in my consciousness and subconscious, I find a multitude of souls and "incarnations," for any in-image-ination [= imagination = *vo-obraz-enie*] is incarnation and any re-collection is a resurrection of sorts. A multitude of souls is living in me, some anonymously and summarily, others in a distinct and individual imagination (heroes, prophets, the Divine Human). All souls potentially live and act in me, if only to an infinitely small extent. Even future individualities can live in my presentiment of them — and this accounts for prophecies, for example, about the Messiah, and even for the positivistic "religion of progress": things will be better for our children. The unique pan-temporality and eternity of the soul consists in this universal permeability of souls, in their conciliarity [*sobornost'*] (and every soul is conciliar, for it gathers up the images and reflections of souls and persons who have lived before us and will come after us). Therefore there is no reason why the soul should "change homes"; or, if one prefers, the soul "changes homes" and is "reincarnated" a countless number of times in its short life; it changes homes and is reincarnated through memory and fantasy. These "reincarnations" are especially vivid to the artist, to the historian. Fantasy is really nothing other than a gift for infinite "reincarnations," and this gift can lay hold of souls who have already existed, or give birth to and anticipate souls who have not yet been. The "transmigration" of souls occurs in love as well: we, as it were, move into the beloved's home and he into ours, we "put ourselves in his place" to the point of complete identification with him, or we take him into ourselves. This is expressed in Paul's words: "yet not I, but Christ liveth in me" [Gal. 2:20]; in Plato's words: "yes and no — there was no such person as Plato, but only Socrates, become young and beautiful again." Finally, Tristan tells his beloved: "You are Tristan, I Isolde!"

There is no doubt, however, that this mutual permeability of souls in love preserves their individuality inviolate. Souls are united in love "without division but without confusion." If Tristan were reincarnated once and for all in Isolde, then he would disappear as Tristan — and consequently love as the harmony of opposites would disappear. We "put ourselves in the place" of the other person while remaining ourselves: this is the wondrous mystery of the mutual permeability of souls. Only under these circumstances will love and the mutual permeability of individualities be an enrichment of being; otherwise, the complete merger of identities would impoverish being. If "there were no such person as Plato," it would be the greatest impoverishment of being, even if Socrates were still alive, "become young and beautiful again." Thus only by taking into ourselves the incarnation of a great person do we enrich and not impoverish ourselves: the other person is still himself and we remain ourselves, and at the same time he develops new potentialities in us and we uncover new potentialities in him.

Of course, there is no doubt whatsoever that this mutual permeability of souls is not reincarnation in the classical Indian sense of the term. The potential infinity of souls even renders such a reincarnation unnecessary: whence and wherefore "change homes" if the soul can thus embrace everyone, albeit with a differing degree of clarity? The only necessary and desirable change might be an increase in the clarity and fullness of the soul in question, the perfecting of the purity of that mirror of infinity that ought ideally to reflect the Absolute (according to the beatitude: "Blessed are the pure in heart, for they shall see God"). But it is absolutely not necessary that one mirror turn into another; all it need do is to become pure, to be "transfigured," and to be restored if it is broken — then every person will appear there in plenitude, and yet in individual plenitude, in his own plenitude. Here again we see the genius of Leibniz. Wouldn't it be true that all souls are really equal and identical, since they reflect the same infinity of the universe and of themselves? No: each soul reflects the entire world, but from its own special shift in perspective. In this shift in perspective, the soul perceives both the world and other souls, each one from the new "viewpoint" of the perceiver.

If every soul preserves its individuality, its vantage point, its shift in perspective, then there is not nor can there be any "reincarnation" whatsoever. Each person remains himself and only in himself and through himself does he perceive other souls and perceive himself through them — but again through this shift in perspective. On the other hand, if the soul does not preserve its individuality, then no reincarnation can take place either: then one shift in perspective is simply replaced by another one.

Who Is "Reincarnated"?

The whole theory of reincarnation depends entirely on how we answer the question: Who is reincarnated? If we are told: the individual, defined by

187

name and surname, is reincarnated, then this answer makes no sense, because the individual is *this* individual, the one who is embodied thus, here and now. Unincarnated beauty, the idea of beauty, is not an individuality: only *this* beauty as it has been imagined and embodied is an individuality. Therefore individuality can be incarnated, transfigured, it can even be resurrected, but it cannot turn into another individual while remaining itself. It cannot be replaced by another individual, for the essence of individuality consists in the fact that it is irreplaceable. It cannot wholly take the place of another individual, for this would mean that another individual could substitute for it, and individuality does not allow for substitutes.

People often say, "Put yourself in my place," and the mutual permeability of souls makes this possible, and love positively requires it. All our relations with people, insofar as they are spiritual, rest on the fact that we put ourselves in another's place, we try to empathize with him. But this putting of ourselves into another's place has its limits. The limits are easy to see in that often expressed desire: "Ah, how I would like to be in his place!" When we say this, we ordinarily have in mind another person's wealth or fame, even another's talent — but all this is given to me myself, to me such as I know myself to be; the other's gifts are given, but my own personality remains. I am standing "in another's place," but I am still myself. Many people are more than willing to agree to this. I am ready to "change places" — but am I ready to be replaced by another creature absolutely and down to the last particle? Most people would answer in the negative. Why so? Because it means that I would be obliged to withdraw and disappear, and a completely different creature would then appear in my place. However charming this creature might be, the least of persons would not agree to be replaced by it. This is why the answer to the question: "Who precisely changes homes and is reincarnated?" is so important. Individuality cannot be reincarnated, for this would mean sending in a replacement for what cannot truly be replaced. Individuality is precisely the concrete incarnation here and now, the incarnation in this spatiotemporal segment, from which is revealed, in this or the other potential plenitude, the whole infinity of being. The individuality, or the monad, can be altered, but not to the point where it turns into another individuality — as Leibniz says, it allows for metamorphosis but not metempsychosis.[4]

---

4. Here we can once again use the comparison with a mirror: it tarnishes, it lightens, it becomes clear and pure, it has its own angle of vision in which the whole of its irreplaceability resides, for the world and other mirrors are reflected in it in a particular individual perspectival stance.

The remarkable thing is that the classical theories of reincarnation, in India or in Greek Orphism, simply had no concept of individual personhood. This concept is typically Christian and realized rather late in Christian culture. With the deviation from Christianity, this concept disappears (e.g., in Marxism, in communism), it loses its meaning and significance, and is replaced by the individual unit: the zoological representative of a species, or the economic representative of a class.[5]

Lacking the concept of a person, the classical theory of reincarnation responds to the question about who changes homes or is reincarnated by claiming that it is the suprapersonal and supraindividual "I," supraindividual selfhood, Atman, Purusha, the Spirit, the Logos, common to everybody and the same in everybody, or even identical (as in Vedanta). It is this supraindividual selfhood that moves into the various bodies that are born or, more precisely, it is this that crowns the summit of the hierarchical, many-leveled structure of the human being. Insofar as Steiner is capable of thinking philosophically, this is roughly how he thinks.

In India, and even in the works of Plato, there is no concept of individuality in the sense of personhood, but there is a concept of selfhood; this selfhood, ideally detached and deincarnated, totally independent from the body and even from the "soul," is a divinely dispassionate eye, an eternal spectator, everywhere identical. The Hindus even call it "the one who surveys the field." Differences exist only in the sphere of the objects surveyed; the subject is always the same. In European philosophy this is the "I think" that accompanies all my ideas; it is Kant's transcendental unity of apperception (the perception that involves recognition): merely the unity of self-consciousness, the same in everybody.

Memory and the Identity of Persons in "Reincarnation"

But is it possible in such a worldview — with such an understanding of the structure of the human being, the person — to talk about the transmigration and reincarnation of Atman, detached selfhood, the pure "I," the abstract unity of self-consciousness? At first glance it might seem obvious that it is indeed possible, and that only in such a worldview is it even pos-

---

5. One must bear in mind that individuum and individuality [*individual'nost'*] are opposites; individuum is a replaceable unit, while individuality is an irreplaceable uniqueness. Personality and individuality should not be confused. The Venus de Milo is an individuality but not a person.

sible to talk about these things. The pure "I" reincarnates again and again, while always remaining the same immutably detached eye of consciousness, the same center of consciousness, the focal point that is everywhere equal. The "one who surveys the field," Atman, "transmigrates" again and again while remaining itself, since it always "surveys" new "fields," new bodies, new souls.

Yet one could claim with equal right that there is no reincarnation here whatsoever, but only a series of identical incarnations, identical only in the sense that they are always flowing through the same form of the unity of self-consciousness. But the qualitative identity of many "I's" in no way entails their numerical identity, just as the qualitative identity of points does not mean their numerical identity, for there are lots of points. The unity of the point and the qualitative identity of all points in no way entails the singularity of the point; and in exactly the same way the unity of self-consciousness in no way entails the singularity of self-consciousness. How can one establish that a self-consciousness with a certain content is numerically identical to a self-consciousness that is living a thousand years later and that possesses a totally different content? Only one answer is possible: numerical identity is established by memory and karma. Indeed, personal identity presupposes memory and at the same time makes memory possible. And the karma of actions is also nothing other than ontological memory, the memory of being, but not the memory of consciousness. An action is preserved in what has been done, and what has been done further determines what the person will do and undergo. Karma is a union of conditionality and freedom, which union gives us "fate."

It must be said that no one has ever succeeded in rigorously and precisely establishing the memory of his previous births, just as no one has succeeded in using that memory to divine his karma and thereby to rationalize the injustice of his fate. The one and the other would presumably be accessible, by order of a miracle, only to a few superior beings, for example, the Buddha or Rudolf Steiner. But even John Locke remarked that without the memory of a previous incarnation there is no personal identity and consequently no reincarnation either — but merely the incarnation from scratch of an entirely new "I." For where there is memory, there is also individual personal identity; where there is personal identity, there is memory.

That the memory of previous incarnations exists can only be an article of faith. Yet is this faith truly reasonable? Is such memory in general possible? Here we would first have to establish that individual memory is linked to the individual subconscious. This has been fully established by modern psychology. The individual subconscious is, undoubtedly, linked to the individual organism, with its capacity to feel sensations, to experience joy and suffering. The pure "I," Atman, selfhood, is not memory. It can construct memory and use memory as a tool, but it exists on a higher level than memory, since it can contemplate the supratemporal and the eternal.[6] It "reads" as it were in the scroll of memory that is kept rolled up in the subconscious: "Recollection silently unfurls its long scroll before me" [Pushkin]. Accordingly, if the pure "I," Atman, selfhood wants to preserve the scroll of its memory in the course of "changing homes," then it must take along with it its individual-personal subconscious and even its individual organism.

This means, in Steiner's language, that the spirit (the "I") must furnish its new apartment with its astral, ethereal, and physical body. But this would in fact be the entire former personality as a whole — it will not be a reincarnation of any sort, but rather a resurrection. Only someone who has been resurrected could remember everything and thereby restore the numerical identity of self-consciousness. Someone who has been reincarnated, that is, transported into another flesh and another subconscious, cannot in principle do so. After all, memory is in fact a partial resurrection and revival, a victory over death and time; and "eternal" or absolute memory — for which we pray and which we desire — would be the full resurrection in eternal life of the divine in-image-ination [i.e., the assumption of the perfect image and likeness of God as the fulfillment of the personality].

We get a strange result: resurrection is miraculous, but possible in principle, and it happens in part all the time (resurrecting the past, resurrecting the fathers [Fyodorov]). As for reincarnation, it is impossible, for it is inconceivable. Besides, no one could possibly desire it. Leibniz's proposition still holds true: the metamorphosis of the monad is possible and conceivable — but not its metempsychosis.

Cosmic Memory, the Idea of Karma, and the Idea of Future Possibilities of Development

We can only surmount a particular theory, however erroneous it may be, when we can point to what is true and worthwhile in it. And only that the-

---

6. The soul in the sphere of the mind has no need of memory, says Plotinus, for noetic contemplation is not memory.

ory which accepts this true and worthwhile material while giving it another explanation, making another hypothesis about it, will triumph. We must follow this principle even when dealing with "reincarnation." What is worthwhile in it and what constitutes the entire force of its argumentation is — in other words, supraindividual and cosmic memory, the idea of karma and the idea of future possibilities of development — the link between past, present, and future incarnations, which are like beads strung on a single thread.

But supraindividual and cosmic memory, as we have seen, has been provided with a much more convincing explanation by the psychological discovery of the collective unconscious and the philosophical discovery of the mutual permeability of souls. This supraindividual memory is much more wondrous and mighty than the individual one: it remembers, in varying degrees, the whole infinity of incarnations that are inscribed in its inheritance. This is why it can say: "I have already been a youth and a maiden, and a bird, and a mute fish, and a bush" (Empedocles). It inherits all the forms of biological development and contains in its present self all the forms of plant and animal life — psychic and spiritual. The myth about the "transmigration of souls" is a symbol of evolution, which the soul divines and reveals by virtue of its potentially infinite memory. This is especially clear in Empedocles, but it is even clearer in Steiner: he is plainly fantasizing on Haeckel's theme [ontogeny recapitulates phylogeny] when he recalls that the human being was once, as it were, a fish or an amphibian.

When the soul descends into the unconscious or rises into the suprapsychic sphere of science, for example, history, it experiences its pantemporality and total permeability; and this mysterious discovery, which baffles the crowd, is expressed esoterically as the capacity to "change homes" and to be born an infinite number of times.

The idea of karma, deeply linked to the idea of memory, which asserts that nothing that has been done is ever forgotten — for vengeance is a sort of cosmic memory of evil — this idea is also much more convincingly explained by the collective unconscious and the mutual permeability of souls. The entire inherited sum total of acts, aspirations, emotions, the nasty ones and the good ones, is living in our collective unconscious and even in our common consciousness. It conditions our unconscious instincts and actions; it even conditions our entire situation and everything that "happens" to us, that is, our "fate" or karma. In this sense "his blood" is always "on us and on our children" — whether we shout about it or hush it up, whether we are aware of it or not. This is the psychological and philosophical foundation of both "original sin" and karma ("for every crime is avenged here on earth" [Goethe]).[7] There is a karma, of course, within the confines of an individual life, but it is far from being limited to this: there is also a karma that is supraindividual, tribal, national, collective. It presupposes, of course, a series of "incarnations" and the link between them, but in no way does it presuppose the "reincarnation" of a numerically identical personality.

Now as for the third valuable idea, contained in the symbol of metempsychosis — namely, the idea of future possibilities of development — this idea, just like the first two, has a solid foundation in the development of the collective unconscious, a development that is continuous and imperceptible. Every one of my acts, every emotion, adds to the inherited stock that operates in the future. My aims, my aspirations, my hopes will be resolved and fulfilled by others, as happens constantly in science, philosophy, the making of culture: my heirs will pay my debts. But in addition to this supraindividual influence on future conciliar creativity, there is also an individual influence that is made possible by the mutual permeability of souls: Pushkin lives and is "reincarnated" in every Russian soul and, what is more, in a new way, and the same thing goes for Peter the Great and Seraphim of Sarov. Geniuses, heroes, and saints participate as individuals in the creation of the historical process, and they participate to an infinitely greater degree; while "simple mortals" also participate, but imperceptibly and to an infinitely lesser degree. Thus every person has his place in eternal or absolute memory, in the kingdom of the spirit, the ideal kingdom, where nothing can ever be lost — not one image, not one value, not one idea, not one individuality.

The Meaning of the Symbol of "Reincarnation"

Such a mutual permeability of souls undoubtedly exists, but it is not the "reincarnation" of one individuality in another one, which is simply impossible, for an individuality is *this* individuality and not another. This mutual permeability is something much more wondrous, precisely because it enables the life and activity of one individuality to be in another

---

7. The problem of the Christian attitude toward karma, toward "fate," cannot be examined here. For Christianity karma exists, but it can be and is overcome through redemption, through the overcoming of both original (i.e., supraindividual) and individual sin.

and through another. Leibniz is wrong about one thing: monads have no "windows and doors" not because they are closed and impenetrable, but precisely the other way round — it is because they are absolutely permeable, and therefore have no need of "windows and doors," that they do not go out or come in nor do they change homes. They are permeable and all-embracing, but every one preserves its singular shift in perspective, its singular angle of vision, which unfolds, surveys, and illuminates the entire world and every soul in it in a new way. It is impossible for these points of view, these individual centers, to be switched around, and therefore it is also impossible for them to "change homes." If one switches into another, then this means that one individuality will perish and another one will spring up. But the mutual permeability of souls enables one individuality to concentrate all its attention, all its imagination, on another: a person can become "obsessed" by another person. Freud uses this kind of "obsession" to explain our infatuation with a woman, our infatuation with a leader, with a teacher: another's "I" takes the place of our higher, ideal "I." It is quite apparent that we are not dealing in these cases with any kind of "reincarnation," since we know that both individuals can remain incarnated simultaneously: for example, Marx and Engels, Tristan and Isolde. The poet is freely transported and "reincarnated" into everyone and everything; even the ordinary man freely "moves into the homes" of those whom he loves. What is more, the unordinary man — Christ — is born and incarnated anew in our minds and hearts, as Origen says. This is the sole genuine meaning of the symbol of "reincarnation." If this symbol means anything great and eternal, then it is only this.

The Immortality of the Soul and the Resurrection of the Dead

We turn now to the third and fourth forms of portraying man's fate after death: the immortality of the soul liberated from the body — "Platonic" immortality — and, finally, the resurrection of both souls and bodies. Here we can note only briefly the meaning of these symbols, since we have focused our attention on the second notion: the idea of reincarnation. A full examination of the third and fourth forms would require another work treating the problem of immortality as a whole.

The problem of immortality can be posed and solved only from the depths of anthropology, from the depths of a unified theory of humanity. Throughout the course of our investigation we have constantly run into the hierarchical structure of the human being. This structure is made up of the levels of "dead" matter, "animate" matter (the body), the unconscious soul, the conscious soul, the spirit and, finally, that mysterious summit that constitutes the human essence, his eternity, his likeness to God — namely, selfhood, Atman, the "deep I," the "hidden man of the heart." We have seen that the human being is "microcosmic," that he contains all the elements of the cosmos, all levels of being, that he is a concentrated total unity and potentially infinite, so to speak, in all directions — vertically and horizontally, like a cross, or a sphere. Every level of his being — his body, his life processes, his subconscious, his consciousness, his creative spirit — every level reveals a specific infinity and a specific "immortality." This fact alone already makes it absolutely impossible to think of the human being as a finite and entirely mortal creature. On the contrary, infinities of various "potencies" dwell in him.

But the supreme, ultimate might of infinity is contained in a human being's selfhood, which is higher than consciousness and higher than the conscious spirit, and ought therefore to be called supraconsciousness. It is precisely this selfhood that is mystical and Godlike, for it is grasped by mystical intuition and is entirely irrational, transcendent, and not of this world, like the Deity himself. This selfhood of ours is rooted in the Absolute, and therefore it is higher than death and birth, higher than time and eternity; and through this selfhood we make contact with the absolute source of being.

Selfhood displays its creative power through incarnation, through imparting form to the lower levels, or their "sublimation." Selfhood subjects everything to itself, and "appropriates" everything; it uses "its" spirit, "its" consciousness, "its" subconscious, "its" body, even "its" matter as tools, as material; it makes everything into an instrument, a means of expressing itself. Individuation, the principle of individuation, starts here; this principle lies in the "uniqueness" of selfhood, which produces a unique combination of all these levels and materials. Selfhood makes everything its own and imparts uniqueness to everything: its spirit, its soul, its body, even its material possessions and dwelling place. Selfhood is, as it were, the vertical axis that runs through all the layers and horizontal levels of the human essence. This intersection provides the unique "angle of vision" that unfurls all of being from one particular shift in perspective. Selfhood creates "its" individual personhood through the transformation of all the levels of being that are included in it, through their "assimilation."

From the viewpoint of such an anthropology, what is the significance of the two Christian notions of immortality — the notion of the "immortal soul" and the notion of bodily resurrection? What, in the final analysis, does each of them signify: what kind of experience, aspiration, postulate? The Platonic-Orphic, the Christian, and, in part, the Indian theory of the immortal soul, liberated from the "dungeon" of the body, signifies an unattainable "Godlike" selfhood, transcendent in relation to all levels of being, freely hovering over everything. This "immortality" is indubitable, but for Christianity it is not sufficient. It is the immortality of the "source of being," the source of the person, but not of that individual person himself as a whole. From the Christian viewpoint, death is the disintegration of the individual person, the distortion of that unique combination of elements and levels of being which is the principle of individuation. Therefore death is a tragedy; it cannot be reconciled with the demand for perfection ("Be ye therefore perfect, even as your Father which is in heaven is perfect" [Matt. 5:48]), since "God is not the God of the dead, but of the living" [Matt. 22:32]. Hence the postulate of resurrection, as the restoration of that distorted unity, and the utter eradication of the source of mortality. The elements are immortal and "I myself" — the artist who created his own "harmony and proportionality" from those elements — am also immortal. Yet the lyre is smashed to bits and the melody does not sound, even if that melody is also immortal in the "eternal memory" of God and humanity, in "ideal" immortality, just as the artist survives in his "biography." But biography is not life; hence the demand is born for the fullness of existence, the full resonance of life, which selfhood will never renounce. Everything must be restored, except for imperfection; and it must be restored for the sake of its perfecting, for the human being can never renounce the postulate of perfection, "even if it were never to be realized." And if life is more perfect than death, then death must be vanquished. The extreme positivism of Ilya Mechnikov and the Christian idea of the triumph over death jointly agree on this basic postulate, this ineradicable aspiration of the human spirit. Death must be vanquished on all fronts: the bodily, the psychic, and the spiritual.

Here is the postulate, the strange hybrid of positivistic science and Christianity's ultimate faith and hope, that was perceived and so powerfully expressed by a most fascinating Russian thinker of the last half of the nineteenth century, Nikolai Fyodorov. The argument from impossibility loses its force here, for human beings by their very nature strive for the impossible. It is impossible for us to be perfect as God is perfect, and yet the postulate of perfection retains all of its meaning and significance.

The Russian philosophical tradition, truncated by a compulsory communism and Marxism, has devoted a great deal of attention to the problem of death and immortality. For Russian thinkers constantly strove for definitive solutions; they strove to grasp the ultimate meaning of everything that exists. The Russian soul, as I mentioned at the beginning, has a real affinity for Hegel's dictum: "the object of philosophy is the same as the object of religion." And Russian philosophy constantly appeals to religion for the solution of philosophical problems. In this sense the problem of death and immortality, which is essentially at the center of all religions, is the central problem for Russian philosophical consciousness.

Index